ARSENAL

ARSENAL
THE STORY OF A FOOTBALL CLUB IN 101 LIVES

ANTON RIPPON

WHITE OWL
AN IMPRINT OF PEN & SWORD BOOKS LTD.
YORKSHIRE – PHILADELPHIA

First published in Great Britain in 2020 by
PEN AND SWORD WHITE OWL
An imprint of
Pen & Sword Books Ltd
Yorkshire - Philadelphia

Copyright © Anton Rippon, 2020

ISBN 978 1 52676 774 5

The right of Anton Rippon to be identified as Author of this work has been asserted by him in accordance with the Copyright, Designs and Patents Act 1988.

A CIP catalogue record for this book is available from the British Library.

All rights reserved. No part of this book may be reproduced or transmitted in any form or by any means, electronic or mechanical including photocopying, recording or by any information storage and retrieval system, without permission from the Publisher in writing.

Typeset in Times New Roman 11.5/14 by
Aura Technology and Software Services, India.
Printed and bound in the UK by TJ International Ltd.

Pen & Sword Books Ltd incorporates the Imprints of Pen & Sword Books Archaeology, Atlas, Aviation, Battleground, Discovery, Family History, History, Maritime, Military, Naval, Politics, Railways, Select, Transport, True Crime, Fiction, Frontline Books, Leo Cooper, Praetorian Press, Seaforth Publishing, Wharncliffe and White Owl.

For a complete list of Pen & Sword titles please contact
PEN & SWORD BOOKS LIMITED
47 Church Street, Barnsley, South Yorkshire, S70 2AS, England
E-mail: enquiries@pen-and-sword.co.uk
Website: www.pen-and-sword.co.uk

Or
PEN AND SWORD BOOKS
1950 Lawrence Rd, Havertown, PA 19083, USA
E-mail: Uspen-and-sword@casematepublishers.com
Website: www.penandswordbooks.com

Contents

Introduction viii
David Danskin 1
George Leavey 3
Harry Bradshaw 5
John Dick 8
Andy Ducat 10
Roddy McEachrane 12
George Morrell 14
Sir Henry Norris 16
Leslie Knighton 19
Bob John 22
Jimmy Brain 24
Dan Lewis 26
Herbert Chapman 29
Jack Lambert 34
Joe Hulme 36
Tom Parker 38
David Jack 40
Herbie Roberts 42
Frank Moss 44
Joe Shaw 46
George Allison 48
George Male 51
Eddie Hapgood 53
Cliff Bastin 55
Alex James 57
Ray Bowden 59
Ted Drake 61

Arsenal: The Story of a Football Club in 101 Lives

Wilf Copping	63
Jack Crayston	65
Bernard Joy	67
Reg Lewis	69
Leslie Compton	71
Bryn Jones	73
Ronnie Rooke	75
Tom Whittaker	77
George Swindin	79
Cliff Holton	81
Doug Lishman	83
Jack Kelsey	85
David Herd	87
Geoff Strong	89
George Eastham	91
Frank McLintock	93
The Hill-Woods	95
Peter Storey	97
Bertie Mee	99
Sammy Nelson	101
Bob Wilson	103
John Radford	105
Pat Rice	107
Ray Kennedy	109
Charlie George	111
George Armstrong	113
Alan Ball	115
Liam Brady	117
Frank Stapleton	119
David O'Leary	121
Graham Rix	123
Malcolm Macdonald	125
Pat Jennings	127
Alan Sunderland	129
Brian Talbot	131
Kenny Sansom	133
Tony Adams	135
Charlie Nicholas	137
David Rocastle	139

Contents

Viv Anderson	141
Paul Merson	143
George Graham	145
Nigel Winterburn	147
Alan Smith	149
Steve Bould	151
Lee Dixon	153
David Seaman	155
Anders Limpar	157
Ray Parlour	159
Ian Wright	161
Martin Keown	163
Dennis Bergkamp	165
David Platt	167
Patrick Vieira	169
Emmanuel Petit	171
Marc Overmars	173
Freddie Ljungberg	175
Thierry Henry	177
Kanu	179
Robert Pires	181
Cesc Fabregas	183
Lauren	185
Sol Campbell	187
Jens Lehmann	189
Robin van Persie	191
Kolo Toure	193
Jack Wilshere	195
Mikel Arteta	197
Laurent Koscielny	199
Arsene Wenger	201
Ivan Gazidis	203
David Dein	205
Stan Kroenke	207
Unai Emery	209
Bibliography	211
Index	214

Introduction

'To say that these men paid their shillings to watch twenty-two hirelings kick a ball is merely to say that a violin is wood and catgut, that Hamlet is so much paper and ink.' So wrote J. B. Priestley in *The Good Companions* in 1929. It is my favourite literary passage.

Ninety-odd years later, football has changed so much. Whereas for Priestley's fan 'it offered you more than a shilling's worth of material for talk during the rest of the week', now you almost need a bank loan to pay for a season ticket to watch Premier League football.

And yet football has also stayed the same. Football clubs are not simply businesses. They go far beyond that, filling a unique gap in the emotional lives of hundreds of thousands of people as 'cheering together, thumping one another on the shoulders, swapping judgements like lords of the earth', they have pushed their way through a turnstile 'into another and altogether more splendid kind of life'.

And it is other people's lives that have made them. Players, managers, directors – down the decades, across more than a century, Arsenal Football Club has been moulded by men whose talents have been revered (and sometimes jeered), management skills applauded (and sometimes criticised), and ownership motives questioned, because supporters care more than anyone who is not a fan can imagine.

In this book, I have attempted to tell the story of the Gunners through the lives of 101 people (it's actually 103 because I couldn't leave out any of the Hill-Woods but I cheated and put them all in 1 entry). It does not pretend to be a list of all the best players because that is too subjective, although you will probably find your favourites here. It is a collection of men whose stories mirror the story of Arsenal.

The information has been drawn from a number of sources, but mainly from contemporary newspapers. You will find that an occasional detail in this book differs from what has been previously published,

Introduction

especially online. An example is the 1920s goalscorer Jimmy Brain who is often mixed up with Joe Brain who plied his trade a decade later; there were two Brains, but Arsenal had only one. For most of the statistics – and the true football fan must have his statistics – I have relied on that exemplary researcher Fred Ollier's *Arsenal: A Complete Record* that I had the pleasure of publishing some years ago.

So here we go. I wonder what David Danskin would have made of Stan Kroenke?

David Danskin

Was he the 'man who founded Arsenal'? He was almost certainly the man who provided the inspiration for one of the world's most famous football clubs. David Danskin was born in Burntisland, Fife, in January 1863. By the age of 18 he was living in Kirkcaldy, working as an apprentice fitter and playing at half-back for Kirkcaldy Wanderers FC, pioneers of the game in Fife. So he already had a record for being in at the start. In 1885, now 22, he moved to Kent to work at the Royal Arsenal munitions factory where he was the driving force behind the formation of a football team raised among men at the Dial Square workshop.

In December 1886, they played their first match, against Eastern Wanderers on the Isle of Dogs. Elijah Watkins, the first secretary of Royal Arsenal FC, remembered the day well. His comments are reported in the book, *Association Football and the Men Who Made It*:

> Talk about a football pitch! Well this one eclipsed any I ever heard of, or saw. I could not venture to say what shape it was, but it was bounded by backyards about two-thirds of the area, and the other portion was ... I was going to say a ditch, but I think an open sewer would be more appropriate. We could not decide who won the game [some accounts credit the visitors with a 6-0 win] for when the ball was not in the back gardens it was in the ditch, and that was full of the loveliest material that could possibly be. Well, our fellows did not bring all of it away with them but they looked as though they had been clearing out a mud-shoot when they had done playing. I know because the attendant at the pub asked me what I was going to give him to clear the muck away.

On 8 January 1887, sandwiched between the report of a man charged with selling hams unfit for human consumption from a cart in Woolwich, and a line advertisement for Cadbury's Cocoa ('beware of imitations') the *Woolwich Gazette* reported that although a meeting of Dial Square Cricket Club had, the previous September, decided to form an 'Association Football team', it had subsequently been agreed to open up membership to all employees. Consequently, the name of the club would be Royal Arsenal Football Club. All this suggests that the game against Eastern Wanderers had been played under the cricket club banner and that there was never a Dial Square FC. Later that month the *Woolwich Gazette* reported that on Saturday, 22 January, Royal Arsenal beat Eastern Wanderers 1-0 at Plumstead to score 'another win against the Wanderers'. There is no mention of any other game between the clubs, so we must assume that the newspaper was referring to the December match played beside an open sewer at Millwall.

On 19 January 1889, playing against Clapton in the semi-final of the London Senior Cup at the Essex County Ground at Leyton, Danskin, the man who started it all, was injured. He turned out only a few more times before retiring. After failing to gain election to the club's committee, in 1893 he joined Royal Ordnance Factories FC, a club founded as a rival to Royal Arsenal FC. That club folded in 1896 and thereafter, Danskin's involvement with football was restricted to refereeing a few local matches and watching Royal Arsenal. By 1901 he was running a cycle shop in Plumstead. In 1907, he sold the business and moved to Coventry where he took a job as an examiner at the Standard Motor Company, which had been founded 4 years earlier. Danskin remained there for the rest of his working life. In failing health, he listened to the wireless broadcast of Arsenal's 1936 FA Cup final win from his sickbed. His football mementos, together with family valuables and photographs, disappeared after his house was damaged during the 1940 Coventry Blitz. Increasingly immobile, he died in a Warwick hospital in August 1948, aged 85. In 2007 Arsenal supporters in Scotland dedicated a blue plaque to him at his Burntisland birthplace. In 2019 a headstone, paid for by Arsenal, was unveiled at Danskin's grave in Coventry. At the Emirates Stadium, David Danskin's image is 1 of 32 depicting some of the club's greatest, figures on 8 giant murals on the stadium's exterior. History certainly records that he was indeed the man who founded Arsenal.

George Leavey

In August 1899, on the eve of the new football season, the *Sporting Life* promised supporters of the now renamed Woolwich Arsenal that 'great things are promised at Plumstead'. Very few of the old players had been retained, the newspaper reported, and the new players were a formidable lot. New manager Harry Bradshaw had free charge of the players, and during the summer 313 upholstered seats had been installed in the Grand Stand and all had been taken up, in addition to 1,200 season tickets. The club had obviously gone to a great deal of trouble on both the ground and the players, the paper said, but then 'their chairman, Mr George Leavey, never does things by halves, and his ambition is to bring the club into the First League if possible.'

George Hiram Leavey ran a small chain of gentlemen's outfitters and opened a branch in Woolwich in 1896. Two years later he joined the Woolwich Arsenal board of directors, and only a year after that he was the club's chairman. Leavey, along with George Lawrance, a newsagent and bookseller, was one of Arsenal's earliest benefactors. Without either man's support the club would have died. Lawrance attended the meeting in 1891 that approved Royal Arsenal adopting professionalism, and he oversaw the change of identity to Woolwich Arsenal in 1893. The same year he paid the deposit that enabled the club to purchase the Manor Field (later renamed Manor Ground). He was still in office when he died in June 1901, of heart failure caused by appendicitis.

Leavey, meanwhile, found that running both his clothing business and a professional football club was too much. He stepped down from the board and was elected president in 1900. He was, though, far more than just a figurehead. In 1910, he became chairman again after liquidating the struggling club – on several occasions he had paid the players' wages – so that it could be taken over by Sir Henry Norris.

In his first spell as Arsenal chairman, Leavey had railed against what he saw was a drink culture in football. At the 1899 annual general meeting he asked the public not to buy drinks for the players. Later that year he told a players' dinner, 'Do not let people stand you drinks ... . No man with a skinful of whisky can play football.'

At an extraordinary general meeting in January 1900, with the club struggling financially during the Boer War, he moved the resolution:

> That this meeting hears with regret of the difficulties of the Arsenal Football Club owing very largely to the continuous pressure of work in the Royal Arsenal, and hereby pledges itself to use every endeavour to assist the club through its present financial difficulties and heartily wishes the old club success and greater prosperity in the near future.

He told the meeting that 'they' – presumably the directors – were disappointed in the team, and the subsequent falling off in gate money. Despite wages being cut, he estimated that with all the liabilities, at the end of the season there would not be much left out of a cheque for £2,000. If 80 members each collected 10 shillings a week until the end of the season it would help things along. A committee was elected to raise funds, and in answer to 1 question Leavey said that the second 11 had been 'a disastrous and expensive failure'.

Between them Leavey and Lawrance, together with the business acumen of Jack Humble – one of the original Dial Square members who was a board member when Woolwich Arsenal became the first club from the south of England to be elected to the Football League in 1893 – steered matters to a point where Leavey could tell the 1903 annual general meeting that finances were 'eminently satisfactory'.

After Norris had taken over, Leavey remained as chairman until 1912. In April that year he announced that he had neither the time nor the resources to continue supporting Arsenal as he would wish, and he resigned. George Leavey, the man who lent the club money that he would never see again, and who saved Arsenal from oblivion, died in Buckingham on 18 January 1950, aged 92.

Harry Bradshaw

In the summer of 1899, 46-year-old Harry Bradshaw was announced as the new manager of Woolwich Arsenal. Bradshaw had never played football as a professional. Appointed Burnley's club secretary in 1891 and chairman 2 years later, he took over the role of manager in 1896. At the end of his first season the Clarets were relegated. However, a year later they were back in the top flight, and the *Burnley Express* described his leaving as a 'severe blow to Burnley Football Club'. The *Kentish Independent*, commenting on his move to Arsenal, felt that 'in the person of Mr Harry Bradshaw a capable man has been found.' He was the third person to be charged with Arsenal's playing fortunes, following in the footsteps of Thomas Brown Mitchell, the club's first professional manager, and George Elcoat, who between them managed less than 2 seasons running the show.

Bradshaw's decision to leave a club third in the First Division for one that had just finished seventh in the Second Division was not easy to fathom. Woolwich Arsenal's financial situation was dire. Attendances at the Manor Ground rarely reached 7,000 and were generally around 4,000. There was a reported 20,000 for the visit of Derby County in the third round of the FA Cup in January 1899 – Arsenal lost 6-0 – but the figure was probably exaggerated.

With money tight, Bradshaw looked around for local talent. Goalkeeper Jimmy Ashcroft came from Gravesend United, and full-back Archie Cross from Dartford. Ashcroft would make 303 appearances for Arsenal and play 3 times for England; Cross would make 149 appearances. Both would help the club win promotion. The new manager looked further afield for defenders Jimmy Jackson, from Newcastle United, and Duncan McNichol, from Scottish club St Bernard's. Jackson would also play in a promotion-winning team.

Arsenal finished 1 place lower than the previous season, but in 1901-02 they were fourth. Better results brought bigger gate receipts.

Roddy McEachrane came from West Ham United and would make 346 appearances. Then an entire forward line was signed: Tommy Briercliffe from Stalybridge; Tim Coleman from Northampton Town; Bill Gooing from Chesterfield; Tom Shanks from Brentford and Billy Linward from West Ham United. They, too, would all win promotion with the Gunners. Coleman would be capped by England while with Arsenal.

In 1902-03 Arsenal finished third and the following season won promotion, but not before Bradshaw had been tempted by a big-money offer from Southern League Fulham. The announcement that he would leave the Manor Ground at the end of the season came as early as 20 February 1904, the day of an FA Cup second-round tie against Manchester City. The *Kentish Independent* said it was the 'sensation of the season ... that Mr Harry Bradshaw is to leave ... . What does it all mean? How much is behind it? Who will be the new manager? These and a hundred other questions have been agitating the public breast ever since.' The *Athletic News* said that 'unfeigned astonishment will prevail in London today'.

Bradshaw had written to the Arsenal chairman, John Humble, on 26 January to hand in his notice, telling Humble that, 'I leave it entirely with you as to the time that this letter shall be made public. I am anxious that nothing shall be done which may be thought to have a tendency to unease the team ... or jeopardise the chances of promotion in the League.'

The *Kentish Independent* said, 'A better or more loyal manager will be very difficult to find.' On 8 April 1904, the *Woolwich Gazette* announced that Phil Kelso, the 33-year-old manager of Hibernian, had taken over and thus 'this weekend will see the completion of Mr Bradshaw's service with the Arsenal club.' But did it? Two weeks later Arsenal ended their season with a goalless draw against Burslem Port Vale at the Manor Ground before a crowd of 20,000. Preston North End still had 1 game remaining (they won that 5 days later, beating Blackpool 1-0 at home to lift the title by a single point), but Arsenal's draw meant that they were promoted whatever the Preston result.

The *Woolwich Gazette* painted the scene:

> The air was alive with bombs, crackers, squibs, rockets ... even a balloon was sent aloft to send the glad tidings far and wide. Round the players' enclosure the crowd gathered in thousands ... the names of Mr George Leavey

and Mr Harry Bradshaw ... were called until the crowd seem to be afflicted with one huge gigantic cold, so hoarse had they become. Kelso sat in the stand for the Burslem match, at the end of which Bradshaw – who had signed eighteen of the twenty players to appear that season – was presented with a medallion upon which was inscribed, 'To H. Bradshaw from the Players of the Woolwich Arsenal Football Club, 1904.' The following day the *Southern Echo* was still referring to Bradshaw as 'the Arsenal manager who will be in charge of Fulham next season'.

At Fulham, he won the Southern League twice before taking them into the Football League and to the FA Cup semi-finals. In 1909 he became secretary of the Southern League, an office he held until his death on 28 September 1924, at the age of 71 after undergoing an operation at Wimbledon Hospital. Harry Bradshaw was buried at Putney Vale Cemetery. He was Arsenal's first truly successful manager.

John Dick

In August 1898, Woolwich Arsenal were involved in a player exchange when 21-year-old half-back John Dick, a stonemason by trade, arrived from Airdrieonians with reserve centre-forward James Devlin going in the opposite direction. Arsenal had the best of the deal. Devlin, who had made only 1 League appearance for the Gunners – he had fallen ill with pleurisy soon after arriving from Sunderland for £80 and never appeared again despite marking his debut with a goal – was soon on his way to Third Lanark and then Albion Rovers before serving in the Army during the Boer War.

Dick, meanwhile, would go on to make 284 appearances for his new club. His debut came against Luton Town in a Second Division match at Dunstable Road on 3 September. Arsenal won 1-0 and the *Luton Times and Advertiser* reported that 'the new centre-half, Dick, of the Airdrieonians, played a steady, useful game and was not as rough as his two partners.' The newspaper also reported that the gate money was rather disappointing 'but the summer-like weather must have tempted many to go out cycling.'

William Elcoat, who in his short tenure as Arsenal manager brought several Scottish players to Plumstead, signed Dick, a centre-half in the days when that position was a link between defence and attack; Herbert Chapman's 'stopper' was some decades away. In his first season Dick missed only 4 Second Division games, and was almost ever-present for the next 6 seasons in 1899-1900, missing only 1 match.

Dick was what we might call today a 'box-to-box-player'. His stamina is perhaps best illustrated by the fact that he also excelled as a cross-country runner. It was reported that he once ran 6½ miles in under 34 minutes, which, if correct, is remarkable even by today's standards. In those days some centre-halves scored plenty of goals. Dick was not 1 of them. He scored just 13, 2 of them coming in Arsenal's record win in a competitive match – 12-0 against Loughborough Town in March 1900.

John Dick

With the arrival in the first team of schoolteacher Percy Sands in September 1903, Dick moved to right-half. As Arsenal won promotion that season he played in every game but 1, with injury ruling him out of the 3-1 defeat at Burton United in January 1904. Dick had been the Arsenal captain but by the time promotion was confirmed, left-back Jimmy Jackson, a fellow Scot, had taken over.

As Arsenal settled in the First Division, Dick remained their first-choice right-half and that season he passed the 200-game mark for the club. In November 1905, however, he lost his place to the former West Ham United player James Bigden. That season Arsenal allowed Dick to play 1 game for Crystal Palace in the Southern League's Second Division. Thereafter he appeared only sporadically in the Arsenal first team, his final League appearance coming in a 1-0 home defeat by Blackburn Rovers in February 1910.

Towards the end of his time at Arsenal, Dick coached young players and ran a confectioner's and tobacconist's business in Pattison Road, Plumstead. In the summer of 1912, however, he went off to what was then part of the Austro-Hungarian Empire. He became player-coach of Deutscher FC Prag, a club founded by German Jews. Arsenal had recently played them in a friendly in Prague. When the First World War broke out in July 1914, Dick found himself in enemy land, but in Czech territory and so escaping internment. After the new country of Czechoslovakia was proclaimed in October 1918, Dick moved to AC Sparta and turned them into a trophy-winning team. In 1922 he moved to Beerschot, who played in Antwerp, home of the 1920 Olympic Games, and over the next 5 years won them 4 Belgian titles. Then it was back to Prague (where 2 of his 6 children had been born) and a second spell with AC Sparta who won their league in 1931-32. But Dick was now seriously ill and the club gave him extended leave. He was suffering from cancer and died in Welling, Kent, on 14 September 1932, aged 55. Remarkably, his death went unrecorded in British newspapers but the Prague-based, German-language *Prager Tagblatt* wrote: 'He enjoyed great popularity everywhere because of his humble nature, and his advice was always well received.'

Andy Ducat

Writing in the *Athletic News* on 13 February 1905, 'Busy Bee' described the Woolwich Arsenal debut of 'a 19-year-old youngster named Ducat' as 'a daring experiment'. As far as Busy Bee was concerned it was an experiment that did not succeed, adding: 'It must be said that the line, as constituted on Saturday, is far from satisfactory.'

Yet Busy Bee saw potential:

> Ducat is young and he will no doubt make headway. Splendidly built, he has the right conception of what constitutes the duties of a pivot, but he lacks experience, and the Woolwich club, rich in patrons – a club with unequalled opportunities of making history – cannot afford to persevere with the undeveloped player. I don't wish it to be inferred that Ducat was a failure. He often showed promise, but he failed to make the most of his chances.

Writing in the same newspaper, another journalist was more positive about the former Southend Athletic centre-forward who, after scoring twice for Arsenal's reserve team in a 5-1 win over Hastings the previous week, had been promoted for the First Division match against Blackburn Rovers at the Manor Ground:

> It was a trying ordeal to be put straight into First Division football practically from a very junior team. But Ducat is made of the right stuff; he showed a surprising amount of confidence; he made some good wing passes; and he was always worrying the backs … . Altogether a very creditable debut for a youngster who is worthy of encouragement. Too much must not be expected from so raw a youth, but Ducat's

good point is his bustle, and the value of bustling centre-forwards is well known.

Arsenal won 2-0 that afternoon. Ducat retained his place for the rest of the season and by the time he was transferred to Aston Villa for £1,500 in June 1912, had scored 21 goals in 188 League and FA Cup games for Arsenal and had won 3 England caps. His goal tally may seem moderate for a centre-forward but the fact is he lost his place the following season and most of his career at the Manor Ground was as a right-half. There he blossomed, becoming a regular as Arsenal struggled to establish themselves in the top flight. His England debut came in a 1-1 draw with Ireland at Cliftonville in February 1910. A month later he scored the only goal of the match against Wales in Cardiff.

Although he broke his leg in September 1912 and missed the rest of the season, his career reached new heights with Villa – 3 more England caps and captaining the 1920 FA Cup winners. However, Ducat much preferred living in London – during the First World War he guested for Arsenal – and in May 1921 he was transferred to Fulham. He retired as a player in 1924 and took over as manager. At that point, all of the Cottagers' managers had Arsenal connections as Ducat followed Harry Bradshaw and Phil Kelso (who had signed him for Arsenal) to Craven Cottage. In 1926, though, he was the first Fulham manager to be sacked – his predecessors had resigned – and he was reinstated as an amateur so that he could play for Casuals FC.

Ducat was also a fine cricketer with 52 centuries for Surrey between 1906 and 1931, and a Test cap against Australia in 1921, making him 1 of the few men to play for England at both sports. He coached in Queensland during the 1929-30 Australia cricket season, and at Eton College, and worked as a journalist, ran a sports outfitter and was a licensee. It was with a cricket bat in his hand that he died, collapsing at the crease while playing for 5th Battalion Surrey Home Guard against Worthing Home Guard at Lord's in July 1942. He was 56 and suffering from heart disease. His obituary in *Wisden* described him as 'a man of delightful disposition, quiet and unassuming, he endeared himself to all who met him.'

Roddy McEachrane

Roddy McEachrane was a midfielder and a deep-lying one at that. Under 3 different managers – Harry Bradshaw, Phil Kelso and George Morrell – he made 346 appearances for Woolwich Arsenal but never scored a goal. That long career encompassed highs and lows and a momentous event in the club's story. McEachrane helped gain promotion from the Second Division in 1903-04, played in 2 consecutive FA Cup semi-finals, was still playing when the Gunners were relegated in 1912-13, and a few months later made his final League appearance during the first season at Highbury.

He was born in Inverness in February 1877, and when he was 20 he moved to Canning Town to seek employment at Thames Ironworks. He joined the football team and the 1905 book, *Association Football and the Men Who Made It*, told the following story:

> Among the workmen was Roddy McEachrane, the Arsenal half-back who came all the way from Inverness to get employment. One day he told somebody that he could play football, and that he had turned out at home for Clac-na-Cudden, a name that everyone could not pronounce. Every Scotsman is supposed to play football well, and so McEachrane was soon included in the Works team. He has gone on playing football ever since and was registered as a professional in 1898 when Thames Ironworks decided to engage paid players.

McEachrane had been a member of the successful Highland League club, Clachnacuddin FC, and in 1898-99 he was an ever-present when Thames Ironworks won the Southern League's Second Division. In September 1899 *The Berkshire Chronicle* noted that, 'Thames Ironworks are a team which will be heard of a good deal this season … McEachrane is a player of more than average ability.' The writer was an excellent judge: McEachrane was again ever-present for each of the next 2 seasons, by which time the club was known as West Ham United.

In May 1902, McEachrane – 'reputed to be the finest half in Southern League football last year' – signed for Woolwich Arsenal. The *Kentish Independent* said that the new man 'had played a wonderfully consistent game for West Ham during the current season.' By coincidence his debut in an Arsenal shirt came against West Ham, in a London League game at the Memorial Grounds on 1 September 1902. Arsenal, supported by a surprising number of travelling fans for a Monday, won 3-1 and it might have been more: 'A furious shot by McEachrane would probably have reached its billet had it not been for the intervention of Eccles [the West Ham right-back].' His Football League debut came against Preston North End at the Manor Ground the following Saturday. It was the beginning of a long Arsenal career.

McEachrane's first 2 seasons saw Arsenal finish third, and then promoted as runners-up, after which he was joined by other West Ham players: Charlie Satterthwaite (April 1904) and James Bigden (June 1904). McEachrane was 33 when he lost his regular place, to Angus McKinnon in January 1912, but he remained with the club, making his final League appearance in a 1-0 win at home to Birmingham in November 1913. His last game in Arsenal's colours came in a South-Eastern League match at Croydon in April 1915, and at the end of that season proper competitive football was suspended for the duration of the First World War. During the war McEachrane worked, appropriately enough, at the Royal Arsenal munitions factory. When the Second World War broke out he was working as a boilermaker and living at Leghorn Road, Plumstead, with his wife, Bertha. He died in Woolwich in 1952, aged 74.

George Morrell

George Morrell was Arsenal's first manager after the Gunners moved to Highbury in 1913. He also has the less enviable distinction of being the only manager in the club's history to see them relegated. He came from the Scottish school – committee member, secretary, treasurer, president and occasional player with a Glasgow junior club called Glenure Athletic. Then he ran Glasgow Rangers' reserve team and also found the time to qualify as a referee before, in 1905, being appointed secretary-manager of cash-strapped Greenock Morton. He helped them to solvency and a place in the Scottish First Division before moving to another club that was struggling financially, and for support – Woolwich Arsenal.

On 8 February 1908, the *Greenock Telegraph and Clyde Shipping Gazette* reported that he was to leave Morton 'tomorrow' and commented, 'This appointment to so important a club is a distinct compliment to Mr Morrell.' According to *The Scottish Referee* he left after the match at Easter Road: 'Parting, we are told, is sweet sorrow ... let us hope that in his new sphere he may be able to influence goals and points galore, and that under his guidance Woolwich Arsenal will prosper and flourish.'

At Plumstead, Morrell took over from Phil Kelso, who had resigned and returned to Scotland to run a hotel in Largs. Within months of Morrell taking over, players of the calibre of Tim Coleman, Peter Kyle, Bert Freeman, Jimmy Ashcroft, Jimmy Sharp and Billy Garbutt had been sold. However, in his first season, Arsenal finished a respectable sixth in the First Division and goalkeeper Leigh Richmond Roose – an amateur but still a Wales international and one of the great celebrity footballers of his day – and former England centre-forward Alf Common, the first player to be transferred for £1,000 when he moved from Middlesbrough to Sunderland in 1905, were signed. In April 1909, the *Yorkshire Telegraph Football and Sports Special* said, 'Evidently Mr George Morrell intends

Woolwich to be "all Scotch". Of the fifteen players signed to date, eleven are Scots! And in London too! What are the Arsenal directors doing?'

In December 1908 Morrell had been the target of the *Woolwich Gazette* that published a heavily sarcastic critique of 'a History of Arsenal Football Club published by a now weekly paper, written by "George Morrell" … . No one knowing anything about the club could have written such weak stuff.'

While Morrell was earning a few extra pounds by allowing his name to be credited with penning a ghost-written series, Arsenal's financial crisis deepened and Common, together with Andy Ducat, had to be sold. In 1911-12 Woolwich Arsenal were relegated, finishing bottom of the table. The following season, the club moved to north London and the fight to regain a place in the top flight continued until the Football League closed down at the end of 1914-15 when it transpired that the First World War was not over by Christmas after all. Morrell resigned in April 1915. He returned to Scotland and from 1917 to 1921 managed Third Lanark. In June 1921 *The Sunday Post* reported that he had been 'the recipient of a beautiful timepiece from the collectors and money-checkers at Cathkin Park. He is due to leave the Warriors shortly and may take charge of one of the leading League clubs in England.' Morrell did not return to England, nor, so far as anyone knows, manage any other club. Even the date of his death is apparently unrecorded.

Sir Henry Norris

Photographs show a man who looked quite like one of those silent film villains that tied young women to railway lines. Indeed, accusations of villainy followed him throughout his adult life. He is forever associated with the storm that surrounded Arsenal's promotion to the First Division in 1919, and he was later accused of embezzlement. The name of Sir Henry Norris is the most controversial in Arsenal's history. He was also perhaps the most influential.

Although born to a working-class family in Kennington in July 1865, his career was anything but ordinary. Privately educated, he joined a firm of solicitors at 14, made a fortune in house building in Fulham and Wimbledon, was a prominent Freemason, served as the last mayor of the old metropolitan borough of Fulham, was a member of London County Council, and Conservative MP for Fulham East from December 1918 to October 1922. He was also chairman of Fulham FC. In 1910, he became the majority shareholder of ailing Woolwich Arsenal, and, 2 years later, its chairman.

Norris set about turning a troubled club into one of the game's most famous and successful, albeit he would not be in office when the peak was achieved. His first move in that direction was a bold one: in 1913, he moved the club from Plumstead, south-east London to north of the capital, to a site at Highbury which housed the recreation ground of St John's College of Divinity. His close friendship with the Archbishop of Canterbury, Randall Thomas Davidson, helped here. It was the archbishop who signed the ground's title deed over to Woolwich Arsenal. Arsenal Stadium opened in 1913, and the following year 'Woolwich' was dropped from the club's name.

When the First World War broke out in July 1914, the Football League continued for another year and Arsenal finished the season in fifth place in the Second Division. Then the League was suspended in favour of regional wartime competitions. When the League resumed in 1919, somehow Arsenal were promoted although Barnsley and Wolves had finished ahead of them behind the champions, Derby County, and the runners-up, Preston North End. More to the point, Tottenham Hotspur, bottom of the First Division, were still relegated even though the division was being extended from 20 to 22 clubs and previous extensions had seen bottom clubs re-elected. Chelsea, who had finished next to bottom, 1 point ahead of Spurs, were spared.

Allegations of undue influence and downright bribery were rife. Critics targeted Norris, and also the owner of Liverpool, John McKenna. At the 1919 Football League annual meeting, McKenna supported Arsenal's claim over Spurs because of Arsenal's longer membership of the Football League, although Wolves, 2 places ahead of Arsenal in the 1914-15 Second Division, were founder members in 1888.

So, Sir Henry Norris had moved Arsenal to north London, and he had engineered their promotion to the top flight of English football in a manner that few would have thought possible. He was to make 1 more major contribution. After the messy sacking of manager Leslie Knighton in 1925, he appointed Herbert Chapman, the manager of Huddersfield Town, to succeed Knighton. Chapman's reign at Highbury would see Arsenal as the dominant team in English football in the 1930s.

Meanwhile, controversy dogged Norris until his death. In 1927 an FA commission ruled that he had improperly taken £539 from Arsenal in order to pay his chauffeur's wages, and £125 for 'a season's use of his car'. The commission ordered him to repay £664 and permanently suspended him from taking part in football or football management. Subsequently Norris brought a libel action against the Football Association. When the case was heard in February 1929, Sir Patrick Hastings, opening for Norris, said that his client 'had a record of which any man in the country might be proud'. Of Sir Henry's association with Arsenal, Sir Patrick said, 'It is not too much to say that he made the club.' Norris had personally guaranteed £50,000 under the covenants of the lease at Highbury, and on another occasion given personal security for £10,000 borrowed from a bank: 'The club was his baby and he managed its finances.'

However, the *Daily Mail* had claimed that in 1925 Norris had made under-the-counter payments to Sunderland's Charlie Buchan as an inducement to sign for Arsenal, and Sir Patrick agreed that 'irregularities committed by Sir Henry as between himself and the League are admitted.'

Buchan was in court to hear all this. Asked if the payment to Buchan was a breach of the rules, Norris said, 'You cannot call compensation for loss of business an increase in wages.' He was referring to Buchan's sportswear shop in Sunderland that would obviously suffer if Buchan was not there.

Asked if he had received payments to himself in advances for expenses to be incurred later, Norris replied, 'There was nothing in me having a cheque for £170 when the club has had thousands of pounds of mine.' Norris lost his action for libel and also failed to secure an injunction restraining the FA from suspending him.

Sir Henry Norris died in Barnes on 30 July 1934, a week after his 69th birthday. He had suffered a heart attack. His estate was valued at £71,000 – almost £5 million today – and now a softer persona emerged. It was said that many of the 2,000 houses he had built were kept to affordable prices for less well-off people. He also left money to many of his former employees including Arsenal staff. Leslie Knighton, the manager he had so acrimoniously sacked, was shocked to receive £100 from the estate. Maybe Sir Henry Norris was not so much a villain after all.

Leslie Knighton

Leslie Knighton was a long-serving manager of Arsenal but one who achieved very little. In his 6 years at Highbury, the Gunners never scored more goals than they conceded, their best finishing position was ninth, and twice they narrowly avoided relegation to the Second Division. According to Knighton's 1948 memoirs, *Behind the Scenes in Big Football*, his task was continually dogged by Sir Henry Norris who dictated how the job should be done, setting guidelines that made progress on the field difficult, if not impossible. We shall see.

Knighton was a native of the South Derbyshire coalfield, born at Castle Gresley in March 1884. His playing career was cut short by injury and in his mid-20s he was managing Castleford Town in the Midland League. In February 1911, he resigned to become assistant-secretary-manager of Huddersfield Town, and 18 months later took a similar job at Manchester City.

In April 1919, the *Manchester Evening News* reported:

> Mr Leslie Knighton, who has for several years acted as assistant secretary to Manchester City, has been appointed team manager of the Arsenal, a post of considerable responsibility now that the London club has been elected to the First Division. Popular alike with officials and players, Mr Knighton will have a greater scope for the exercise of that keen judgement he has long been known to possess and should be a decided acquisition to his new club.

The new manager soon found himself hamstrung by yet another Arsenal financial crisis. but he ploughed on. In November 1919 'Custodian', writing in *The Globe*, told of a chat he'd had with Leslie Knighton 'the enterprising manager of the Arsenal Football Club who has introduced many innovations into London team management.' Knighton told his interviewer:

> Football is not just a case of one match and then an easy life. Players have to keep in the pink of condition for a whole season … . Many footballers spend the close season at the seaside or in the country and live a healthy open-air life … . We have probably the most conscientious team in England. Every member of the Arsenal realises his club's as well as his own standpoint, and none of them ever shirks training, though it is left so much to his own judgement and inclinations.

The new manager was certainly popular with reporters. In December 1919, *The (Sheffield) Star Green 'Un* wrote, 'Arrangements for the Press on the Arsenal ground are capital and so on behalf of Pressmen we take the opportunity of recording our appreciation of Mr Leslie Knighton's kind attention to the requirements of the Fourth Estate.'

According to his autobiography, Knighton's 6 years at Highbury were handicapped by Sir Henry Norris setting a transfer fee cap of £1,000, and banning the signing of any player who stood less than 5ft 8in tall or weighed less than 11 stone. It was claimed that when, in 1923, Knighton signed a 5ft-tall outside-right called Harold Moffat from North-Eastern League club Workington, Norris was furious and quickly moved him on to Third Division South Luton Town. This was despite the fact Moffat had done well in that summer's end-of-season tour of Scandinavia. He certainly never played for the Gunners in a League game but there are no newspaper accounts of an instant move. In August 1923, *The Sportsman* reported that 'H. Moffat is a nippy little executant on the wing'. In September, reporting on Arsenal Reserves' London Combination game against West Ham United, the *Athletic News* said, 'The feature was the display at outside-right by the diminutive player, Moffat.' At the end of that season Moffat moved to Guildford and from there joined Luton in May 1925. Far from being too small for Norris, Moffat was probably just not good enough for the top flight. In May 1926 he was transferred to Everton but managed only 2 First Division appearances before they moved him on to Second Division Oldham Athletic, for whom he did not play before dropping back into the third tier with Walsall and QPR.

Leslie Knighton

There is little or no supporting evidence for any of Knighton's claims, although at the 1923 Football League annual meeting Norris did propose, unsuccessfully, that transfer fees be capped at £1,650.

Whatever Norris did or didn't do, Knighton's time at Arsenal saw modest progress at best, and a struggle for much of the time, although he did sign Bob John, Jimmy Brain and Alf Baker, all of whom played in trophy-winning Arsenal teams in the 1930s. In May 1925, after Arsenal had finished twentieth out of 22 clubs in the First Division, the Press Association reported: 'Mr Knighton and his directors have not seen eye to eye on the conduct on the affairs of the conduct of the organisation, and they have decided to part company on terms of mutual respect.'

Two months after leaving Arsenal, Knighton took over as manager of Bournemouth. He took Birmingham to the 1931 FA Cup final, and from 1933 he managed Chelsea for 6 years up to the Second World War. He managed Midland League Shrewsbury Town from 1945 to 1948, and was later secretary of a golf club in Bournemouth. He died in hospital in Bournemouth in May 1959, aged 72, after undergoing major surgery.

Bob John

The *Athletic News* reporter 'Achates' was not impressed by the Arsenal debut of 23-year-old left-half Bob John against Newcastle United at Highbury in October 1922. He said, 'Baker is a wonderful utility man, but he was sadly missed from the half-back division in which Milne thoroughly justified his selection, but John was weak.' The *Daily Herald* was equally critical, saying, 'John was a source of great weakness.'

That day the Gunners went down 2-1, having the previous week earned a creditable draw at St James's Park. John's debut, according to the *Athletic News,* had come in a game 'at times poor enough to make one sigh for the days of old, but more frequently sparkling with incidents of brilliance in attempts to score and prevent a score.'

John, who Leslie Knighton had signed for Arsenal from Caerphilly for £750 the previous January, had been given his chance because the regular left-half, Tom Whittaker, was injured. Whittaker returned the following week but by the beginning of December, John was back in the side and then missed only 1 game to the end of the 1922-23 season in which Arsenal finished eleventh in the First Division. There was a further hiccup – in 1923-24 John lost his place – but after being switched to left-back he was almost an ever-present in 1924-25, and then, back at left-half, he remained a regular in the first team switching between full-back and half-back.

First impressions were obviously misleading. The player who had had a 'weak' debut for Arsenal went on to clock up 467 appearances (13 goals) before his final League game, at home to Birmingham in March 1937. No other pre-war Arsenal player played more times for the club as he sailed past the record – 350 – set by Percy Sands before the competitions were suspended in 1915.

John's career spanned the greatest period in Arsenal's history: football League champions in 1930-31, 1932-33, 1933-34 and 1934-35, albeit in the latter season he managed only 9 appearances having lost his place to Wilf Copping. He played in Arsenal's first FA Cup final, in 1927, and in their first FA Cup-winning team, in 1930, as well as gaining another runners-up medal in 1932 when he scored the Gunners' goal in their controversial 2-1 defeat by Newcastle United. Photographic evidence later showed that the ball was clearly out of play before Newcastle's Jimmy Richardson crossed it back into play for Jack Allen to equalise John's 15th-minute opener. VAR was still more than 85 years away.

John was a ball-winner who passed it well. He won 15 caps for Wales while with Arsenal, a good return in the days when there were few international matches beyond the 3 in each season's Home Championship. Reporting on his first selection, against Scotland at Love Street, home of St Mirren, in March 1923, Achates of the *Athletic News* wrote:

> John got on the ladder of progress when the Arsenal management decided on the drastic course of practically scrapping their recognised first team at a period when the outlook was dark indeed … . I well remember John's debut in the League team, and he could not be written down as a success. Yet there were signs that he possessed football ability, and as he improved a lot with each game it is not surprising that he has kept his place. He is not the complete half-back yet, although his play in some recent games has reached a high standard. I am convinced that this young Welshman will become a notable player.

John's final 3 years at Highbury were spent mainly in the reserve team and mentoring younger players. His final League appearance resulted in a 1-1 draw when John saved the day with a goal-line clearance. His career at Highbury had started with Jock Rutherford, Jack Butler and Alf Baker as teammates; it ended in the company of Eddie Hapgood, Ray Bowden and Denis Compton.

After leaving Arsenal, Bob John was a coach at West Ham United, and after the Second World War he coached and managed Torquay United, was trainer at Crystal Palace and worked as a coach and a scout for Cardiff City. He died in his birthplace, Barry, on 17 July 1982, aged 83.

Jimmy Brain

When in May 1923, Arsenal signed a 22-year-old centre-forward from Welsh League football, *The Sportsman* told readers that 'Brain of Ton Pentre has the reputation of cleverness as leader of the attack.' Just over 2 years later Jimmy Brain was embarking on a record-breaking season that would bring him 34 League goals, up to then the most any Arsenal player had scored in 1 campaign.

Brain was not quite ready to step up to the top flight of English football immediately, but he was a quick learner. He made his League debut against Spurs at Highbury on 25 October 1924 and scored the only goal of the game. By the end of the season – Leslie Knighton's last as Arsenal manager – Brain had scored 12 goals in 28 League games, a vital contribution in the fight to avoid relegation.

In 1925-26, with Herbert Chapman now at the helm, it seemed that Brain just could not stop scoring. There were hat-tricks against Everton home and away, Cardiff City and Bury. The following season he scored 31. Twice there were 4 goals in a game, against Sheffield Wednesday and Burnley, and another hat-trick against Cardiff. In those 2 seasons Arsenal finished runners-up and then eleventh. Twice they also managed to lose 7-0, first at Newcastle and then at West Ham.

Brain was Arsenal's outright leading scorer 3 seasons in a row – in 1924-25 he tied with Harry Woods – and he played in the 1927 FA Cup final defeat by Cardiff. When Arsenal finally won the Cup, in 1930, Brain missed out. David Jack, Jack Lambert and Dave Halliday were all recognised ahead of Brain who managed only 6 League appearances that season. The following season of 1930-31, when the Gunners won the Football League title for the first time, he made 16 League appearances and scored 4 goals. Three of them came in the 7-1 win over Blackpool at Highbury in December. His final League appearance was in a 2-0 win over Sheffield Wednesday on 21 March 1931.

Jimmy Brain

The following September, Brain was transferred to Spurs for £2,500. For Arsenal, he had scored 139 League and FA Cup goals in 231 appearances. It was a remarkable strike rate. Yet he never played for England; the nearest he got was an international trial. He was 31 when he joined Tottenham, for whom he scored 10 goals in 47 games.

In April 1935 Spurs released Brain and the following month he took over as player-manager of Eastern Counties League club King's Lynn Town. In the summer of 1936 he was back at Highbury as a member of the Arsenal coaching staff and in April 1937, he became secretary-manager of Southern League Cheltenham Town. He remained in that job until January 1948. His last piece of business was to transfer young centre-forward Peter Goring to Arsenal for a Cheltenham Town record fee of £1,000. Jimmy Brain died in Barnet in 1971.

Note: Many football historians have Jimmy Brain playing for Swansea Town and Bristol City. They confuse him with Joe Brain, the former Sunderland, Norwich City, Barrow and Preston North End centre-forward who ended his career with those clubs.

Dan Lewis

He will always be remembered as the goalkeeper whose slip sent the FA Cup out of England for the first – and so far only – time.

Dan Lewis was a coalminer playing part-time football for Mardy in the Welsh League when Second Division Clapton Orient signed him in April 1924. Or did they? Lewis's career, if it can be called that, with Orient was short and apparently not very sweet. He was on their retained list in May 1924, but on 2 August the Football League announced that it had refused his registration, and on 24 August it fined Orient £20 for playing him – although he never appeared in the first team – without first having registered him as a professional. The subsequent registration was cancelled and Orient were banned from registering him again. For his part in whatever had transpired, Lewis was fined £5.

On 30 August, an agency report read:

> The full story of the cancellation of Lewis, the ex-Mardy goalkeeper, as a Clapton Orient player and his subsequent signing for the Arsenal may never be known outside official circles. We have tried to get to the root of the business but have failed. Yet it is certain that the Arsenal have obtained a goalkeeper of undoubted ability, and one who is going to rise in the game.

Lewis's League debut for the Gunners came in the fifteenth game of the 1924-25 season, at Goodison Park where he replaced the 5ft 8in-tall Jock Robson. Arsenal beat Everton 3-2 but his debut received mixed reviews: 'Lewis in the Arsenal goal was none too safe with high shots,' according to *The (Sheffield) Star Green 'Un*; 'Perhaps it was the foggy outlook that made Lewis pick up badly from Irvine ... Lewis left his charge untenanted

Dan Lewis

and 3 minutes later he didn't handle a Chedgzoy centre properly,' said the *Liverpool Echo*, but later reported that 'Lewis improves'.

He must have improved because he played in the next 13 matches and at the end of the season had made 19 appearances altogether, including 3 in a long-running FA Cup-tie against West Ham. After Herbert Chapman took over, Lewis found himself sharing the goalkeeping duties with first Robson and then Bill Harper before finally establishing himself as the number 1 choice in December 1926. At the end of that season came the match that would ensure that the name of Dan Lewis stands out in the history of Arsenal. The facts are simple enough; the 1927 FA Cup final between Arsenal and Cardiff City was a moderate affair but one made memorable by the only goal of the game when, in the 74th minute, Cardiff's Hughie Ferguson hit a tame-looking shot that Lewis failed to collect cleanly and then knocked into his own net.

The People reporter described 'Lewis's dreadful ordeal' adding:

> Lewis caught the ball as cleanly as could be, and when he half-rose in order to punt clear, he saw the possibility of being rushed by Irving. On one knee and one foot, the goalkeeper turned from his opponent and towards his own goal-line with a view to preventing the possibility of the Cardiff man kicking the ball out of his arms.
>
> To place his body between the ball and the opponent was a good idea – but he dropped the ball as he was turning, and – well, there was the tragedy, for the ball rolled over the goal-line. It was an awful moment for poor Lewis. He looked as if he could have sworn off goalkeeping for good.

Lewis said later that the ball had slid off his brand-new jersey – apparently ever since that day Arsenal goalkeeping jerseys are washed before they are first used – and at the end of the game he allegedly hurled his runners-up medal away. He also had to deal with totally unfounded allegations that, as a Wales international, he had handed the game to a Welsh club. On a much sadder note, Hughie Ferguson, scorer of 1 of the most famous goals in FA Cup final history, took his own life on 8 January 1930 at the age of 34.

Lewis, meanwhile, kept his place for the next 3 seasons, although he missed Arsenal's 1930 FA Cup final victory when Charlie Preedy replaced him at Wembley after Lewis aggravated an old injury in a 6-6 draw in a League game at Leicester.

That proved to be the last of his 167 appearances for Arsenal. In May 1931, he was transferred to Gillingham but made only 6 appearances for them before injury forced him to retire at the age of 28. He went to work at Kodak at Harrow. Dan Lewis was 63 when he died in Scarborough on 17 July 1965.

Herbert Chapman

Seldom in the history of football can the appointment of a new manager have had such a profound effect. In 1924-25 Arsenal finished twentieth in the First Division. In 1925-26 they were runners-up. The difference was Herbert Chapman.

Yet so the story goes, Chapman entered football management almost by chance. Legend has it that a colleague at Tottenham Hotspur was offered the post of player-manager at Northampton Town but suggested that Chapman applied instead. Thus began one of the most influential managerial careers the game has ever seen.

Born near Sheffield, at Kiveton Park, in January 1878, Chapman played as an amateur for several non-League clubs while qualifying as a mining engineer. He made a few appearances for Northampton Town, Grimsby Town and Sheffield United before signing for Tottenham in 1904. He scored 16 goals in 43 Southern League games for Spurs. Apparently he was sitting in the team bath after a match against QPR when Tottenham centre-half Walter Bull, Northampton's pick as player-manager, said that he was going to have another season with Spurs and that Chapman should contact them instead. Things must have moved fast because the QPR match was on 27 April 1907 and Chapman was appointed on 1 May. His application letter is alleged to have included the words 'pay me what you like,' so perhaps that clinched the matter. Newspaper reports said that 'he can play at inside-forward but this season has often appeared at centre-forward, a position for which he does not care.'

Chapman remained at Northampton for 5 years. There was no ill-feeling when he left; he simply felt that he had taken them as far as he could. In the 2 seasons before he took over, Northampton finished bottom of the Southern League; in his second season, they won the title. His playing career now over – he was 34 – in May 1912 he became secretary-manager of Second Division Leeds City; Northampton agreed to release him from his contract 'due to the remunerative nature of the offer.' They had every reason to be accommodating. During his time at Northampton, season ticket sales had increased from £1,800 to £5,300, money had been spent on the ground and outstanding liabilities wiped off.

Chapman's first job at Leeds was to canvas for their re-election to the Football League. That was successful – Gainsborough Trinity were voted out – and in his first season Leeds City missed promotion to the First Division by only 2 points, gate receipts were up and the club recorded a profit. Chapman encouraged players to speak their minds, and he introduced weekly golf sessions to boost comradeship. But in 1914-15 Leeds failed to live up to early promises and again struggled financially. When the Football League closed down for the duration of the First World War, Chapman took a managerial job at Barnbow munitions factory in East Leeds. He returned to Elland Road in 1916 and took City to successive Midland Section titles, in 1917 and 1918. But he was caught up in a scandal over illegal payments to wartime guest players. Five club officials and, surprisingly, Chapman were banned for life. Leeds City were disbanded, their players auctioned off at the Metropole Hotel in Leeds, and Leeds United eventually took their place, ignoring a suggestion that they should amalgamate with Huddersfield Town.

During his ban, he worked as an industrial manager at a Selby oil and coke company but in September 1920, having successfully argued that he had been absent from Elland Road when the illegal payments had been made, his ban was lifted and he took over as secretary of Huddersfield. Within 5 months he was assistant manager and in March 1921 replaced Ambrose Langley as manager. The following year he took Huddersfield Town to their first – and so far only – FA Cup final win, and then oversaw 2 Football League championships, in 1923-24 and 1924-25. It was the start of a hat-trick of titles – the first ever recorded – for Huddersfield but Chapman was not there to see the third. In June 1925, the *Shields Daily News* reported that:

> The Huddersfield people moved heaven and earth to induce Mr Chapman to reconsider his decision, but having given his word to the Arsenal he refused to be tempted by an offer that even exceeded in amount that of the London club [reportedly £2,000 per annum]. The matter was not irrevocably settled until midnight.

Chapman's staff presented him with a gold pencil to mark his time at Leeds Road, and he left for Highbury. Arsenal's fortunes were about to undergo a spectacular improvement. In Chapman's first season at Highbury the Gunners finished runners-up as Huddersfield completed their hat-trick. The following year they reached their first FA Cup final. In 1930, they won the Cup for the first time – their first major trophy, – and in 1931 became the first southern club to win the Football League championship.

In 1932 there was another FA Cup final, lost to Newcastle by a controversial goal, and a sensation in January 1933 when Third Division North Walsall knocked Arsenal out in the third round. But there were also consecutive League titles, in 1933 and 1934. Chapman had brought glory after glory to Highbury. Arsenal were *the* team of the 1930s. David Jack, Alex James, Eddie Hapgood and Cliff Bastin followed Charlie Buchan, Tom Parker, Bill Harper, Joe Hulme and Jack Lambert.

As he brought success to Arsenal, Chapman also changed the face of football itself. Since the 1860s, the offside law had required at least 3 defenders to be between the last attacker and the goal at the moment the ball was played. Full-backs could go further forward. As long as they maintained a diagonal line, an opponent would be offside if he got behind the more advanced full-back.

By the 1920s an offside trap had been honed to perfection by men such as Newcastle United's Irish international defender Bill McCracken. More significantly, it threatened to kill the game as a spectator sport. Stoppages for offside increased enormously. Football was becoming monotonous. In 1925 the law was changed so that only 2 men were needed between the goal and the attacker to play him onside. The immediate result was a flood of goals as defenders failed spectacularly to come to terms with this new-found freedom for forwards. For a season at least, football anarchy ruled.

From the opening day of 1925-26, football rained goals. By the following April, the Football League had seen a staggering increase in the number scored. The First Division alone produced 1,703 – 511 up on the previous year.

Chapman's reign at Highbury had hardly begun when the Gunners suffered a humiliating 7-0 defeat at Newcastle, all the goals coming inside a 50-minute spell. The day was 3 October 1925 and it was a disaster that convinced the new man at Arsenal that he must shore up the defence. Chapman moved centre-half Jack Butler – like all his centre-half brothers, Butler had hitherto enjoyed a versatile, attacking role – deep into defence, and dropped inside-forward Andy Neil, a pastry cook by trade, back to link up in midfield. Two days after their hammering at Newcastle, Arsenal won 4-0 at West Ham. Chapman's theory was vindicated. From narrowly avoiding relegation the previous season, the Gunners finished runners-up. Moving the centre-half led to the old 2-3-5 system being dismantled in favour of what became know as the W-M formation. In his autobiography, *A Lifetime in Football*, Charlie Buchan wrote: 'The novelty of Arsenal's new methods took the other League clubs by surprise.' It certainly did: by Christmas Arsenal were top of the table and probably only injury and illness prevented them from lifting the title in Chapman's first season.

Nonetheless, Arsenal's 'Chapman Era', with its FA Cup success and its own League championship hat-trick, was soon under way. By then, everyone had followed their lead. The attacking centre-half was dead; the 'stopper', the soccer 'policeman' – the man who stayed to block the middle – soon to be personified by Herbie Roberts, was born, although it should be said that a few clubs were already experimenting with that and Arsenal's new style was more 'zonal marking', something that Buchan had apparently been promoting.

Alas, Herbert Chapman did not live to see another of his teams achieve a hat-trick of League championship titles. On the morning of 6 January 1934 he died at his home in Haslemere Avenue, Hendon, from pneumonia, an appparent legacy of the round of hectic scouting trips on which he had embarked. He had been at a match at Guildford the previous afternoon. The Arsenal director and radio commentator George Allison said:

> Herbert Chapman was an extraordinary man – a man of amazing vitality and energy. He lived for football, not only for the club with which he was associated but for the players under his care and in whom he took the deepest personal interest. Their welfare was his chief consideration. He was such a master of the psychology of the players that he could make a moderate player into a good one ... . He really was the most remarkable man, head and shoulders above everybody else.

On the day of his death, newspapers throughout the country treated his passing as a major story. The Portsmouth *Evening News* wrote, 'The famous Arsenal manager was an ornament to his profession. He was a sportsman who lived for the game … it was his astuteness, tact, geniality and fearlessness that brought the Arsenal, the League champions, to the proud position they now occupy.' The *Liverpool Echo* recalled that 'he was never afraid to urge his directors to pay his price – sometimes running into five figures – when he wanted his man.'

Alex James said, 'Mr Chapman was the most popular manager a team could have. All the boys would do anything for him. I don't suppose there will be anybody like him in the game again.'

That afternoon 4 trumpeters sounded the *Last Post* at Highbury before the League game against Sheffield Wednesday as 45,000 spectators stood bareheaded in tribute to the man who had revolutionised Arsenal and football.

Jack Lambert

In April 1923 Second Division strugglers Rotherham County gave 21-year-old former miner Jack Lambert his Football League debut, away to Bradford City. The young centre-forward marked his first appearance with a goal – the only 1 of the game – after 7 minutes, but Rotherham had erred. Lambert was still on Leeds United's retained list. The club was fined £25 and Lambert was returned to Elland Road. He played only once for Leeds, in a 2-0 defeat at Leicester, before being transferred to Doncaster Rovers in January 1925 in exchange for goalkeeper David Russell. With Doncaster, Lambert finally came to prominence, and scored 11 goals in the Third Division North in 1925-26, despite missing 3 months of the season after being injured against Bradford Park Avenue in November. That form encouraged Herbert Chapman to pay £2,000 to sign Lambert for Arsenal in June 1926.

A robust centre-forward from Greasbrough near Rotherham, who had been turned down by Sheffield Wednesday after a trial, Lambert made his League debut for Arsenal at Bolton on 6 September but in 16 matches that season he managed to score only once. Another 16 appearances in 1927-28 produced 3 goals, and he scored once in 6 games in 1928-29.

In 1929-30 Lambert at last repaid Chapman's faith in his ability. After Christmas, he won a regular place and scored 18 goals in only 20 First Division appearances. His 4 goals in the FA Cup took Arsenal to Wembley where he scored again as the Gunners beat Huddersfield Town. *The (Sheffield) Star Green 'Un*, taking a special interest in a local lad made good, commented, 'Lambert thus justified the faith which caused him to be preferred to Halliday, though the latter got four goals in a match this week. We know that Mr Herbert Chapman has a very high opinion of Lambert's reliability.'

The following season was even more spectacular. As Arsenal won the League championship for the first time in their history, Lambert set a new club record with 38 goals, including 7 hat-tricks, in only 34 matches. He played in another FA Cup final – the 1932 defeat by Newcastle – and when Arsenal won the First Division again, Lambert weighed in with 14 goals from only 12 appearances, 5 of them coming in the 9-2 hammering of Sheffield United at Highbury on Christmas Eve 1932. By now Lambert was 31, and after Jimmy Dunne was signed in September 1933, his Arsenal career was over. He made his last appearance in a 1-0 defeat at West Brom that month. He had scored 109 goals in 159 League and FA Cup games for Arsenal and his 12 hat-tricks equalled Jimmy Brain's club record.

In October 1933 Lambert was transferred to Fulham for £2,500. He had lost much of his pace and made only 34 Second Division appearances for the Cottagers before joining Arsenal's 'nursery' club, Margate. In January 1936, he took over as player-manager after the resignation of James Ramsay, himself a former Arsenal forward. Despite steering the Southern League club to the third round of the FA Cup, the *Thanet Advertiser* said that Ramsay had 'a difference of opinion with the directors'. Margate's chairman, Mr A. A. Stickels, assured the *Thanet Advertiser* that 'our relations with the Arsenal are not affected in any way by what has happened and they are on the friendliest of footings.'

Jack Lambert remained in the job until he returned to Arsenal in 1938 to coach young players. He was 38 when he was killed in a motoring accident on the Great Cambridge Road at Enfield on Saturday, 7 December 1940.

Joe Hulme

On the Friday night of 5 February 1926, at York, Herbert Chapman made one of his first major signings for Arsenal. His target was Joe Hulme, a 21-year-old outside-right who had been earning rave reviews with Blackburn Rovers. Actually, by then Hulme had been out of the Rovers first team for almost a month. After returning from injury he had then been replaced by Jack Crisp. His last game in a Blackburn shirt was a Central League match against Manchester City Reserves at Ewood Park, 5 days before Chapman took him to Arsenal.

In reporting the transfer, the *Lancashire Evening Post* said, 'Hulme, who is an exceptionally fast and very tricky winger, has, of late, not been altogether too satisfactory in his finishing.' None of that deterred Chapman from paying £3,500 for Hulme's skills, or from playing him at Leeds just 24 hours later. It was the first of 372 appearances for Arsenal.

Hulme was born in Stafford in August 1904 and joined Blackburn in February 1924 after 2 years in the Midland League with York City. He went straight into the first team and stayed there for a run of 64 consecutive appearances until he was injured. In his 2 years at Ewood Park he scored 8 goals in 82 appearances, a record that would be eclipsed by his figures with Arsenal.

He remained in the team for the rest of the season as the Gunners finished First Division runners-up. The first of 9 full England international caps came against Scotland at Hampden Park in April 1927. At the end of that month Hulme played in his first FA Cup final, against Cardiff City, and he was now Arsenal's first-choice outside-right. In Hulme and Cliff Bastin the Gunners now had 2 high-scoring wingers. In 1931-32, Hulme scored 14 League goals, and the season after that he hit 20 with hat-tricks against Leicester City, Middlesbrough and Sunderland. With all this came medals – FA Cup winner in 1930 and runner-up in 1932, and League championships in 1930-31, 1932-33 and 1934-35. He missed out in 1933-34, playing only 8 times that season because of injury.

Joe Hulme

His final Arsenal honour came in the 1936 FA Cup final win over Sheffield United, making him the only player to appear in all of Arsenal's first 4 Cup finals. He did play in a fifth FA Cup final. After making only 10 appearances in his last 2 seasons – 7 of them coming when Arsenal won the League again in 1937-38 – in January 1938, after scoring 124 League and FA Cup goals for the Gunners, he was transferred to Huddersfield Town for £2,000 and appeared for them in that season's Wembley defeat by Preston North End, after which he announced his retirement.

Joe Hulme was also a fine all-round cricketer, an aggressive middle-order batsman (average 26.56; 12 centuries) and medium-fast bowler (89 wickets at 36.40 each) who played 225 times for Middlesex between 1929 and 1939. During the Second World War, Hulme served as a reserve officer in the Metropolitan Police.

In February 1944, he was appointed assistant to Tottenham Hotspur's Arthur Turner, the secretary who was looking after the club during wartime. Hulme was appointed manager at White Hart Lane on 18 January 1946, halfway through the interim season before the Football League resumed. In December 1948, he was admitted to hospital suffering from a stomach complaint. When he returned to work on 7 March 1949 he was sacked. He said:

> Without wishing to boast, I did well at Tottenham. I took them into the FA Cup semi-final last season, and when I went into hospital in December the club were virtually top of the Second Division. I am puzzled to understand why I have been dismissed. I told the club, in reply to their inquiry, that my health was equal to the strain of the job and asked to resume my duties. In answer I received a month's notice, and was told that the club were making other arrangements.

He was perhaps unlucky: he had assembled almost all the players who would take Spurs to their first-ever League championship in 1950. Instead of seeing that job through, he became a sports journalist, 'taking the lid off soccer' for the *Sunday People* until his retirement in the 1960s. In September 1949, he told how he had tried to sign Tommy Lawton for Spurs but the Tottenham board refused because 'they said he had bad knees'. Lawton later played 38 times for Arsenal and scored 15 goals.

Joe Hulme died at Winchmore Hill on 26 September 1991, aged 87.

Tom Parker

On Saturday, 3 April 1926, the *Derby Evening Telegraph* wrote:

> It would be quite interesting to know what Southampton think about the Arsenal not having promoted Tom Parker, their international full-back, to the League side as yet. Manager Chapman took the player because he wished to be ready for all emergencies, but the form of Mackie and John is such that they cannot be disturbed. It does seem funny to think of red-haired Tom Parker as a reserve.

On 28 December 1929, the Portsmouth *Evening News* reported:

> It is very bad luck for the Arsenal, and also for the player, that the club's captain, Tom Parker, received a leg injury against Pompey at Highbury on Boxing morning, and could not take his place at right-back at Leeds today … . For a player of the forceful type who gives and receives hard bumps and never shirks a tackle it is a wonderful record.

In fact Tom Parker made his Arsenal debut on that first Saturday of April 1926, in a 4-2 win over Blackburn Rovers at Highbury. He did not miss another match until the last Saturday of 1929, meaning that he had played in 172 consecutive games since his debut. His was certainly a wonderful record.

Born in Woolston, Southampton, on 19 November 1897, Parker played as an amateur for Sholing Rangers, Sholing Athletic and St Mark's before his first game for Southampton, in 1917-18 in the South Hants War League. The following season the young full-back was Saint's second-highest scorer with 12 goals, most of them penalties, and with peacetime football restored, in 1919-20 he made 40 Southern League appearances. In 1920-21 Southampton finished runners-up in the new Third Division of the Football League, and the next season they were champions of what was now the Third Division South. By the time Parker became 1 of Herbert Chapman's first major signings – Arsenal paid Southampton £3,250 – he had played in 206 Football League matches for the Saints and in May 1925 won an England cap against France in Paris.

Once his Arsenal career was launched, Parker was not to be shifted from the right-back position. He was the first player to captain Arsenal in an FA Cup final, in 1927, and the first to lift the Cup, in 1930. He captained the side that won Arsenal's first-ever Football League championship, in 1930-31, and the team that lost the 1932 FA Cup final to Newcastle's 'over-the-line' goal. But by the time the Gunners embarked on the first of 3 consecutive League titles, Parker was 35. George Male took his place. Parker's final League appearance came against Derby County at Highbury on 8 October 1932. Altogether he had made 292 appearances and scored 17 goals, again most of them penalties.

In February 1933, he was coaching the Isthmian League club Nunhead. Parker then applied for the manager's job at Kent League club Tunbridge Wells Rangers – their former secretary-manager, Richard Hendrie, was on trial for alleged theft of money from players' insurances, wages and bonuses – but the former Arsenal skipper, who reportedly asked for £10 a week in wages, was not granted an interview.

In March 1933, however, Parker received a much better offer: he took over as manager of Norwich City and the following year saw the Canaries to the Third Division North title. In March 1937, he was back at Southampton, this time as manager. Then war intervened and in June 1943 he took a job outside football, as a ship's surveyor at Southampton docks. In the 1950s he managed Norwich City for a second spell but in 1956-57 the cash-strapped club finished bottom of the Third Division South and he resigned. He returned to his job as a ship's surveyor until he retired in 1962. For 10 years after that he was Southampton's chief scout. Tom Parker died in Southampton in November 1987, aged 89.

David Jack

On 13 October 1928, football woke up to the news that Arsenal had paid a British record transfer fee of £10,890 – some accounts gave the figure as £10,340 – for the Bolton Wanderers forward David Jack. Whatever the precise amount, the first 5-figure fee eclipsed the previous record set when Bob Kelly moved from Burnley to Sunderland for a reported £6,500 in December 1925.

The sensational sum that Arsenal had paid for the man who scored the first-ever goal in a Wembley FA Cup final, when Bolton beat West Ham in 1923, drew scathing comments from some quarters. Speaking at the Lancashire FA's jubilee celebrations the FA president, Sir Charles Clegg, declared that no player was worth £10,000 but added that 'he could not supply the remedy'.

Commentators up and down the country had an opinion. The *Nottingham Evening Post* felt it 'curious to recall' that in 1922 Arsenal had proposed a transfer ceiling of £1,650, had tried again to introduce a limit the following year, and had made yet another attempt in 1926. The newspaper said everyone had heard that Jack was one of the few players that Bolton were not prepared to sell but 'the Wanderers must have fallen for Mr Chapman's tempting bait.'

Writing in the *Sporting Times*, QPR's Jack Boyer – 'Soccer's Youngest Director' according to his byline – reminded critics that 'the money is still left in the game, merely being changed from one club's coffers to another.' He added, 'Nothing is said when a foreign entertainer is paid a huge salary to amuse a theatre audience, then leaves the country much wealthier than when he arrived at the expense of a profession that can ill bear the competition.'

On the same day in the same newspaper 'The Scribe' commented, 'Few will agree that a player, however good he may be, is worth such an enormous sum, but from what we have seen of Jack's play it certainly looks as if Arsenal have got the right man.' Indeed they had.

David Jack

David Bone Nightingale Jack was Bolton-born, the son of former Bolton, Preston, Glossop and Plymouth Argyle forward Bob Jack. When Jack senior managed Plymouth, David, along with his brothers, Rollo and Donald, progressed through the junior ranks there. David Jack served in the Royal Navy during the First World War, and in February 1919 he guested for Chelsea against Arsenal in a London Combination match at Stamford Bridge.

In December 1920, when Plymouth were halfway through their first season as a Football League club, in the Third Division South, he signed for Bolton for £3,500. His brothers also played professionally for the Trotters – and by the time Arsenal came calling he had scored 161 goals in 324 League and FA Cup matches for Bolton including the winner in the 1926 FA Cup final, and played 4 times for England.

In his first season at Highbury, Jack finished leading scorer with 25 goals in 31 League games. He played in the 1930 FA Cup-winning team, in the 1932 Wembley runners-up side, and in 3 League championship-winning seasons: 1930-31 (when he scored 31 goals in only 35 League appearances), 1932-33 and 1933-34, and he won another 5 England caps while with Arsenal.

In April 1932 newspapers linked him with 'a leading French club' who, it was said, had offered him 4 times his Arsenal salary to become their player-manager, but it came to nothing. In 1933-34, now aged 35, Jack managed only 14 League appearances and at the end of the season he retired. His return for Arsenal was 123 goals in 206 League and FA Cup matches, giving him a total of 287 goals in 544 games including his brief Plymouth career. He went straight into management, first with Southend United where he stayed until 1940. He was managing Sunderland Greyhound Stadium when he was offered the job of Middlesbrough manager in September 1944. He left Ayresome Park in April 1952 to return to London because of his wife's ill-health. He ran a pub in Islington and wrote articles for *The People* in which he said he had become disillusioned with football, especially the transfer market 'one of the most unsavoury features of the game'. The man who was once the game's most expensive footballer said, 'If I had my way there would be a limit to the sum which any club was allowed to spend in buying a player.'

There was a final stint managing Shelbourne United in the League of Ireland, from August 1953 to April 1955, after which he took a job at the Air Ministry. David Jack was only 59 when he died in St Thomas's Hospital, London, on 10 September 1958.

Herbie Roberts

'No Roberts! No Arsenal.' That was the headline in the *Daily Herald* on Monday, 1 November 1937. 'Middlesbrough won at Highbury because Arsenal lost their centre-half, Roberts, during the first minute of the second half. He tore a ligament in a leg and had to be carried off the field,' reported the paper's football correspondent T. J. Raymond.

Arsenal were winning 1-0 when Herbie Roberts was injured. Reduced to 10 men they lost 2-1, giving Middlesbrough their first victory at Highbury since the 1910-11 season. 'Their rearguard lose a great stopper when they lose Roberts,' concluded Raymond. In fact Arsenal had lost him for good. Following that bad knee injury, the centre-half, who had played a pivotal role in Herbert Chapman's tactical formation that changed the way footballers defended, would never play another League game.

Roberts was a 21-year-old right-half when he joined Arsenal in December 1926. A gunsmith by trade, he had been playing for 5 seasons with his local club, Oswestry Town, in the Birmingham League. Herbert Chapman paid £200 for him and his debut came at Villa Park on 18 April 1927. It was the first of 333 appearances for the Gunners – he scored 5 goals – during which time he won League championship medals in 1930-31 and in the hat-trick seasons of 1932-35, as well as an FA Cup winners' medal in 1936 and a runners-up medal in 1932. He missed the 1930 Wembley final because of a back injury suffered at Upton Park in mid-March that saw him sidelined for the remainder of that season. There was also a single England cap, against Scotland at Hampden Park in March 1931.

Herbie Roberts became synonymous with the term 'football policeman', after Herbert Chapman countered the 1925 alteration to the offside law by withdrawing his centre-halves from their former roles as link players between attack and defence.

Herbie Roberts

Chapman used Roberts in other ways, too. In December 1933 'Corney', writing in the *Nottingham Journal*, recalled a recent goal he witnessed:

> A free-kick just outside the penalty area. As usual the defenders line up between the ball and the goal. But lo, Herbie Roberts, the Arsenal centre-half, slips in between them! A rather mysterious intrusion but one to which the rules raise no objection. Now Roberts is in line with one side of the goal, Bastin takes the kick and aims not at the goal itself, but at Roberts. As the winger shot, the Arsenal pivot swung quickly aside, the ball went hurtling through the space left vacant and was in the net before the goalkeeper even saw it go! And that is why Mr Chapman is the highest paid manager in the game.

As a 'spoiling' defender, Roberts often came in for boos and jeers from opposing fans but he took that, and everything else, in his stride. In September 1936, he suffered a broken nose during the 4-1 win over Sunderland at Highbury. After some rudimentary first-aid he returned to the field, scored a goal, and delayed his trip to hospital until the final whistle.

After his last appearance in the First Division, Roberts remained on the staff at Highbury, as trainer to the reserve team. On the outbreak of war, he enlisted in the Royal Fusiliers (City of London Regiment) as a physical training instructor and was serving as a lieutenant when he contracted the skin infection erysipelas, a form of cellulitis that affects only the upper layers of the skin. He died on 17 June 1944 in the North Middlesex Hospital and was buried in Southgate Cemetery. He was 39.

Frank Moss

After half an hour of the First Division match at Goodison Park on 16 March 1935, Arsenal goalkeeper Frank Moss dislocated his shoulder in fisting away a Jimmy Cunliffe corner. Eddie Hapgood took over between the posts – no substitutes, not even for goalkeepers, in those days – and Moss made his way to the dressing room. Moments later, reported the *Liverpool Echo,* 'the funniest thing … Hapgood taking a goal-kick and then forgetting himself and beginning to run up the field to his usual position.' But then Hapgood made a brilliant save from a Cunliffe header and got his fingertips to another header, from Joe Mercer, before Ted Drake gave 10-men Arsenal the lead against the run of play.

When the teams emerged for the second half, Moss was back on the pitch, but now on the left wing. Everton pressed but Arsenal weathered the storm. In the 69th minute Moss wrote his name into the record books. Drake put in a fast, low centre and there was Arsenal's usual goalkeeper sending the ball past his opposite number, Ted Sagar, to ensure an unexpected victory: Everton 0 Arsenal 2. Struggling with his injury, Moss left the pitch again before the final whistle but more than 50,000 spectators made their way home with something to talk about. It isn't every day you see a goalkeeper score a goal.

Frank Moss was 22 when he joined Arsenal in November 1931. Born in the Lancashire town of Leyland, he played for a year with Preston North End and for a season and a half with Oldham Athletic before Herbert Chapman paid £3,000 to bring him to Highbury. He made his League debut at Stamford Bridge only 24 hours after signing, and his last appearance at Ewood Park in February 1936, when he again dislocated his shoulder. Moss played in the controversial 1932 FA Cup final defeat by Newcastle, and was Arsenal's first-choice for their hat-trick of League championship titles, missing only 15 League games in those 3 seasons. He played 4 times for England, all in 1934. His final cap came in the notorious 'Battle of Highbury' against Italy in November when no less than 7 Arsenal players were in the England line-up.

After dislocating his shoulder at Goodison, Moss managed only 5 more League appearances for Arsenal – his comeback match was a 5-4 defeat at Roker Park in December 1935 – taking his total games to 159 in League and FA Cup (with that 1 goal, of course) before calling it a day.

He had been helping top coach Arsenal's reserve team but in March 1937, at the age of 27, he became the youngest manager in the history of Heart of Midlothian. A few days before the start of the 1937-38 season the *Dundee Evening Telegraph* reported:

> Probably no other club can afford to make such big investments as Arsenal, but other Arsenal examples may be freely copied. Hearts' manager, Mr Frank Moss, formerly goalkeeper at Highbury, yesterday had twenty-two Tynecastle stalwarts, attired in flannels and polo sweaters, walking through the streets of Edinburgh, just as the Arsenal staff do in the Highbury district.

In 1937-38 Moss managed Hearts to runners-up in the Scottish League First Division, 3 points behind Celtic and 7 ahead of third-placed Rangers, and to fourth place in 1938-39. Hearts were in third place when the competition closed down in September 1939, and in July 1940 Moss resigned and returned to England.

The only goalkeeper ever to score a goal for Arsenal – if you don't count Graham Stack's in a 2003 League Cup penalty shootout against Rotherham United – he later ran a pub in Chorley. He died on 7 February 1970, at the age of 60.

Joe Shaw

After the sudden death of Herbert Chapman in January 1934, it was inevitable that several names from across the country would be mentioned as his possible replacement. They included David Pratt, the former Celtic and Liverpool player who had recently resigned as manager of Clapton Orient. Instead the job went, temporarily at least, to someone even closer to Highbury than Lea Bridge Road. Arsenal turned to one of the club's longest-serving and most faithful employees.

Born in Bury in May 1883, Joe Shaw played for Bury Athenaeum before signing for Accrington Stanley, then in the Lancashire Combination, in 1905. He played for Stanley against Crewe Alexandra in the FA Cup in January 1907. Five months later Phil Kelso signed him for Woolwich Arsenal. The *London Daily News* heard that the left-back was 'a well-set-up-lad and is spoken of highly in Lancashire'.

Kelso gave Shaw his debut at Preston on 28 September 1907 but he did not appear in the first team again until the following April, at home to Bolton. In 1908-09 he gained a regular place and was first choice at left-back – he was ever-present in 1914-15 – and then at right-back until 1920-21. During the First World War, Shaw worked at the Royal Arsenal munitions factory and played in as many matches as that would allow. He was selected for a London Combination match against Reading at Highbury on 19 February 1916 but could not get away. Pre-war, England full-back Bob Benson – who was also working in a munitions factory – volunteered to take Shaw's place but 20 minutes before the end of the game Benson left the pitch because he was feeling unwell and died in the dressing room at 5.40 pm. It was reported that he had not played for a year, had been working 15-hour shifts, and that his death had been caused by a burst blood vessel due to a longstanding medical condition. He was buried in his Arsenal shirt.

In 1919 Shaw succeeded Percy Sands as club captain. He made his last appearance at Old Trafford in March 1922. Thus, he won no honours with Arsenal – they were relegated in 1912-13 – but he was with the club when they moved to Highbury, served through some of the most unsettling years in the club's history, and tasted First Division football again after the controversial promotion of 1919. He made 326 appearances but never scored a goal. Had war not interrupted his career then he would surely have topped 500 appearances and might even have found the back of the net.

After his playing days ended, Shaw coached Arsenal's reserves and then managed the second team. But it was in January 1934 that he faced his biggest test when, following Chapman's untimely death, the directors asked him to take over as first-team manager until the end of the season. It was Chapman who had appointed Shaw reserve-team manager in 1925. Together with Tom Whittaker he became the linchpin of the backroom staff at Highbury. Bernard Joy said that their personalities 'helped fashion the club.' Eddie Hapgood found Shaw 'always ready to lend an ear to a player's troubles.'

At the point where the entire club was shaken by Chapman's death, Arsenal had lost only twice in 24 League matches. Shaw's first game in charge was a 1-0 FA Cup win over Luton Town but then Arsenal lost 3 League matches in succession – at Manchester City and at home to Spurs and Everton. Shaw steadied the ship. Arsenal won 11 of their last 15 matches and lost only twice. Although they scored only 75 goals – 43 fewer than the previous season – they conceded only 47 as against 61 in 1932-33. In March, Shaw completed the signing of Ted Drake from Southampton. Drake scored 7 goals in the last 10 games of the season as Arsenal won their second successive title.

When George Allison was appointed Chapman's long-term successor, Shaw returned to managing the reserve side but, again, it was he and Whittaker who were the real influence in the dressing room as Arsenal completed their hat-trick of championships. In 1939 he was living close to Highbury, in Avenell Road, his occupation 'assistant manager Arsenal Football Club'. He remained with Arsenal right up until the end of the Second World War before spending 2 years as a coach at Chelsea. In 1947, he returned to Highbury as assistant to new manager Tom Whittaker, and the old coaching team was back in business. When Joe Shaw left the club in 1956 he had given a remarkable 49 years' service to Arsenal. He died, aged 80, in September 1963.

George Allison

On Friday, 4 May 1934 a statement that William Struth, the manager of Glasgow Rangers, had been offered the job of managing Arsenal was 'emphatically denied by Arsenal's managing director, George Allison, who said that, at present, nothing had been done to appoint a successor to the late Herbert Chapman.' The following day Struth issued a statement: 'I have decided not to leave the Rangers.' It was now reported that, 2 days earlier, Allison, a journalist and broadcaster, had been in Glasgow to interview Struth. 'So now you know the position in regard to a successor to Mr Herbert Chapman,' commented no less an authority on the matter than the *Sunderland Daily Echo and Shipping Gazette*.

There had been 150 applicants for the job but it went in-house. On 30 May, speaking on the telephone from Dublin 'where he had gone in connection with the Irish Sweepstake Draw,' Allison said:

> Yes, it is quite true that I have been appointed successor to the late Mr Herbert Chapman ... Arsenal under my managership will continue their progressive policy. Arsenal have a very high position to maintain and we intend to maintain it. So far as paying big fees for players are concerned we will be guided by the necessities of the money. We hope to continue as in the past to keep up the level of ability which is expected of Arsenal.

On 31 May, the *Coventry Evening Telegraph* reported:

> Mr George Allison no longer denies that he is the new secretary-manager of the Arsenal club. In his appointment he will receive the warm congratulations of everybody interested in football. He is the right age – 51. He has a

mass of experience which few men can boast, and all those qualifications of temper and spirit which will go to consolidate all that is best in the great Arsenal club.

Asked if he would continue his journalistic activities, Allison said:

> In my agreement with the Arsenal board it has been agreed that I shall continue certain of these activities and also my broadcasting. I have had thirty-two years' experience of professional football ... and Arsenal will carry on in the best traditions ... . I am fortunate in having under my control the finest and most loyal band of players that ever represented any club. Perfect harmony and happiness is the only way in which one can describe the Arsenal family.

Writing in *The Bystander* on 12 June 1934, 'Mark Over' said:

> So, George Allison has burnt his boats and become manager of Arsenal ... . A remarkable man, in his way, is genial George. He makes you feel, as you listen to that deep, confident voice of his, that Association football really is important. George is a thick-set, versatile, vastly energetic, with a laugh like Niagara Falls. He is a journalist at heart, and a first-rate one at that, and his stories of the peculiarities of American millionaires are worth hearing.
>
> They say his salary is to be £3,000 a year. I've no doubt he will earn it. This is the day of the sporting impresario, and George Allison may well become the Cochran of the football world. His journalistic training and connections will help him. We shall undoubtedly hear more of George.

After the sudden death of Herbert Chapman, former Arsenal defender Joe Shaw had taken over the team until the end of the season and, such was Chapman's legacy, guided the Gunners to another League title. John Peters resumed the post of club secretary he had held before Chapman joined, and George Allison, already a director, assumed overall management duties.

Allison was a native of Hurworth-on-Tees, a village near Darlington. A young amateur footballer who wrote reports on matches in which he played, his early adult career combined journalism and football administration. In March 1906, after working on a newspaper in Plymouth, he became assistant to the secretary-manager of Middlesbrough, Alex Mackie. Two months later Mackie resigned after being suspended for his involvement in a financial scandal at his previous club, Sunderland, and Allison also left and went to London where he reported on Woolwich Arsenal matches. He became the club's historian and editor of Arsenal's programme and yearbook. During the First World War, he worked for the War Office and the Admiralty, and joined the Royal Flying Corps. His journalistic career covered such diverse briefs as greyhound correspondent of the *Sporting Life* and London correspondent of the *New York Post*. As a BBC radio broadcaster, he commentated on the Derby, the Grand National, the annual England-Scotland Home International Championship match, and on the 1927 FA Cup final between Arsenal and Cardiff City, a year after he had joined the Arsenal board.

As Arsenal's manager Allison concentrated on bringing in new players – Ted Drake, Jack Crayston and Wilf Copping were among those who joined under his watch, as well as Bryn Jones for whom he paid a British record transfer fee of £14,000 in August 1938. Almost 15,000 came to see Jones play in Arsenal's pre-season public practice match – while Joe Shaw and Tom Whittaker took training and coaching. Eddie Hapgood later wrote, 'The new manager, Mr George Allison, had the hardest job in the world following a man like Chapman. But Tom [Whittaker] knew the methods which had made us a great team, and to him it was we turned in the weeks which followed.' Hapgood admitted to having 'a few ups and downs' with Chapman's successor.

Under Allison, 2 more League titles and another FA Cup were won before war intervened. Overall, he maintained the success started under Chapman, and it was only after a difficult first season when the Football League resumed for 1946-47 and most of the pre-war stars had retired, that he stepped down, by now in his mid-60s. After several years of failing health, George Allison died of a heart attack at his Golders Green home on 13 March 1957. He was 73.

George Male

George Male could not have asked for an easier introduction to First Division football. It came on 27 December 1930, against relegation-threatened Blackpool at Highbury. David Jack and Jimmy Brain each scored a hat-trick, Arsenal won 7-1, and at the final whistle Male earned a handshake from his captain. It was a very happy Christmas for the Gunners. On Christmas Day they beat Manchester City 4-1 at Maine Road, and on Boxing Day won the return fixture 3-1 at Highbury. Fourteen goals in 3 matches. The *Daily Herald*'s C. A. Hughes wrote, 'Incredible speed in a morass of mud, quick thinking and tactics that differed with every attack filled Arsenal's Christmas stocking with points.'

At the end of the season Arsenal were champions (Blackpool just avoided the drop by 1 point) and Male had made 2 more appearances, switching from left-half to left-back for the final 1; a 2-1 win at Elland Road in a midweek game on a March afternoon after the original fixture had been postponed due to January fog. A native of West Ham, he was 19 when he signed amateur forms for Arsenal in November 1929 and the *Daily Herald* pointed out, 'It is not anticipated that Male's services will be entirely lost to Clapton FC and he is expected to play in their Isthmian League and Amateur Cup games.' That was the case and Male was included in the Isthmian League XI that met the Corinthians in the annual Christmas holiday match. He finally signed professional forms in May 1930.

In 1931-32 Male made 9 League appearances and 1 in the FA Cup. But that happened to be after Alex James missed the last few games of the season through injury and the team was reshuffled for Wembley. It was, of course, runners-up medals for Male and his teammates. There were, though, winners' medals galore to follow. In 1932-33, with Tom Parker now in his mid-30s and his career drawing to a close, and his replacement, Leslie Compton, never looking like a convincing replacement, Chapman made the seemingly bold move of switching Male from left-half to right-back. It was a masterstroke and the start of a glorious Arsenal career. In November 1932 *The People* declared, 'Male is making a big difference. He improves with every game.' For the next 7 seasons Male hardly missed a game as the Gunners won the League championship 4 times, with an FA Cup in 1936 for good measure. He made his England debut, alongside 6 Arsenal teammates, against Italy in the infamous 'Battle of Highbury' in November 1934. Altogether he won 19 caps and captained England in 6 internationals.

Male was 29 when the Football League closed down because of the Second World War, during which he served with the RAF in Palestine. He managed 181 wartime appearances for Arsenal, however, and was still good enough at the age of 37 to make 8 appearances when the Gunners won the title yet again in 1947-48. He was just a week short of his 38th birthday when he made his final appearance, an 8-0 defeat of Grimsby Town at Highbury on 1 May 1948. He had made 314 appearances, plus 3 League games in the aborted 1939-40 season.

Thereafter he worked as a coach for Arsenal, and also scouted for the Gunners, in 1966 bringing a talented schoolboy footballer called Charlie George to Highbury. Male was still working for Arsenal when they won the Double in 1970-71. After retiring in 1975 he emigrated to Canada where he had family. George Male, the only footballer to play in 6 League championship-winning teams, died in Ontario on 19 February 1998, aged 87.

Eddie Hapgood

Eddie Hapgood had a choice: sign for Bristol Rovers on £8 a week and earn extra during the summer by driving a coal cart, or join Kettering Town for £4 in the football season, £3 in the summer, and keep his job as a milkman. 'I figured there was a social distinction between driving a coal cart and a milk float,' he wrote later. So he signed for Southern League Kettering.

According to a local newspaper account, in his first game for Kettering Hapgood was 'appalling', but in October 1927, after only a handful of games, he was signing for Arsenal for 'a four-figure fee' – actually £750 down and the guarantee of £200 from a friendly match. Bristol Rovers supporters were disappointed. Writing to the *Athletic News* in November 1927, William J. Sibley of Barton Hall, Bristol, asked:

> How many players have had a rise so rapid as Hapgood? Last year, at the age of 18, he was playing … in the junior division of a Bristol local league. After a trial with Bristol Rovers Reserves … he was recommended to Kettering. He played there a matter of five or six weeks at the end of which time Kettering had apparently been deluged with enquiries as to his transfer, and at the finish the Arsenal just beat Aston Villa on the post, parting with a substantial cheque. In these days of high transfers it does seem a pity that local lads in many parts of the country find fame elsewhere.

Edris Albert – Eddie – Hapgood made his First Division debut in a 1-1 draw at Birmingham on 19 November 1927. His final appearance was on 6 May 1939, at home to Brentford. The 3 League games of the aborted 1939-40 season did not count so that brought his total number of appearances for Arsenal to 434 – he scored 2 goals – during which he played in 5 League championship-winning seasons – 1930-31, the hat-trick seasons of 1932-33-34-35, and 1937-38 – and the 1930 and 1936 FA Cup winning teams as well as the 1932 runners-up. For most of his career he was Arsenal's captain.

Hapgood won 30 England caps and captained his country 21 times, the first when he was 1 of 7 Arsenal men who played in the 'Battle of Highbury' against World Cup holders Italy in November 1934. After only 2 minutes Italy's centre-half Luis Monti broke a small bone in a foot, in a tackle from Ted Drake. Italy played the last 73 minutes with 10 men. Although Manchester City's Eric Brook missed a first-minute penalty, he atoned with 2 goals. Drake added another and after 12 minutes England led 3-0. In the second half Italy pulled back to 3-2 and, but for the intervention of the crossbar, might have equalised. The game had long generated into violence. Drake was punched in the face, Brook fractured an arm and Male broke a bone in a hand. The following day the *Daily Herald* reported, 'In the matter of injuries Hapgood was the worst sufferer … . His nose had been broken, so one can truthfully say that the Arsenal left-back played a gallant game.'

Hapgood was captain when England were forced by the Foreign Office to give the Nazi salute before a game in Berlin in May 1938.

It was the Second World War that ended his career. He was 30 when it broke out. He served in the RAF as a physical training (PT) instructor, attaining the rank of pilot officer; played for Arsenal whenever he could; guested for Luton Town, West Brom, Southampton, West Ham and Chelsea; and won 13 wartime caps. In January 1946, he took over as manager of Blackburn Rovers where his philosophy of introducing younger players at the expense of seasoned campaigners saw him fall out with the club's directors. In February 1947 he resigned. He played for Midland League Shrewsbury Town before managing Watford and Bath City. In November 1957 at Bristol Assizes, he was awarded £1,500 damages for libel and £10 for slander against the Bath City chairman.

Later he ran YMCA hostels in Berkshire and Dorset. He died on Good Friday, 20 April 1973, at Honley Hall, near Kenilworth, where he was taking part in an international youth football training conference. He was 64.

Cliff Bastin

'There is no confirmation of a rumour associating the name of C. Bastin of Exeter City FC with the Arsenal Club.' So said the *Exeter and Plymouth Gazette* of 22 May 1929. It was 4 June before the *Western Morning News* could tell supporters of the Grecians that their starlet would henceforth be shining elsewhere: 'Exeter City have transferred Clifford Bastin, their clever inside-left, to Arsenal at a fee which is said to run into four figures.'

Four days later a supporter signing themselves 'Bridge' complained to the *Exeter and Plymouth Gazette*, 'The City's followers have been wonderfully loyal in view of the wretched fare that has been served up … . Now we get news of Bastin's transfer … . Selling the best men is a funny way of building up a team.'

Born in Exeter on 14 March 1912, Bastin was capped by England Schoolboys against Wales in 1926. He made his Third Division South bow against Coventry City in April 1928, and after only 17 games – and 6 goals – Herbert Chapman paid £2,000 to take him to Highbury. Chapman made many astute signings but none more so than Cliff Bastin. Five League championships and 2 FA Cup final victories later he had scored 176 goals in 392 appearances for the Gunners. He scored 12 goals in 21 games for England and by the time he was 19 had won every major honour then available to a professional footballer. The peak came in 1932-33 when Arsenal won the first of their hat-trick of titles and 'Boy' Bastin weighed in with 33 goals from outside-left, a record number for a winger. When Alex James found age and injuries catching up with him, Bastin moved inside. Although he scored only 13 League goals in 1933-34 he was still Arsenal's joint leading scorer with Ray Bowden. Twenty goals in 1934-35 saw him well behind Ted Drake's total of 42, and in 1935-36, when Arsenal dropped to sixth place, he scored 11 to Drake's 24, but netted 6 times in the run to another FA Cup final win.

Arsenal: The Story of a Football Club in 101 Lives

There seemed to be no end to his versatility. When in 1936-37 Jack Crayston was injured, Bastin moved to right-half. Restored to the left wing in 1937-38 he scored 15 times as Arsenal won their fifth League title in 8 seasons, but in September 1938, 5 games into the new season, Arsenal announced that he had been given a month's leave. 'Bastin has not been at all well for some time and we are hoping that a complete rest will restore his enthusiasm for the game.' In December it was reported that Second Division Plymouth Argyle had tried to sign him but Bastin remained at Highbury and in that final post-war season made 23 appearances – a leg injury did not help – and scored 3 goals.

That injury curtailed Bastin's wartime appearances. He was excused military service after failing a hearing test; instead he became an air raid precaution (ARP) warden at Highbury – Italian radio's 1941 claim that he had been captured in Crete being way off the mark. After 6 appearances in the first post-war season he played his final game, against Manchester United on 28 September 1946. 'I've had a good run,' he told *The People*, 'and there's no point in hanging on. No doubt I could get good wages from other clubs, but what's the point in struggling for another season or two?' He ran a café on the North Circular Road and then took over the Horse and Groom pub in Exeter. He spent his final years in the house he'd lived in as a child. Cliff Bastin died on 4 December 1991 at the age of 79 in the Royal Devon and Exeter Hospital.

Alex James

When 27-year-old Alex James from Mossend in Lanarkshire signed for Arsenal in May 1929, the Football League wanted to know why Preston North End had accepted a fee of £8,750 when Manchester City had reportedly offered £9,000 for the Scotland international forward, and Liverpool had apparently been willing to go as high as £9,500. The transfer eventually went ahead after an enquiry ruled that James's new job as a 'football demonstrator' at Selfridges store in London did not amount to an inducement to sign. The *Liverpool Echo* commented, 'He will earn nearly as much in his "outer ring of influence" as he will in football wages. This is how the game of football is developing these days.'

It was not the first James transfer to attract the League's attention. When he signed from Raith Rovers, for £3,000 in September 1925, Preston were fined 10 guineas for an irregularity on the form. It was at Deepdale that his career blossomed with 4 Scotland caps including 2 goals when the 'Wembley Wizards' beat England 5-2 in April 1928. However, his goals for Preston – 53 in 147 Second Division appearances – could not help them win promotion, and they would not always release him for international duty either. Frustrated, he looked elsewhere and to a path that eventually led to Highbury.

His debut came at home to Leeds United on the first day of the 1929-30 season. Arsenal finished 14th but when James scored his first FA Cup goal for the club, it was in that season's Wembley victory over Huddersfield Town. The following season he missed only 2 League games as Arsenal added their first title to what would be an ever-growing honours list. In the League championship hat-trick seasons he made 92 League appearances and scored 10 goals, and in 1936 he captained the Gunners against Sheffield United at Wembley. In 1931-32, Arsenal might have won the Double but for an injury to James that ruled him out for the last 9 games. Without their playmaker Arsenal finished runners-up and also lost the FA Cup final to that controversial Newcastle goal.

In March 1934 Derby County, whose trainer Dave Willis was James's father-in-law, were on the brink of signing James for £2,000. The Derby secretary called it a done deal, waiting only for the player's signature. But the best opportunities to earn money outside of football lay in London, not the East Midlands. James stayed at Highbury.

The Bystander touched on his financial worth:

> James, I suppose, makes about £1,500 a year ... not out of his playing abilities for the maximum salary of a footballer is £386 a year, which seems to me very poor pay. James supplements his income by journalism, and by his work in the sports department of a big London store, but very few of his fellow players are as fortunate as he is, and for most of them a four-figure income is very nearly beyond their dreams of avarice.

In the summer of 1937, at the age of 36 and struggling to shake off injuries, he retired. He had made 259 appearances and scored 27 goals. Unlike his earlier career at Raith and Preston, with Arsenal James – who won 4 more caps while with the Gunners – played a more withdrawn role, creating chances for Bastin, Lambert, Jack, Hulme, and later Drake. He went to coach in Poland for a short time, and in 1938 applied to become a manager but the FA ruled that his association with a pools firm prevented that. In 1942 he suffered a fractured rib while serving on a Royal Artillery gun site. In the post-war years he continued with journalism, and in 1949 returned to Highbury to coach junior players. Alex James – the player famous for his baggy shorts that were said to hide the long johns that protected rheumatic knees – was only 51 when he died, from cancer, at the Royal Northern Hospital in London on 1 June 1953. The Gunners' manager, Tom Whittaker, said, 'He did as much as anybody to make Arsenal what they have become.'

Ray Bowden

Despite scoring more than 100 goals in just 1 season for Looe, Ray Bowden's frail physique made Plymouth Argyle manager Bob Jack wonder whether the 17-year-old solicitor's clerk, the son of a signal porter, would withstand the rigours of football as played in the Third Division South. So his introduction was gradual: 1 appearance in 1926-27; 2 more games in 1927-28. But then Jack was convinced. In 1928-29 Bowden played 29 times and rewarded the manager's faith with 21 goals. By the time Herbert Chapman paid £5,000 to bring the player to Arsenal in March 1933, Bowden had scored 87 times in 153 games and helped Argyle to win promotion to the Second Division in 1929-30.

Even then it took Arsenal officials 3 trips to Plymouth before Bowden could be persuaded to forsake Argyle for a life in London. After all, the maximum wage of £8 per week was still £8 per week wherever it was earned. Or perhaps Argyle didn't want to let go of their star, even for an amount of money that would make a huge difference to the club's finances – although, despite reports to that effect, it was hardly a record for Arsenal who, 5 years earlier, had paid £10,890 for Bolton's David Jack, son of the Plymouth manager who sold them Bowden.

Bowden made his Arsenal debut shortly after signing, at inside-right at home to Wolves. Arsenal lost 2-1 but Bowden scored their goal. *The Staffordshire Sentinel* reported: 'Bowden, like many a man when playing for a new club, scored a good goal, his left-foot effort, taken when the ball reached him unexpectedly, was most praiseworthy.'

He played in 7 of the last 9 games – and scored twice – as Arsenal won the First Division for the second time in 3 seasons. As the Gunners completed a hat-trick of titles, Bowden scored 27 goals in 56 games through 1933-4-5. In the first of those seasons he was joint top scorer with Cliff Bastin.

While he was with Plymouth he had toured Canada with an FA party, from May to July 1931, and in September 1934 he won his first full England cap, against Wales at Ninian Park. Nineteen-year-old Stanley Matthews of Stoke City was also making his England debut that day, and scored from a Bowden pass in the 64th minute. Bowden had earlier laid on a goal for Manchester City's Fred Tilson. England won 4-0. Two months later Bowden was 1 of 7 Arsenal players who lined up against Italy in the 'Battle of Highbury'. Altogether he played 6 times for England, scoring against Wales in February 1936 at Molineux. Wales won 2-1. His final England appearance was at Highbury, in a 6-2 win over Hungary in December 1936.

Bowden played in the 1936 FA Cup final win over Sheffield United – he scored 5 goals in the Cup run – but the ankle that he had first injured against Italy was beginning to bother him more. In 1936-37 he missed 14 League matches, and although he played in 10 of the first 13 games of 1937-38, by the time Arsenal had won yet another title Bowden was a Newcastle United player. He signed for the Magpies in November 1937, for £5,000. He had scored 47 goals in 136 appearances for the Gunners. Newcastle narrowly escaped relegation in his first season at St James's Park and he retired in 1940, after the Football League closed down due to the war. He scored 6 goals in 48 League games for the Magpies.

He returned to Plymouth where, with his brother, he ran a sports shop in Mayflower Street. Ray Bowden died on 23 September 1998, aged 89. He was the last surviving link with the Chapman era.

Ted Drake

'The Arsenal Football Club should adopt the motto of the Canadian North-West Mounted Police. Like the famous force it always gets its man.'

Clifford Webb, writing in the *Daily Herald* in March 1934, was reporting on the transfer of centre-forward Ted Drake from Southampton, for £6,500. 'Arsenal have spent more than £20,000 on centre-forwards alone during the past few seasons,' wrote Webb. 'In all there is something like £50,000-worth of forwards at Highbury.'

Although born in Southampton – on 16 August 1912 – Drake might have become a Tottenham Hotspur player before he ever arrived at The Dell. A talented schoolboy footballer, he missed a trial match for Spurs because of injury and was playing for Winchester City and working as a gas meter inspector when Saints manager George Kay spotted him and signed him as an amateur in November 1931 when he was 19. After 1 season at The Dell, he travelled to Highbury for talks with Arsenal but returned to play 1 more season with Southampton before Arsenal finally got their man, although even then he almost changed his mind at the last minute.

Drake made a spectacular start with the Gunners. In 1934-35 he broke the club's individual scoring record for 1 season with 42 goals in 41 matches, and the following season set a First Division record of 7 goals in 1 match, at Villa Park on 14 December 1935. Despite fielding 6 internationals Villa found themselves 3-0 down at half-time to a Drake hat-trick. By the hour mark he had doubled his tally and with a minute to go scored yet again. He had earlier hit the crossbar with a shot that a linesman ruled had not crossed the line. Jackie Palethorpe scored for Villa, who lost 7-1 before a home crowd of 58,469. That afternoon Drake had just 9 shots: 7 goals, 1 saved and 1 disallowed. 'As Easy As Shelling Peas' said a headline in that afternoon's Birmingham *Sports Argus*.

With Arsenal Drake won 2 League championship medals, in 1934-35 and 1937-38 (his 7 goals in the last 10 games of 1933-34, although vital, did not qualify him for a medal) and an FA Cup winners' medal in 1936 when he scored the only goal of the final against Sheffield United. Injury had meant that he was a doubt right up to the day. He was the Gunners' leading scorer for 5 consecutive seasons – 1934-35 to 1938-39 – and by the time war was declared, he had scored 136 goals in 182 League and FA Cup matches. He also scored 6 goals in 5 appearances for England.

He made his last appearance for Arsenal in a Football League South match at Upton Park in May 1945 before retiring because of a spinal injury suffered earlier against Reading. On 28 August 1945, the *Daily Herald* reported:

> For some time Drake was on his back in a plaster cast. Mr George Allison, Arsenal manager, said yesterday, 'I am afraid that Drake is finished with more vigorous sports [Drake had also played first-class cricket for Hampshire], although he may be able play a little goal.' Drake, in civilian clothes – he is on his discharge leave from the RAF – watched Arsenal's game yesterday with West Ham at Upton Park.

In October 1946 he was coaching Hendon. He managed Reading to runners-up position in the Third Division South in 1948-49 and 1951-52 but only the champions were promoted, and then in May 1952 he took over as Chelsea manager and guided them to their first-ever Football League championship in 1954-55. Thereafter, things went downhill with many of the title-winning team past their best. In September 1961 Drake was sacked, the board citing 'a general lack of success'. He was Vic Buckingham's assistant at Fulham and Barcelona, and then coached Fulham's reserve team and scouted for the Cottagers. He became a Fulham director and life president. He was a member of the pools panel in 1963, worked as a bookmaker and a life assurance salesman. Ted Drake died at Raynes Park in May 1995. He was 82.

Wilf Copping

On 2 June 1934 *The (Sheffield) Star Green 'Un* reported:

> With the appointment of Mr G. Allison as manager of Arsenal FC there is evidently to be no change in the policy of the club – in effect, it is determined to get the really first-class men it desires, if money can achieve that object and the players are willing. Following the acquisition of Crayston, the big Bradford centre-half-back, Arsenal today made the biggest close season capture, securing the transfer from Leeds United of Wilfred Copping, the English international left-half-back.

The Yorkshire Post said that Copping 'at first gave the impression of having little more to recommend him than an extraordinary spirit of tenacity' but had since 'acquired sufficient polish to be picked for his country.' The paper added:

> Copping undoubtedly possesses a temperament for the big occasions, and his knowledge of tactics, his ability to vary his methods and to adapt himself to the requirements of his forwards have been outstanding features of the progress he has made ... the way he supported Bastin in the international match against Scotland at Wembley will long be remembered, and his association with the brilliant young forward at Highbury should make the Arsenal left wing the best in the country.

The paper also commented that Copping was 'a very keen tackler and this quality has, no doubt, endeared him to the selectors of representative teams, for he was never content to be a mere exhibition player.'

Indeed, Wilf Copping daunted opponents even before kick-off. He never shaved before a match and his stubble helped fuel the menace that came with a reputation for bone-jarring tackles. Herbert Chapman had identified him as a target, and after Chapman's sudden death George Allison kept on the trail and signed him for £8,000.

Copping was born at Middlecliffe, a hamlet close to Barnsley, on 17 August 1907 and joined Leeds from Middlecliffe Rovers in March 1929. Copping was an ever-present in his first season with Leeds, part of a formidable half-back line along with Willis Edwards and Ernie Hart, both of whom also played for England. In 5 seasons at Elland Road Copping won 6 caps and made 162 League appearances. His Arsenal debut was at Portsmouth on the first day of the 1934-35 season and thereafter he was a regular until he injured a knee at Goodison Park in mid-March and missed the last 9 games of the season, Scottish international Frank Hill taking over as Arsenal completed their hat-trick of First Division titles.

Copping recovered to play in most of Arsenal's games for the next 4 seasons. He played in another championship-winning season, 1937-38, and in the 1936 FA Cup-winning team, and added another 13 England caps including the 'Battle of Highbury' when he was England's enforcer against Italy. For the Gunners, he made 185 appearances before he rejoined Leeds in March 1939, for £3,500, telling Arsenal that he could see war coming and wanted to take his wife and family back up north before he joined up. He played 12 more times for Leeds and won another cap, his twentieth, against Romania in Bucharest in May 1939.

After war was declared, Copping became a reserve policeman in Leeds before joining the Army. He served in North Africa as a sergeant. He played a few games for Leeds when home on leave, as well as making guest appearances for Arsenal and Hartlepool United. In 1945 he coached an Army XI in Dusseldorf, then Beerschot AC in Antwerp. In January 1946, it was reported that he was manager of the Belgium national team that had arrived to play England and Scotland. The following July he was appointed trainer-coach at Southend United. He later had similar positions at Bristol City and Coventry City before retiring from football in 1959, to work at Ford in Dagenham. He retired from there in 1972. Wilf Copping died in Southend in June 1980, aged 72.

Jack Crayston

When Jack Crayston signed for Arsenal in May 1934 the *Yorkshire Evening Post* commented that:

> Good half-back though the local soccer fraternity knew him to be [there was] no recognition in the metropolitan columns; no more in fact than was accorded to any Second Division man. Attached to the Arsenal playing staff he at once becomes a 'star' and is given the full benefit of large headline print ... it is really funny how soon a player is placed high in the football world when translated to the select precincts of Highbury.

The *Daily Herald* reported that the fee was 'pretty substantial because Arsenal were not the only pebbles on the beach ... . Backed another winner, too, for Crayston is a fine, natural footballer ... . Consistency is the former Bradford six-footer's middle name. Seldom, if ever, been known to have an off-day. That's how the clubs like 'em.'

Crayston was born at Grange-over-Sands on 9 October 1910 and played for Ulverston Town in the North-Western League before joining Barrow in 1928. He made 77 Third Division North appearances for them before signing for Bradford in May 1930. Four years and 97 League games later he was on his way from Park Avenue to Highbury for £5,250, despite having suffered both a broken wrist and a broken leg with Bradford the previous season.

Few players could have enjoyed a more comfortable League debut. On 1 September 1934, Arsenal beat Liverpool 8-1 at Highbury and Crayston marked his first appearance with a goal. It was also Wilf Copping's home debut and the *Daily Herald* reported that they 'created a deep impression and are likely to make the Arsenal defence stronger than ever.' In July the same paper had reported the signing of inside-right James Marshall from Glasgow Rangers, expressing the view that 'Arsenal may have said to have made the catch of the season.' A Scotland international who averaged better than a goal every 2 games in over 250 appearances for Rangers, Marshall was also a doctor who made only 4 League appearances for Arsenal before moving to West Ham United and then giving up professional football altogether in 1937 for a job with Bermondsey Borough Council.

Crayston, though, went from strength to strength. Altogether he made 184 appearances for Arsenal, scoring 17 goals. He won 2 League championship medals, in 1934-35 and 1937-38, and an FA Cup winners' medal in 1936. He was capped 8 times for England between December 1935 and December 1937. The Second World War put a premature end to his Football League career, although he continued to play in wartime matches until an injury sustained in a Football League South match against West Ham in December 1943 forced his retirement. He had made 93 wartime appearances and scored 26 goals. In July 1945, with the rank of flying officer, he was a sports instructor at RAF Henlow in Bedfordshire.

After his demobilisation Crayston joined the Arsenal coaching staff and in 1948 became assistant manager to Tom Whittaker. On Whittaker's death in October 1956, Crayston was promoted. Arsenal were eleventh in the table when he took over, went up to third after a run of 10 unbeaten games, and finished fifth. The following season, however, the Gunners finished twelfth with their lowest points total since 1930. There was also a sensational exit from the FA Cup: in the third round at the hands of mid-table Third Division South club Northampton Town. At a board meeting in May 1958, frustrated by the lack of money to buy new players, Crayston resigned after 24 years' service to Arsenal.

He moved back to Yorkshire that summer, and took over as manager of Doncaster Rovers until March 1959 when he became secretary-manager with Jackie Bestall as team manager. Crayston left Belle Vue when his contract expired on 1 July 1961. He then ran a newsagent's and general store in Streetly, Sutton Coldfield. He lived in retirement in that area until his death on Boxing Day 1992, aged 82.

Bernard Joy

Imagine a football club resting 5 of its players so that they would be fit for an international match 3 days hence. It happened on Wednesday, 1 April 1936 when Arsenal left out George Male, Eddie Hapgood, Jack Crayston, Ray Bowden and Cliff Bastin, all of whom had been selected to play against Scotland at Wembley that Saturday. As it happened, Bowden did not play due to injury. The Gunners also had centre-halves Herbie Roberts and Norman Sidey injured, which meant a debut for England amateur international Bernard Joy, who had signed for Arsenal a year earlier.

The midweek afternoon game against mid-table Bolton Wanderers attracted only 10,485, Highbury's lowest attendance for many years. It was a sad afternoon. Ronnie Westcott, who had given Arsenal a second-minute lead, collided with Bolton goalkeeper Fred Swift and, in only his second League game, damaged a knee so badly that his playing career ended there and then. The *Daily Herald*'s Clifford Webb said that Bernard Joy 'obviously felt strange trying to play the recognised Arsenal role of stopper, but he used his head extremely well and, in the second half, gave quite a useful of exhibition of cool defence.'

Joy had a memorable year in 1936. He also skippered Casuals to victory in the FA Amateur Cup final against Ilford at the Crystal Palace, captained the Great Britain football team at the Berlin Olympics and became the last amateur footballer to win a full England cap. In Vienna, on 6 May, England lost 2-1. Then it was on to Brussels where Joy made his debut. England lost again, which meant that in 5 games abroad between 1934 and 1936 they had been beaten 4 times. Newspapers were scathing but excused Joy from criticism. One agency report said:

> England's footballers' prestige on the Continent suffered another severe blow when Belgium, a team that do most of their training and playing in the evenings, won by three goals

to two ... . The Englishmen were obviously a tried team ... apart from Bernard Joy, the amateur international, the other defenders were very leg weary long before the finish.

Belgium's *L'Étoile Belge* said that Joy 'had created a favourable impression.'

Joy was born in Fulham on 29 October 1911, the son of a Metropolitan Police officer. After the University of London, he worked as a schoolteacher and played as an amateur with the Corinthians and Casuals clubs, Southend United and Fulham, for whom he made 1 appearance in the Second Division in 1933-34. In 1935, he played in the unofficial jubilee international between an England XI and an Anglo-Scots XI at Highbury, watched by a crowd of 8,944.

Despite winning that full international cap in 1936, it was 1937-38 before he became an Arsenal regular, winning a Football League championship medal that season. In 1937 he captained the FA team that toured Australia, New Zealand and Ceylon.

By the time war was declared Joy had made 92 appearances for Arsenal. He made 205 wartime appearances for the Gunners while serving as an RAF PT instructor. He also guested for Southampton and West Ham and played in 1 wartime international, a 6-2 win against Scotland at Wembley in 1944. His last League game was against Sheffield United at Highbury on 2 November 1946. That month the *Daily Herald* reported that:

> [Joy], one of the most outstanding amateur players to grace football, is to revert to his old love – the Isthmian League club, Corinthian-Casuals [the clubs had merged in 1939]. During his stay with Arsenal, when he earned the highest honours the game can bestow, Joy always paid his 'sub' to the old amateur club. And so automatically goes back to them. At 36 he has decided it is time to make room for the younger professionals on Arsenal's book, but he will always be available if required at Highbury.

In 1948 Joy retired from playing altogether. He became a national newspaper journalist and wrote the book *Forward Arsenal*, a history of the club. Bernard Joy died from cancer in Kenton, London, on 18 July 1984. He was 72.

Reg Lewis

Looking ahead to Arsenal's third-round FA Cup-tie in January 1938 the *Illustrated Police News* commented:

> Much depends upon the sort of team that Arsenal can field. Will Drake play? Lewis looked good as his deputy on Saturday, when he made his debut in League football. In fact, with what was his first big kick he found the net. But this cup-tie will be a different matter. If Lewis leads the line again and plays as cool a game as he did in Saturday's League match, Mr Allison's faith in him will prove well-founded. The Arsenal manager says he is a world-beater in the making.

Ted Drake did play – Arsenal beat Bolton 3-1 – and Reg Lewis made only 3 more appearances that season, scoring a goal in a 3-0 home win over Derby County to set Arsenal further on the way to another Football League championship.

Lewis's League debut had come against Everton at Highbury on New Year's Day 1938. Arsenal won 2-1 and the *Daily Mirror* wrote, 'Arsenal and Everton played so tamely that the game afforded no true guide. Fact is, though, that Arsenal were only second-best. Lewis, 17-year-old centre-forward, scored and played fairly well, but Arsenal can't get on so well without Drake.' Lewis's goal had come 12 minutes after the start of a game against a team that would lose 14 away games that season.

Just over a year earlier, on 14 November 1936, 16-year-old Reg Lewis had scored Margate's goal when they lost 2-1 to Dulwich Hamlet in the fourth qualifying round of the FA Cup at Hartsdown Park. It was the first time that the amateurs of Dulwich had beaten a professional side. It was also the last FA Cup match that Margate played under its nursery arrangement with Arsenal. On 15 March 1937 Reg Lewis signed professional forms for the Gunners. Thirteen years later he would be a Wembley hero.

Lewis was born in Bilston, Staffordshire, on 7 March 1920 but was raised in south London and would spend his entire professional career with Arsenal. If it wasn't for the Second World War, he would surely have added many more official appearances and goals to his name. In 1938-39 he scored 7 goals in 15 League matches, and for the Reserves 43 goals in 31 London Combination games including 6 and 5 in successive matches.

Ironically, it was during the war that his career blossomed. After 2 appearances and 1 goal in the aborted 3-match First Division season of 1939-40, he had the remarkable record of 142 goals in only 128 wartime matches, including 4 in the 7-1 defeat of Charlton Athletic in the 1943 Football League Cup South final. After serving with the British Army of the Rhine in occupied Germany, in 1946-47 he scored 29 goals in 28 appearances, and in August 1946 replaced the injured Tommy Lawton in the Bolton Disaster Fund match between England and Scotland at Maine Road. In 1947-48 he scored 14 goals in 28 games as Arsenal won the Football League championship again with Ronnie Rooke scoring 33 times in 42 matches. That season Charlton again had reason to rue meeting Lewis who scored another 4 when Arsenal won 6-0 at Highbury in September.

The 1949-50 season was particularly memorable for Lewis. He had 19 goals in 31 League matches, won 2 England 'B' caps, and, most memorably, scored both goals as Arsenal won the FA Cup by beating Liverpool 2-0 at Wembley. Thereafter injuries severely restricted his appearances and in the summer of 1953, at the age of 33, he retired, having missed an entire season. His final appearance had come in a 6-1 away defeat at the hands of Manchester United on 26 April 1952. Altogether he scored 116 goals in 175 League and FA Cup matches for Arsenal, despite missing 6 seasons due to the war. He ran a public house in south London before going into the insurance business. Reg Lewis died on 2 April 1997 in Chadwell Heath. He was 77.

Leslie Compton

For their visit to Villa Park on 25 April 1932, Arsenal made 4 changes to the team that had lost the FA Cup final to Newcastle United 2 days earlier. Among the replacements was 19-year-old Leslie Compton, a former Hampstead Town player who had recently signed professional forms although he had been on Arsenal's books as an amateur since 1931. Compton replaced injured skipper Tom Parker at right-back. Villa's Jack Mandley opened the scoring after only 8 minutes, and former England schoolboy international Ray Parkin equalised for Arsenal. The 1-1 draw took the Gunners up to second place in the First Division behind Everton. That was how the season would finish: Everton champions; Arsenal runners-up.

On that Monday evening in Birmingham, though, all eyes were on Arsenal's newest recruit. 'Brilliant' was how the *Daily Herald* described Compton, who 'played with the coolness and anticipation of the man for whom he deputised.' An agency report to regional newspapers said that Compton 'played a magnificent game … and was given an ovation at the close.'

It was, however, a somewhat stuttering start to what would eventually become a long and distinguished career. Leslie Compton held his place for what remained of that season and for the first few games of the next. But as Parker's career ended, so George Male took his place. Compton filled in whenever needed before war intervened, during which he served in the Army and continued to play for Arsenal. He was converted to a makeshift centre-forward with astonishing success: 92 goals in 131 games including 10 in a 15-2 win over Clapton Orient in February 1941, the first 7 of them coming in a row. Guesting for Chester in February 1943 Compton scored a hat-trick in a 5-4 win over Everton at Goodison Park.

It was after the war that Leslie Compton's career really took off, and as a centre-half. After missing the first 6 games of 1947-48 because of cricket commitments (for Middlesex between 1938 and 1956 he scored 5,814 first-class runs, averaging 16.75 with 1 century; kept wicket taking 468 catches and making 131 stumpings; and took 12 wickets at 47.41 apiece), he missed only 1 more match – the last of the season – as Arsenal won the First Division. For 5 seasons Compton was the rock at the centre of the Gunners' defence, but still found time to score the occasional goal, none more vital than against Chelsea in the 1950 FA Cup semi-final at White Hart Lane. Arsenal were 2-1 down when Leslie Compton scored a late equaliser, a header from a corner taken by his brother Denis. In the final minute the pair might have won it. Denis collected a clearance from Leslie and, according to *The People*, 'sent the Chelsea crossbar a-shuddering while Medhurst merely looked on hopefully.'

The Comptons duly collected their winners' medals when Arsenal beat Liverpool at Wembley, and 7 months later Leslie, at the age of 38, became the oldest outfield player to make an England debut when he played against Wales at Roker Park. One week later he was capped again, against Yugoslavia at Highbury.

After playing only 4 times for Arsenal in 1951-52 he retired with a total of 270 appearances and 6 goals to his name. He might have played in that season's FA Cup final against Newcastle United but Ray Daniel was declared fit. It would have been a fine reward for Compton who, earlier in the season, had turned down a move because he would 'rather be a reserve team player at Arsenal than a first-teamer anywhere else'.

He worked as a coach and scout for Arsenal before taking over the Prince of Wales pub in Highgate and was a representative for a wines and spirits business. Leslie Compton was born on 12 September 1912 at Woodford. He died at his son's home in Essex on 27 December 1984, aged 72, following complications with diabetes after a foot had been amputated 2 years earlier.

Bryn Jones

It was a saga that engaged football followers for over a year. In March 1937, the *Coventry Evening Telegraph* announced, 'Bryn Jones not for the Arsenal … . Mr Allison offered a transfer fee that would have been a record for the Wolverhampton club, but it was declined by the Wanderers directors.' Allison was looking for a replacement for Alex James, and when he did finally get his man, on 4 August 1938, Arsenal had to pay a British record fee of £14,000 to prise Jones away from Molineux.

A native of Merthyr Tydfil, born on 14 February 1912, Jones played for Merthyr Amateurs and Glenavon before moving to Aberaman in October 1933. He demanded a share of the £250 that the Irish League club received for his registration but the system of accrued benefits existed only in England. The Welsh League club, though, did well out of the deal: 3 weeks' later Jones moved to Wolves for a transfer fee reported to be £1,500. Five years, 10 Wales caps, 163 League games and 52 goals later he was the talk of football when Arsenal parted with that record fee. The rights or wrongs of paying such a large sum of money for a footballer spilled over into the news pages. After all, the Depression was still a painful and very recent memory, and war clouds were already gathering over Europe.

In the meantime, Jones made a good start to his Highbury career, scoring on his debut, at home to Portsmouth on the first day of the new season. 'Fortune favoured the expensive,' said the *Liverpool Echo*, after the opener was an own goal before Jones made it 2-0. He scored twice more in his next 3 games but then the goals dried up and he added only 1 more all season. By November Allison found himself defending his new signing: 'I am definitely fully satisfied with Bryn Jones who will be an indefinitely more valuable player to this club once he has become accustomed to his new surroundings and his colleagues. I do not expect him to be Alex James. It will be quite enough if he is himself.'

At Wolves, along with most the first team – 2 refused – Jones had found himself being injected with monkey glands, an alternative therapy introduced by Major Frank Buckley who felt that it would rejuvenate the players faster. In October 1938, the *Sunderland Daily Echo and Shipping Gazette* said advocates of the treatment pointed out that since he moved to Highbury, Jones had not been receiving monkey gland treatment 'and so far this season has scarcely been worth 14,000 pence to Arsenal let alone £14,000.'

The Second World War broke out before Jones could begin another season. He joined the Royal Artillery and served in Italy and North Africa. He was 34 when the Football League resumed. When Arsenal won the League again, in 1947-48, he made only 7 appearances. He scored when Arsenal won the 1948 FA Charity Shield match against Manchester United but made his final appearance on 16 April 1949, at Goodison Park. He added another 7 caps to his tally while at Highbury but altogether had made only 74 appearances for Arsenal, scoring 7 goals. Even allowing for the war it was a miserly return for the money he cost. He scored 6 goals in 25 wartime games for the Gunners and played in 8 wartime internationals.

In June 1949, he was transferred to Norwich City and scored once in 23 Third Division South games for them, ending his Carrow Road days as player-coach. After football he ran a newsagent's and tobacconist's business in Stoke Newington. A genuinely modest man who was always surprised when anyone asked him for his autograph, he retired in 1979 and died in north London on 18 October 1985, aged 73. He was 1 of 5 brothers – Shoni, Ivor, Emlyn and Bert were the others – to play professional football.

Ronnie Rooke

Ronnie Rooke was most people's idea of a rugged centre-forward. Craggy face surmounted by a Roman nose, wavy black hair, bandy legs, shirt sleeves flapping – he certainly looked the part. Most importantly, he scored goals – lots of them. In fact, he was a goalscoring sensation, even as a schoolboy. He scored 17 in 1 match for his school team against a Pick of Guildford XI. And he continued to score goals throughout his career.

Born in Guildford in December 1911, when he left school he lied about his age and joined Stoke City but could not settle in the Potteries and returned to London. After a spell with Guildford City, for whom he scored 16 goals in 14 games, in March 1933 he signed professional forms for Third Division South Crystal Palace. Rooke scored regularly for the reserve team but after 2 goals in 6 League appearances in 1933-34, and 4 in 7 matches in 1934-35, the goals dried up. He played only 4 times in 1935-36 but failed to find the net, and in November 1936 he moved to Fulham. The fee was reported to be £300.

At Craven Cottage he made an immediate impact. He scored a hat-trick on his debut, against West Ham, hit 3 more trebles that season, and ended 1936-37 as the Cottagers' leading scorer with 19 goals in 22 Second Division appearances. The hat-tricks kept coming – 10 in all – and in an FA Cup game against Bury in January 1939 he scored all Fulham's goals in a 6-0 win.

Rooke probably deserved more than his solitary wartime England cap, awarded against Wales at Molineux in October 1942, and in November 1945 he guested for Arsenal in their friendly match against Moscow Dynamo at White Hart Lane. Like so many of his fellow professionals, he had served as an RAF PT instructor during the war.

In December 1946, after 64 goals in only 92 League and FA Cup matches for Fulham, Arsenal took him on permanently, for £1,000 and two reserve players, David Nelson and Cyril Grant. The *Coventry Evening Telegraph* was singularly unimpressed:

> Rooke ... rarely had a kick at Highfield Road last week. Rooke is a good player, but if Coventry City had paid good and heavy money for any man of that age they would have been wrong in my estimation. Admittedly the City are not so desperately placed as Arsenal but even if they were I could not agree to the wisdom of the move.

In fact, although he was by now 35, Rooke took the First Division by storm. He scored on his debut, at home to Charlton Athletic on 14 December 1946, and ended that season with 21 goals in 24 League games, and with Reg Lewis's 29 goals in 28 matches between them, the pair probably saved Arsenal from a fate much worse than the Gunners' eventual finishing position of thirteenth.

The following year Rooke was magnificent – 33 goals in 42 games as Arsenal won the title. It made him the leading scorer in the whole of the Football League. He made his final appearance for the Gunners at Goodison Park on 16 April 1949, ending the season with another 14 goals from 22 matches to bring his overall Arsenal tally to 69 goals in only 93 appearances.

He returned to Crystal Palace as player-manager, and in October 1949 was sent off in a match at Millwall. He had, however, lost none of his scoring touch despite being in his late 30s, and hit 21 goals in 39 League games in 1949-50. The Palace directors made £20,000 available for new players but Rooke enjoyed little success. In November 1950, with Palace bottom of the table, he resigned, but was still top scorer at the end of the season, albeit with only 5 goals (from 6 games). He managed Bedford Town in 2 spells before taking a job at Heathrow Airport. Ronnie Rooke died from lung cancer in July 1985, aged 73.

Tom Whittaker

Football has rarely seen the sort of dedication that Tom Whittaker gave to Arsenal. In a career that spanned 37 years, from the end of the First World War until the mid-1950s, he served the Gunners as player, trainer and manager.

Whittaker was born in Aldershot on 21 July 1898, the son of a regular soldier, but grew up in Newcastle upon Tyne where he trained as a marine engineer. In 1917, he joined the Royal Garrison Artillery as an ordnance engineer and then transferred to his first choice, the Royal Navy, before being demobbed in November 1919.

There was a letter waiting for him, from Arsenal's new manager Leslie Knighton, to whom Whittaker had been recommended by someone who had seen him playing Army football. When he travelled for a trial at Highbury, he found Knighton waiting for him at the tube station and together they walked up Avenell Road, Knighton doing most of the talking and Whittaker wondering if he really wanted a football career or whether to rejoin the Navy.

He chose football and made his League debut at the Hawthorns on Easter Tuesday, 6 April 1920. Arsenal lost 1-0 and the *Yorkshire Post* reported, 'Whittaker had a couple of excellent chances of shooting for the Arsenal who really deserved to draw.'

It was at half-back that he established himself, playing in 36 matches in 1921-22 before finding himself once more in and out of the team. He made only 1 appearance in 1924-25 – the regular half-back line was now Billy Milne, Jack Butler and Bob John – but was chosen for that summer's FA tour to Australia. The tour started well. On 6 June, at Wollongong, 52 miles south of Sydney, the FA XI beat South Coast 8-1 and Whittaker injured a knee so badly that his playing career had ended after 70 appearances and 6 goals for Arsenal.

For the rest of the tour Whittaker acted as assistant to masseur Moses Atherton. It was the beginning of a new career. Back at Highbury he was appointed assistant trainer to George Hardy, and then when Hardy retired in February 1927 Whittaker took over. He worked with Arsenal throughout their glory years of the 1930s and acted as trainer to the full England team and on several FA tours.

When war was declared in September 1939, along with several others on the staff at Highbury, he became an ARP warden before joining the RAF. Ordered to undertake PT duties he argued that his engineering background could see him better used. In the months approaching D-Day he worked day and night helping to make damaged aircraft battleworthy. Awarded the MBE in the 1945 New Year's Honours List, he was demobbed with the rank of squadron leader and returned to Highbury, this time as assistant manager to George Allison. With the inspired signings of Ronnie Rooke and Joe Mercer they steered Arsenal clear of relegation in 1946-7.

In June 1947 Whittaker succeeded Allison. He signed Don Roper and Archie Macaulay, and in 1947-48 Arsenal romped away with the League title. After declining an offer to manage Milan, or take over Italy's national team – £8,000 a year for as long as he liked, bonuses, a car, an interpreter and a house in Rome – Whittaker managed Arsenal to victory in the 1950 FA Cup final. With 10 men – Wales international full-back Walley Barnes had to go off injured after 35 minutes – they lost a gallant battle in the 1952 Wembley final against Newcastle, and in 1952-53 won their last match of the season to lift their seventh League championship. But now an ageing team was breaking up and some indifferent seasons followed. An attempt to sign Stanley Matthews failed. Suffering from nervous exhaustion Tom Whittaker was ordered to take a complete rest. He was admitted to hospital and died on 24 October 1956, aged only 58. Jack Crayston, the man who replaced him as Arsenal manager, said, 'He was a great man, and more than a boss to us … . In all my years with the club I never heard him say an unkind thing.'

George Swindin

Some thought that George Allison had erred when he paid £4,000 for Bradford City's goalkeeper George Swindin in April 1936. One year earlier Swindin had collided with West Ham's Jackie Morton 10 minutes from the end of a Second Division match at Upton Park. He limped off but returned for the final few moments and was powerless to stop Dave Mangnall score the only goal of the game. Swindin collapsed again and was carried off. The *Leeds Mercury* said, 'He had played a brilliant game and the 31,000 gave him an enthusiastic ovation.'

A cartilage operation followed and it was 16 September 1935 before Swindin appeared again, at Leicester. Injured once more, he was out of the side again until the end of February before enjoying a run of 10 games in which Bradford went undefeated. Arsenal were looking for goalkeeping cover for Alex Wilson who had taken over from the injured Frank Moss. Swindin had made only 26 Second Division appearances for Bradford but Allison thought he had his man, despite his injury worries.

Wilson finished the season as Arsenal's first choice, which meant that he collected an FA Cup winners' medal when the Gunners beat Sheffield United in the 1936 final. Swindin's debut came in the second game of the following season, at Brentford on 3 September 1936. He made 19 appearances that season, sharing the goalkeeping spot with Frank Boulton. In 1937-38 he came in for the final 17 games, enough to guarantee him a League championship medal.

Swindin, who was born at Campsall, near Doncaster, on 4 December 1914, was on Rotherham United's books as an amateur when Bradford City signed him in 1934. During the Second World War, in which he was an Army PT instructor, he made 44 appearances for Arsenal and in 1943-44 guested 14 times for Derby County. When peacetime football resumed for 1946-47, after recovering from being on the wrong end of a 6-0 scoreline at Upton Park in an FA Cup third-round first-leg match in

January 1946, and then a 6-1 defeat at Molineux on the opening day of the new season, he was the Gunners' regular choice and in 1947-48 was ever-present as Arsenal won the First Division. He played in the 1950 FA Cup final victory over Liverpool and in the losing 1952 Wembley team. When Arsenal won the League Championship again, in 1952-53, Swindin suffered a back injury and made 14 appearances with future Wales international Jack Kelsey his replacement.

In February 1954 Swindin became player-manager of Peterborough United. He had made 294 appearances for the Gunners. After taking the Posh to the first 3 of what would be 6 consecutive Midland League titles before they were elected to the Football League, Swindin returned to Highbury in July 1958 as manager following the resignation of Jack Crayston.

In his first season he brought in Tommy Docherty, Jackie Henderson, Billy McCulloch and Len Julians, while Derek Tapscott, Cliff Holton, Stan Charlton and Jim Fotheringham all left Highbury. After heading the table for part of the season, Arsenal finished third after injuries to key players took their toll. In 1959-60 injuries again hit hard, including Welsh international Mel Charles, who was signed from Swansea Town for £42,250 plus 2 reserve players.

In November 1960 George Eastham was signed for £47,500 from Newcastle United, and Laurie Brown (from Northampton Town for £35,000) and John MacLeod (from Hibs for £40,000) joined Arsenal for the start of 1961-62, although free-scoring David Herd went to Manchester United at the same time.

This, alas, was Tottenham's era, and in April 1962 Swindin left Highbury for the last time. Critics said that he made too many changes in personnel and tactics but some were forced upon him by circumstances. He managed Norwich City for just 5 months, then Cardiff City (for whom he signed John Charles from Roma), and Kettering Town and Corby Town before emigrating to Spain. He returned to England and died in Kettering on 26 October 2005, aged 90.

Cliff Holton

Cliff Holton, young Arsenal centre-forward just out of the Services, took some Army discharge papers into Tom Whittaker's office for the manager's signature. Then, jokingly, he came running into the dressing room to tell his teammates, 'Here I am, out of the Army 5 minutes and Tom's transferred me to Korea United.'

So said *The People* newspaper on 13 August 1950.

Holton had been on Arsenal's books since October 1947, joining them as an 18-year-old full-back from Oxford City – he was born at Headington on 29 April 1929 – but spent his time in the reserves and on National Service. It was only after Whittaker converted him to a centre-forward that he began to progress, and on Boxing Day 1950 he made his First Division debut at Stoke City, where Arsenal went down 2-1.

His next appearance was probably more daunting – Manchester United at Old Trafford on 3 March 1951. Another former National Serviceman made his debut that day: 23-year-old Reuben Marden from Chelmsford City. Both had been scoring regularly for the reserve team: Holton 27 goals in 31 games; Marden, an outside-left, 21 in 26 games.

Again the Gunners lost, this time 3-1, but Holton marked his second appearance with a goal, the first of 88 he was to score in 216 League and FA Cup matches for Arsenal. United also fielded youngsters that day – 17-year-olds, centre-half Mark Jones and right-half Jeff Whitefoot. United were 2-0 after 32 minutes before Holton replied 6 minutes later following a fine move between Jimmy Logie and Ian McPherson, who had won the Distinguished Flying Cross (DFC) and Bar as an RAF flying officer during the Second World War.

At the end of a season in which Arsenal finished fifth, Holton had scored 5 goals in 10 games. He was now a regular and in 1951-52 his

17 goals in 28 games went a long way to Arsenal climbing to a final position of third. When the Gunners won the League championship in 1952-53 he had 19 goals in 21 games.

He was now one of the great characters in the Arsenal dressing room, and as time went on and Arsenal began to fall away, he was happy to play wherever he was needed. In 1955-56 he made most of his 31 appearances as a wing-half, returning to centre-forward for the last 9 games when, again, his goals helped Arsenal back to fifth. On 6 October 1956, he scored 4 times in a 7-3 win over Manchester City at Highbury from centre-forward.

His final appearance for Arsenal was at Turf Moor on 2 September 1958, after which the Gunners sold him to Watford for £10,000, which was a surprisingly big fee considering that Watford were mid-table in the newly formed Fourth Division, although it was reported that he was the first player to be sold with a hire-purchase agreement attached to the deal. At Vicarage Road he formed a successful partnership with Dennis Uphill, and when Watford were promoted in fourth place in 1959-60, Holton scored a club record 48 goals. That made him the leading scorer in the entire Football League, outscoring even Brian Clough at Middlesbrough.

In September 1961 Watford sold him to Northampton Town. He scored a hat-trick on his debut for the Cobblers, at Selhurst Park, and ended the season with 36 goals to break their club record, too. In December 1962, Holton moved to Crystal Palace and helped them to promotion to the Second Division in 1963-64 with 20 goals in 43 games. Manager Dick Graham sold him back to Watford in May 1965. He also played for Charlton Athletic and Leyton Orient before a knee injury ended his career.

Retired from football, he ran a precision engineering business until 1989, then organised golf tournaments before he retired altogether. Cliff Holton was only 67 when he died while on holiday in Spain in May 1996.

Doug Lishman

Two telegrams were delivered to the Arsenal dressing room at Bramall Lane on Saturday, 4 September 1948. They carried good luck messages to 2 debutants who formed an experimental left-wing pair for the Gunners against Sheffield United. The new boys were Stanley Matthews's brother-in-law, winger Tom Vallance, son of Jimmy Vallance, a former Stoke City player and now the Potters' trainer; and former Royal Marine commando Doug Lishman, newly signed from Walsall for £10,500 with outside-left Alf Morgan going to Fellows Park.

Vallance had served as an RAF pilot during the Second World War and on this day he replaced another RAF man – former Flying Officer Ian McPherson DFC and Bar, who was recovering from an operation on his toenails. Lishman, meanwhile, had been spotted by Walsall manager Harry Hibbs, a former England goalkeeper, while playing in a trial match at a local park. His 29 goals in 59 Third Division South matches for the Saddlers had now attracted the attention of bigger clubs. Lishman's debut game for the Gunners ended in a 1-1 draw, and Arsenal manager Tom Whittaker gave a cheerful verdict in the *Daily Mirror*: 'The team looked much more promising.' He described his new left-wing as 'quite effective after a nervous start'.

Lishman's third appearance, at home to Aston Villa on 11 September, was described by the *Daily Mirror* as:

> A nonsensical, scrappy mockery of football, played at walking pace with both teams like slow creaking walking machines lacking polish and finish … . Arsenal supporters are still looking to their team to turn the corner … but although they gathered the points by winning 3-1, this display, lacking polish, left much to be desired … Lishman, sadly lacking in experience, did not bring about the looked-for improvement.

Lishman and Vallance played together 15 times before Vallance made his final appearance in August 1949. That November he suffered a double fracture of a leg, and at the end of the 1952-53 season he was given a free transfer. Doug Lishman, meanwhile, went on to score 12 goals in 23 First Division games as Arsenal finished fifth in 1948-49. His next 2 seasons were marred by injury and after being passed over for the 1950 FA Cup final, on Christmas Day 1950 he too broke a leg, in the 3-0 defeat by Stoke at Highbury. For the return at the Victoria Ground on Boxing Day, Reg Lewis replaced Lishman, and Cliff Holton made his debut, at centre-forward. Lishman returned for the last 2 games of the season and finished as the Gunners' top scorer with 17 goals from 26 League matches.

In 1951-52 he was leading scorer again with 23 goals in 38 matches including hat-tricks in successive home games, against Fulham, West Brom and Bolton Wanderers. He played in that season's injury-hit FA Cup final defeat by Newcastle. Back to full fitness, in 1952-53 Lishman's goals – 22 in 39 games – saw Arsenal win the League championship once more, but this time by a goal average that was just 0.099 better than that of runners-up Preston.

Despite all this, Lishman never won a full England cap – he played in a 'B' international against Scotland in March 1953. He was Arsenal's top scorer for another 2 seasons, making 5 in all, and altogether had scored 135 goals in 243 appearances for the Gunners before he was sold to Nottingham Forest for £8,000 in March 1956. He was now 32, and Derek Tapscott had picked up his mantel. In April 1957 Lishman scored a hat-trick against Sheffield United that saw Forest promoted to the First Division behind champions Leicester City.

That summer he retired from football to join his father-in-law in a furniture business in Stoke, eventually taking over the business himself. Doug Lishman was born in Birmingham on 14 September 1923. He died in Stoke on 21 December 1994, aged 71.

Jack Kelsey

'You have to go back to the 1928-29 season to find Arsenal beaten 5-2 at Highbury,' said *The People* on Sunday, 25 February 1951. 'And that was the year their goalkeeper debutant – 22-year-old Alf Kelsey – was born.' The day before, the former crane driver and National Serviceman had conceded 2 goals in the first 17 minutes against Charlton and 3 before half-time. A poor back-pass by Lionel Smith led to number 4, and a minute from time Charlton's Sweden international Hans Jeppson floated past Smith and Walley Barnes before pushing the ball through Kelsey's legs and into the net.

No matter. Manager Tom Whittaker said, 'Kelsey is like a pilot who crashed on his first flight, but we've such faith in the lad that he'll be there next week.'

Jack Kelsey (he was named Alfred John) was still in Arsenal's goal 7 days later for the trip to Old Trafford where the ball was in the Arsenal net after 17 minutes and they lost 3-1. Kelsey made 2 more appearances that season, eventually being on a winning side against Wolves on 24 March. The following season was spent entirely in the reserves as George Swindin was ever-present, but when Arsenal won the First Division in 1952-53 Kelsey played in 25 matches after Swindin injured his back and then Ted Platt was also hurt.

Kelsey was Arsenal's first-choice goalkeeper for the next 9 seasons, with only a broken arm sustained against Sheffield United in an FA Cup replay at Bramall Lane in February 1959 sidelining him for long. He won no further honours with Arsenal but he was in goal when a London XI lost 8-2 on aggregate to a Barcelona XI (actually represented in full by FC Barcelona) in the 1958 Inter-Cities Fairs Cup final. Arsenal's Vic Groves and Dave Bowen also played.

Kelsey's first full cap for Wales came in March 1954 against Northern Ireland at Wrexham, and in 1955 he also played for Great

Britain against the Rest of Europe. He won 41 caps in total and played in the 1958 World Cup finals in Sweden. Kelsey, whose secret, he said, was to rub chewing gum on his hands to help the ball stick, had a brilliant game against Sweden in a Group 3 game at the Rasunda Stadium in Stockholm, thwarting attack after attack to earn Wales a 0-0 draw. In the quarter-finals at the Nya Ullevi Stadium in Gothenburg, Kelsey defied Brazil almost single-handedly for 73 minutes. Then, with the scoreline still goalless, Stuart Williams tried to block a shot from Pelé. The ball caught the right-back's studs before rolling slowly past Kelsey who was on the wrong foot. It was 17-year-old Pelé's first World Cup goal and sent Brazil into the semi-finals. Wales's reserve goalkeeper Ken Jones thought it would have gone in with or without the deflection. He said, 'It was a tame effort but there were about nine players all with a few yards of the ball. It was a nightmare for any goalkeeper.'

It was a back injury sustained while playing for Wales against Brazil in a friendly in Sao Paulo in May 1962 that ended Kelsey's playing career. Attempts to overcome it proved unsuccessful and in the November, he announced his retirement. He had made 351 appearances for Arsenal. A testimonial match for him against Glasgow Rangers at Highbury in May 1963 realised £7,000. He became the club's commercial manager, retiring from that post in 1989.

Jack Kelsey was born in Llansamlet, Swansea, on 19 November 1929 and joined Arsenal from the Swansea and District League club Winch Wen, where his father was chairman, in August 1949. He died at his home in Friern Barnet, north London in March 1992. He was 62. He had arranged for Arsenal to play at the Halfway Park, Winch Wen, to celebrate the 60th anniversary of his first club but died before the match took place. Arsenal honoured that commitment on 31 July 1993.

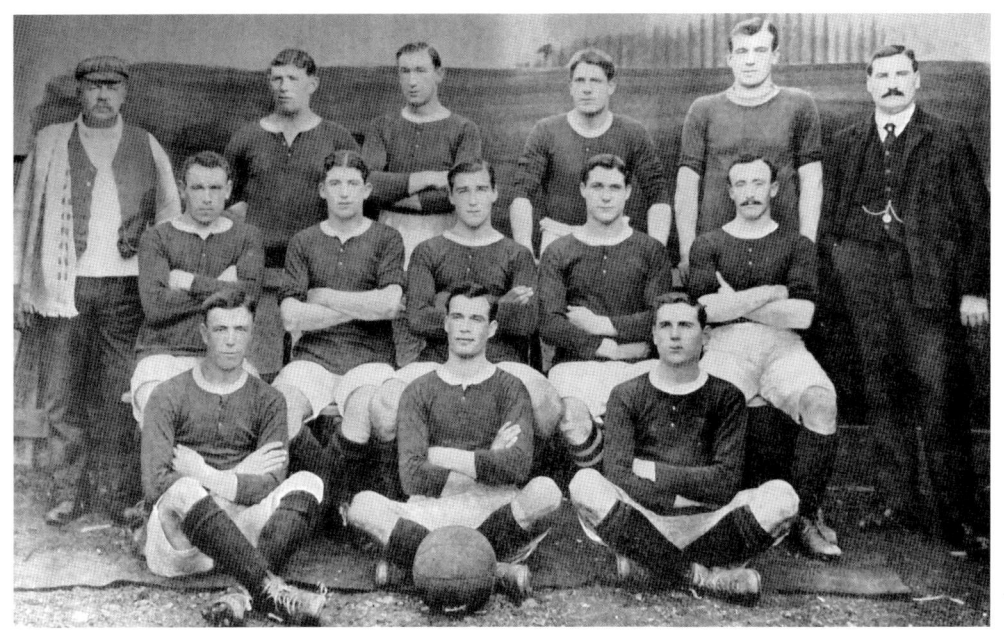

Woolwich Arsenal in 1905-06. Back row (left to right): Bob Dunmore (trainer), Jimmy Sharp, Jimmy Ashcroft, Percy Sands, Archie Cross, Phil Kelso (manager). Middle row: Archie Gray, Bobby Templeton, Andy Ducat, Tom Fitchie, Roddy McEachrane. Front row: Jimmy Bellamy, John Dick, Jimmy Blair. (Author's collection)

John Dick skippered Arsenal to promotion in 1904. (Author's collection)

Phil Kelso left Hibernian to take over from Harry Bradshaw as Arsenal's manager in 1904. (Author's collection)

Woolwich Arsenal's playing staff 1910-11. Back row (left to right): George Hardy (trainer), John Dick, Stephen Thomas, Edwin Bateup, Alf Common, Willis Rippon, Tom Hedley. Middle row: Archie Gray, Andy Ducat, John Grant, Duncan McDonald, Tim Rogers, Percy Sands. Front row: Charlie Lewis, Angus McKinnon, David Greenaway, Frank Heppinstall, George Morrell (manager), Harry Logan, David Neave, Joe Shaw, Roddy McEachrane. (Author's collection)

Charlie Buchan, whose transfer to Arsenal in 1925 was the subject of a libel action. (Author's collection)

Action around the Cardiff City goal in the 1927 FA Cup final. (Author's collection)

Above left: Arsenal paid a British record transfer fee of more than £10,000 to sign David Jack in 1928. (Author's collection)

Above right: Arsenal might have won the Double much earlier had it not been for an injury to their 'Wembley Wizard' Alex James. (Author's collection)

Left: George Male, the only footballer to play in 6 League championship-winning teams. (Author's collection)

Rival captains Tom Parker (Arsenal) and Tom Wilson (Huddersfield Town) shake hands before the 1930 FA Cup final. (Author's collection)

Cliff Bastin scored a record number of goals for an Arsenal winger. (Author's collection)

Eddie Hapgood, England's most capped player between the 2 world wars. (Author's collection)

Ninety years on, the statue of the great Herbert Chapman stands proudly outside the Emirates (Jonathan Wright)

Arsenal manager George Allison – 'thick-set, versatile, vastly energetic' with 'a laugh like Niagara Falls'. (Author's collection)

Herbie Roberts – 'No Roberts, no Arsenal' said one newspaper after the Gunners' centre-half was injured. (Author's collection)

England v The Rest of Europe at Highbury in 1938. Arsenal's Wilf Copping watches an aerial battle. (Author's collection)

Former Arsenal trainer Tom Whittaker – seen here with footballer-cricketer Arthur Milton – took over as manager in 1947. (Author's collection)

George Swindin punches clear from a Chelsea attack during the 1950 FA Cup semi-final. (Author's collection)

Leslie Compton clears from Liverpool's Albert Stubbins in the 1950 FA Cup final. Joe Mercer and Walley Barnes are in the background. (Author's collection)

David Herd was Arsenal's leading scorer for 4 consecutive seasons, 1957-58 to 1960-61. (Author's collection)

Bertie Mee, another former Gunners' trainer who became their manager, in his case winning the club's first Double in 1971. (Author's collection)

Winning goalscorer Charlie George does a forward roll while Liverpool's Larry Lloyd hugs Ray Kennedy at Wembley after the Gunners complete the Double in May 1971. (Ed Lacey/Popperfoto/Getty Images)

Liam Brady in front of the famous Arsenal Clock at Highbury. (Author's collection)

Pat Rice, Liam Brady and Malcolm Macdonald are in jubilant mood. (Author's collection)

George Armstrong's Arsenal career spanned 15 years, from George Swindin's managership to that of Terry Neill. (Author's collection)

Derby County's Bruce Rioch challenges Alan Ball at Highbury in April 1974. Rioch later managed the Gunners. (Author's collection)

Don Howe. A broken leg playing for Arsenal ended the playing career of the former England full-back. He became a highly respected coach and managed the Gunners between 1983 and 1986. (Author's collection)

Arsene Wenger and his staff watch intently during the Champions League match against Spartak in Moscow, November 2000. (Ross Kinnaird/AllSport via Getty Images)

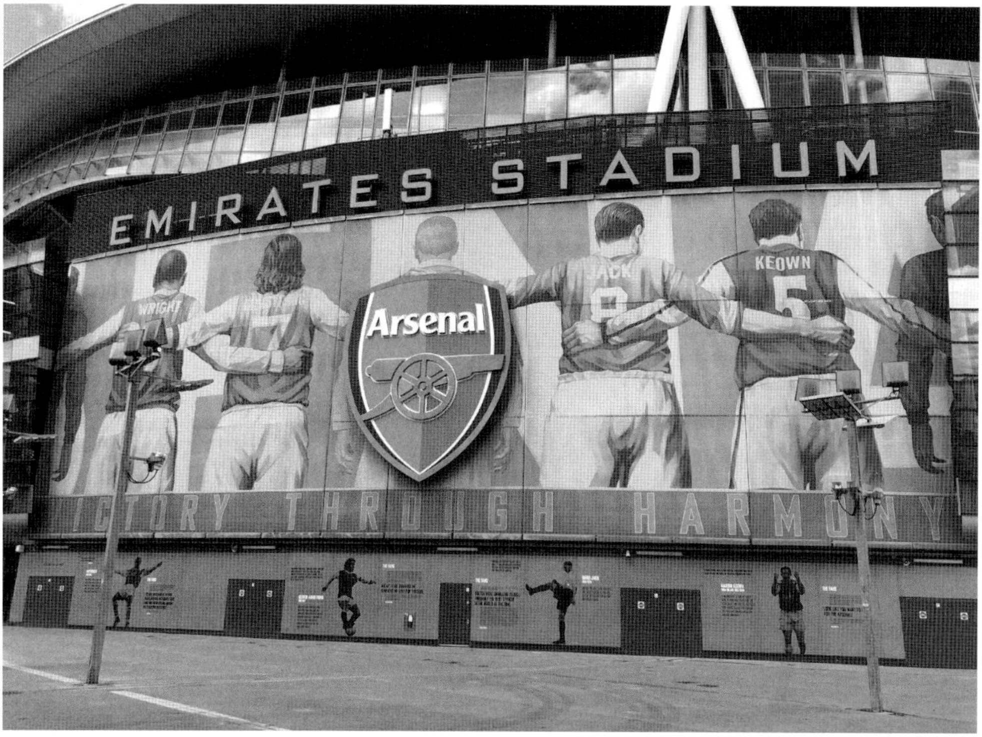

Some of the great Arsenal names commemorated on the walls of the Emirates Stadium (Jonathan Wright)

In typical pose, the statue of Thierry Henry at the Emirates. (Jonathan Wright)

This statue of Arsenal's long-serving Ken Friar OBE – it shows him playing football as a youngster outside Highbury in 1945 – pays tribute to his 60 years' plus service to the Gunners. (Jonathan Wright)

Ready for the new season. Unai Emery addresses the media at London Colney in August 2019. (Stuart MacFarlane/Arsenal FC via Getty Images)

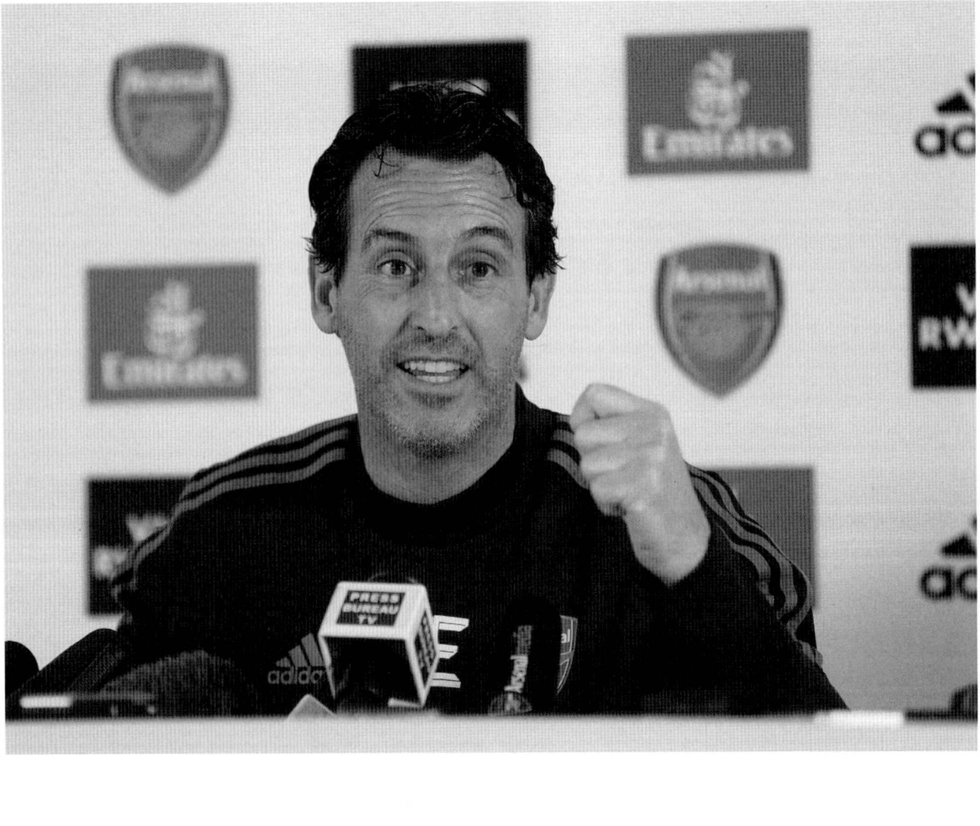

David Herd

Former Arsenal winger Joe Hulme was optimistic. He wrote:

> Arsenal had been playing good football. Don Roper, doing his 'Revie' in the middle, was spraying passes to his forwards. It was only inexperienced finishing by the four youngsters around him that stopped the Gunners from going ahead. I have a hunch that we will be hearing a lot more of the right-wing Arsenal paraded yesterday – Danny Clapton and David Herd. The Herd boy had two or three attempts at goal. If he had the finishing punch his father used to show he would have notched up more than his one goal. But it will come. I think he is made of the right Arsenal material. And he hasn't done badly so far – three games in the first team – one goal.

Hulme was reporting for *The People* on Arsenal's 2-1 defeat at Fratton Park on the final day of the 1954-55 season. David Herd, son of former Manchester City and Scotland forward Alex Herd, had joined Arsenal on 24 August 1954, the day after he had been demobbed from his National Service in the RAF Regiment. From Catterick he travelled straight to a Manchester hotel to sign from Stockport County for £10,000. Although his military service had severely interrupted his football career, Tom Whittaker had seen enough to convince him that this would be an excellent signing.

Writing in the *Daily Mirror* that day, Chris Bale said:

> When Arsenal's Tom Whittaker gets cracking he doesn't waste any time … . Whittaker made up his mind after seeing Herd score three goals in Stockport's trial match last

Saturday week. Three years ago young David created soccer history when both he and his father were in the Stockport attack in a League match against Hartlepool – and David scored one of the winning goals!

David Herd's Arsenal debut came on 19 February 1955 at Highbury where Don Roper scored the Gunners' goal in a 1-1 draw against Leicester City. The match was watched by the Shah of Persia and Queen Soraya, who saw the 21-year-old almost mark his debut with a 10th-minute goal when his shot struck the underside of the crossbar and bounced out. In his first two seasons Herd made only 8 appearances but after he scored twice in a 3-1 win over Spurs at Highbury in October 1956, he never looked back. In 22 League games that season he scored 12 goals, and netted 6 times in Arsenal's run to the sixth round of the FA Cup. After that he was the Gunners' leading scorer in 4 consecutive seasons – 1957-58 to 1960-61 – but in July 1961, apparently unhappy with Arsenal's lack of silverware, he moved to Manchester United for £35,000. His last appearance for Arsenal was in a 4-1 defeat at Goodison Park – and, naturally, he marked his final game with a goal. His overall tally for the Gunners was 107 goals in 180 League and Cup games.

Although born in Hamilton, Lanarkshire, on 15 April 1934, he had grown up in Moss Side and was completely at home in Manchester. With United he found that missing silverware. He scored twice in the 1963 FA Cup final defeat of Leicester City and won League championship medals 1964-65 and 1966-77, although he suffered a broken leg in March of the latter season, against Leicester at Old Trafford. He was not selected for the 1968 European Cup final, and in July that year he went to Stoke City on a free transfer. In December 1970, after injuring a knee, he moved to Waterford in the League of Ireland, and managed Lincoln City between 1971 and 1972. Herd won 5 Scotland caps, all of them while with Arsenal. After football, he managed a garage in Manchester. He once told writer Andy Mitten, 'My business partner mainly ran the garage and I trained in the morning and returned in the afternoon to work. I wouldn't imagine a top footballer doing that now.'

David Herd died on 1 October 2016, aged 82.

Geoff Strong

Tommy Docherty was not pleased. Stabbing his foot into the carpet of his Barnet home he told a *Daily Mirror* reporter:

> This is the first time I've been dropped in twelve years. Of course, I'm annoyed. George Swindin told me that I'm not good enough. I've been playing no better – and certainly no worse – than any other member of the defence. We've conceded only ten goals in eight games and that isn't a bad average is it?

Swindin told the reporter, 'Tommy has been feeling the strain of recent defensive errors. He needs a rest.' The report also said:

> Geoff Strong, 22, the centre-forward who turned down the chance to sign for Newcastle, his local club, so that he could join Arsenal, leads the Gunners today. A week ago he was in the third team. On Tuesday he was promoted to the Combination side and got a hat-trick against Watford. That brought his total to 17 goals in 7 games!

It was Saturday, 17 September 1960 and the Gunners were at home to Newcastle. And what a debut it was for Strong. As Tommy Docherty sat fuming at the indignity of being dropped, Arsenal did not concede a goal – and they scored 5.

While the Magpies' rebel, George Eastham, sat in the stand at Highbury, Arsenal ran riot. He told Ralph Hadley of *The People*, 'I'll never play for Newcastle again.' The Gunners led 1-0 at half-time, went 2-0 ahead shortly after the restart, then 3-0 before Strong made it 4 when he smacked in a lucky rebound. Hadley wrote, 'Arsenal had practically nothing to beat, but Geoff Strong, their newcomer centre-forward, has one or two of the answers.'

Strong held his place, and on 15 October, the Birmingham *Sports Argus* reported on how 'Arsenal's lively young leader snatched a winner with a headed goal 6 minutes from time' against Aston Villa at Highbury.

Born at Kirkheaton, Northumberland, on 19 September 1937, Strong came to Arsenal's notice after scoring goals for Stanley United in the Northern League. He signed amateur forms for the Gunners in November 1957 and after National Service in the Royal Army Ordnance Corps turned professional – Stanley United received £100 – in April 1958. In 1962-63, together with Joe Baker, he formed a strike partnership that ran riot against First Division defences. Baker scored 29 League goals that season, Strong 18. In 1963-64 they were even more prolific – 26 goals apiece in the First Division – although in the second season under Billy Wright's managership, the Gunners could still finish only eighth.

In November 1964 Wright sold Strong to Liverpool for £40,000. He had scored 74 goals in 133 League and Cup games for the Gunners, and without his goals Arsenal finished thirteenth and then fourteenth in the table, and Wright lost his job.

Strong had made it clear that he wished to play for a more successful club, and he got his wish. With Liverpool, he won the FA Cup in 1965 and a League championship medal in 1965-66 as well as playing in a European Cup semi-final, and, despite being injured, heading the winner against Celtic in a European Cup-winners' Cup semi-final, although he missed the final.

When Bill Shankly decided that changes had to be made to his playing staff, Strong was one of those moved on despite the fact that he had now become a utility player who had appeared in almost every outfield position. In July 1970, he was sold to Coventry City for £30,000. He spent 1 season at Highfield Road before ending his playing days.

He co-owned a pub with former Liverpool teammate Ian Callaghan, and ran a hotel furnishing business. Geoff Strong died at a Southport care home on 17 June 2013. He was 75.

George Eastham

On Friday, 18 November 1960 England under-23 international George Eastham posed on the famous mosaic gun in the marble entrance hall to Highbury to signal the final act in the most protracted transfer quarrel in football history. 'I'm not bitter about the wages I've lost,' he told the *Daily Mirror*. 'I've made my choice and I've got what I wanted.' Then the Gunners' club record £47,500 signing looked forward to playing against Leicester City Reserves the following day.

It was the end of Eastham's 158-day battle to leave Newcastle United. He was the son of George senior, an England international who played for Bolton Wanderers and Blackpool, where George junior was born on 23 September 1936. He played alongside his player-manager father in the Irish League, for Ards, before signing for Newcastle in May 1956. But after 4 seasons with the Magpies he refused to sign a new contract. The state of his clubhouse and the suitability of the outside job that the club had arranged to get around the footballers' maximum wage had unsettled him. Newcastle also made it difficult for him to play for England under-23s. Under the retain-and-transfer system then operating, Newcastle refused to release him so Eastham effectively went on strike and moved to Surrey to work for an old family friend – future Fulham chairman Ernie Clay – selling cork. Newcastle eventually relented and sold Eastham to Arsenal but the player still wanted redress against what he viewed as an unfair system. In 1964 in the High Court, Mr Justice Wilberforce ruled that the retain-and-transfer system was unreasonable. Eastham might have lost £400 in unpaid wages and £650 in unpaid bonuses, but he had succeeded in reforming the way that players were employed, bought and sold.

He made his League debut for Arsenal on 10 December 1960, at inside-left in a 5-1 win over Bolton Wanderers – who included 16-year-old Francis Lee – at Highbury. Eastham scored twice and according to

Maurice Smith in *The People* 'made Arsenal almost look a good team.' Smith continued: 'Eastham is probably the cleverest passer of a ball among contemporary inside-forwards. He spots an opening like a small boy gate-crashing a fairground.'

Later in the season, when he scored in a 3-3 draw at Newcastle, Eastham was the object of scorn from home fans, who called him a 'Judas'. One particular memory for older Arsenal fans is his 2 goals in a 4-4 draw with Spurs at Highbury in October 1963.

Eastham played for Arsenal for 6 seasons, making 220 League and Cup appearances, scoring 41 goals, and winning 19 full England caps, although he did not play in the 1966 World Cup despite being in Alf Ramsey's squad. His time at Highbury, though, under first George Swindin and then Billy Wright, brought no club honours – Arsenal never finished higher than seventh – and there was friction when, after the abolition of the maximum wage, he asked for a pay rise which Arsenal at first refused but then relented on. He also lost the captaincy and found his ball-playing style out of favour with new manager Wright.

In August 1966, now aged almost 30, he was transferred to Stoke City for £30,000 and at last won a club honour when he scored the winning goal against Chelsea in the 1972 League Cup final, at the age of 35. He had left Stoke for South African football in February 1971, and then returned to the Victoria Ground in the October. After assisting Tony Waddington, he took on the manager's job for a year before returning to South Africa after Stoke were relegated to Division Two in 1977 and then failed to sustain a quick return to the top flight.

In South Africa, Eastham, who was awarded the OBE in 1974, set up a sportswear business, coached black children – he was a fervent opponent of apartheid – and founded the Arsenal Supporters Club of South Africa.

Frank McLintock

Frank McLintock's debut for Arsenal was memorable, mostly for the wrong reasons. It was a Tuesday evening, 6 October 1964, and the visitors to Highbury were Nottingham Forest. Right-half McLintock had signed the previous day from Leicester City for £80,000 to help silence the grumbles of Arsenal supporters unhappy with the way that Billy Wright's team had begun the new season – albeit things had recently picked up with 3 successive wins, over Sunderland, Blackburn and Leicester, before a 3-1 home defeat at the hands of Chelsea the previous Saturday.

Against Forest, Arsenal were a goal down after only 5 minutes. In the 19th minute McLintock locked into a challenge with John Barnwell, who Arsenal had sold to Forest for £30,000 the previous March. As Barnwell tried to intercept a back pass, McLintock got to the ball first and tried to play it back to goalkeeper Jim Furnell. The new man's pass was short on pace, and Barnwell was upon it to put Forest into a 2-goal lead.

The Gunners now faced an uphill task. At the start of the second half they had a goal ruled out for offside; with 15 minutes remaining Eastham was limping with an ankle injury, and in the last 5 minutes Colin Addison scored a third for Forest. McLintock's first game had been a disaster. He had occasionally linked up well with inside-left George Eastham, but often found himself overwhelmed in the middle of an indecisive Arsenal midfield.

It got better, though. By the time he was transferred to QPR, for £25,000 in April 1973, Frank McLintock had made 384 League and Cup appearances (and scored 31 goals) for the Gunners. He had also captained them to a Fairs Cup triumph in 1970 and to the 1970-71 League and FA Cup double.

Born in Glasgow on 28 December 1939 and brought up in the Gorbals, he was working as a painter and decorator and playing for junior club

Shawfield when Leicester City signed him in December 1956, on his 17th birthday. At first he was a part-timer who continued his painting and decorating apprenticeship. His Leicester debut was against Blackpool at Bloomfield Road in September 1959, and he made his mark as a probing wing-half. McLintock made 200 appearances, scored 28 goals, and was on the losing side in the 1961 and 1963 FA Cup finals before Arsenal paid Leicester what was a record fee for the selling club.

Further Wembley disappointment followed with Arsenal in the 1968 and 1969 League Cup finals, and there was a change of manager, too, when Bertie Mee replaced Billy Wright. During Wright's time, McLintock had asked for a transfer but the request was refused. Under Mee, and the coaching of first Dave Sexton and then Don Howe, McLintock's fortunes improved along with that of the team. He assumed the captaincy and switched to centre-half, forming an effective partnership with Peter Simpson. The Double was achieved, and McLintock was named the 1971 Footballer of the Year and was awarded the MBE in 1972.

But then Howe went to manage his old club, West Bromwich Albion, and McLintock felt that Arsenal were never the same force after that. Midway through the 1972-73 season McLintock was dropped by Mee. He returned to the side but it was only temporary and in March 1973, asked for a transfer and moved to QPR that summer. He helped them finish First Division runners-up before retiring in May 1977. Two months later he was manager of Leicester City, leaving Filbert Street in April 1978 with Leicester on their way out of the First Division. He coached at QPR, managed Brentford and was assistant manager of Millwall before becoming a players' agent and football media pundit. Frank McLintock won 9 Scotland caps, 6 while with Arsenal.

The Hill-Woods

The 1927 annual meeting of Arsenal Football Club was a stormy affair. After a proposal to elect Sir Henry Norris – until recently club chairman – as chairman of the meeting was defeated, Sir Samuel Hill-Wood presided. A shareholder caused a stir when he demanded that he and his accountant should scrutinise the club's accounts, and another shareholder denied that he had been guilty of plotting against Sir Henry or the club.

Some 70 years later Sir Samuel's grandson, Peter Hill-Wood, when also Arsenal's chairman, asked a supporter who posed a tricky question whether he was a shareholder. 'No,' said the fan. 'If I come back as a shareholder, will that make a difference?' Not really,' said Peter Hill-Wood. 'You will still find out bugger-all – but quicker.'

Peter was the son of Denis Hill-Wood, the son of Sir Samuel. All 3 were club chairman through glorious eras. The Hill-Wood family certainly has a special place in the story of Arsenal.

Sir Samuel's time saw the start of it all. Under Herbert Chapman in 1930, Arsenal won the FA Cup for the first time, and in 1931 the Football League championship for the first time, following that up with the hat-trick of First Division titles under Chapman and George Allison. Sir Samuel, whose family had made their fortune in the cotton industry, captained Derbyshire at cricket, owned Glossop North End FC whom he saw promoted to the First Division in 1898, held the High Peak parliamentary seat for the Conservatives from 1910 to 1929 and was created a baronet in the 1921 New Year's Honours List.

In 1936, he stepped down as Arsenal chairman to be succeeded by the Earl of Lonsdale. That made 3 peers on the Arsenal board. Sir Samuel returned as chairman in 1938, replacing Lord Granard, and held the role until his death at Eaton Place, Westminster, on 4 January 1949, aged 75. Tom Whittaker said, 'We have lost a great sportsman.'

Denis Hill-Wood had played inside-right for Clapton in the Isthmian League and for Arsenal's second team. During the Second World War he saw action with the Royal Armoured Corps in Libya, winning the Military Cross and being wounded. He joined the Arsenal board when his father died, and became chairman in October 1961, succeeding Sir Bracewell Smith, a former lord mayor of London who stepped down because of ill-health. Denis, too, was a first-class cricketer, with Derbyshire, Oxford University and MCC. The 1960s proved to be a decade of disappointment for Arsenal, but it was under Denis Hill-Wood's chairmanship that the Double was won in 1970-71. A season earlier the Gunners had won the Fairs Cup with an aggregate victory over Anderlecht in the 2-legged final. Denis Hill-Wood died on 5 May 1982, like his father aged 75.

Peter Hill-Wood – who had joined the board in August 1962 – was now chairman and another glorious era followed. He presided over the appointments of George Graham and Arsene Wenger, and during his time Arsenal won 5 League championships, 5 FA Cups, 2 League Cups and the European Cup-winners' Cup, and reached a European Champions League final. He was also one of the prime movers in the formation of the FA Premiership.

Following a heart attack in December 2012 he retired in June the following year, after 31 years as chairman and thus ending a span of more than 90 years of a Hill-Wood in the Arsenal boardroom. A former Coldstream Guards officer and a merchant banker, he was quite definitely 'old school' in appearance and manner, and he faced fierce criticism from supporters who were concerned at the destination of much of his family's holdings in Arsenal, to David Dein and Stan Kroenke.

Yet when Peter Hill-Wood died on 28 December 2018, aged 82, executive director Ken Friar told Steve Stammers from the *Daily Mail*:

> He was very instrumental in the move from Highbury to the Emirates. A huge decision and Peter did so much to make sure it was a success. What he did for Arsenal Football Club was massive. It is as simple as that. Arsenal have lost a man who played such a huge part in getting them to their current status. And I have lost a great friend.

Peter Storey

In November 1965, the *Belfast Telegraph* said that Northern Ireland international Billy McCullough, hitherto an Arsenal regular, now 'has a fight on his hands. His place has been taken by 19-year-old Peter Storey who was an instant success.'

In fact, Storey was 20 but otherwise the Belfast newspaper was spot on. After replacing the out-of-form left-back McCullough for Arsenal's match at Filbert Street on 30 October, the former England schoolboy international from Farnham, who had signed professional forms for Arsenal 3 years earlier, held his place for the remainder of the season at the end of which McCullough was transferred to Millwall. Storey, meanwhile, went on to make 501 League and Cup appearances for Arsenal and win 19 full England caps.

It was another poor season, 1965-66. Arsenal finished fourteenth – 1 place lower than the previous season and only 4 points above relegated Northampton Town and Blackburn Rovers (who had knocked Arsenal out of that season's FA Cup) – and manager Billy Wright was sacked.

New manager Bertie Mee continued to believe in Storey, who could play in either full-back position or as a defensive midfielder. He was, however, earning a reputation as a rough player. When in September 1966, at Maine Road, Manchester City's Mike Summerbee limped off after only 15 minutes with a badly bruised ankle – the result of an earlier Storey tackle – the Arsenal player, who was now being lectured after an ugly challenge on Glyn Pardoe, was roundly booed by home supporters. The *Daily Express* reporter thought that 'Storey … is overdoing the tough-guy act.'

With Bob McNab claiming the left-back spot midway through 1967-68, Storey switched to the left. In December 1967, along with Frank McLintock he was sent off in a bad-tempered League game at Turf Moor, although on this occasion Storey's dismissal was for using bad language, not for foul play. A few days earlier McNab had suffered a broken nose before being sent off in a League Cup match against Burnley. 'What has happened to Arsenal's proud tradition of gentlemanly conduct?' asked Peter Batt of *The People*.

Whatever had happened to it, results were to improve dramatically. There were consecutive League Cup finals, albeit both were lost, and then Arsenal won the 1970 Fairs Cup. The following season it was the Double, and Storey missed only 2 games. In the first FA Cup semi-final match against Stoke City at Hillsborough he scored twice (1 an injury-time penalty) to rescue a 2-goal deficit.

After being injured and losing his place to Alan Ball, Storey, along with other first-teamers, demanded a pay rise when they learned that Ball was being paid twice as much as his teammates. Arsenal's fortunes declined, and so did Storey's. In February 1977, he was suspended and transfer-listed after refusing to train with the first team the day after playing for the reserves. He had been in similar trouble before: in March 1966 Bertie Mee suspended him for refusing to train with the reserves. Now new manager Terry Neill, who was Arsenal's captain when Storey made his debut, said, 'Storey has made it quite clear that he does not want to play with the reserves. He said he would rather move somewhere else.'

In March 1977, he was transferred to Fulham for £11,000 but retired that November after only 19 League and Cup appearances for the Cottagers. He was already running a pub, the Jolly Farmers, just over a mile down the road from Highbury, and now his life began to fall apart. Over time he was convicted of keeping a brothel, importing pornography and counterfeiting money. In March 1982, his legal bid in the House of Lords to overturn his conviction to counterfeit gold sovereigns failed, although his 3-year sentence was reduced to 2 years.

In his autobiography, *True Storey: My Life and Times as a Football Hatchet Man*, he said, 'I was never a criminal mastermind, but rather a foolish former footballer with more money than sense.'

Bertie Mee

In May 1966 only 4,554 bothered to turn up for Arsenal's home game against Leeds United. It was raining and Liverpool's Cup-winners' Cup final against Borussia Dortmund was on television. Arsenal lost 3-0 before the smallest crowd ever to watch a competitive first-team match at Highbury. The next game, the last of the season, saw 16,435 watch a 1-0 home over Leicester City, but it was too late. Arsenal, though, did not wish to heap the indignity of the sack on one of English football's most famous names so, in June, Billy Wright was called into Denis Hill-Wood's office and invited to resign, which he did.

Wright's 4-year reign was one of the most disappointing periods in Arsenal's history: seventh, eighth, thirteenth and fourteenth in the First Division and never beyond the fifth round of the FA Cup. The former England captain – 105 caps – had no previous managerial experience of any kind. He was also the first post-war Arsenal manager with no previous association with the club.

Now Bertie Mee stepped in to hold the fort. Born in Bulwell, Nottinghamshire, on Christmas Day 1918, Mee joined his older brother and fellow winger, George Mee, on the books of Derby County. George, already a star in his Blackpool days, had a good career at the Baseball Ground but Bertie moved to Mansfield Town without playing a game for the Rams. His career at Field Mill was cut short by injury. After 6 years in the Royal Army Medical Corps, he qualified as a physiotherapist and spent 12 years rehabilitating injured servicemen. In August 1960 he replaced Billy Milne, who retired, as Arsenal's physio and trainer.

At the end of his first season in charge of the team, Arsenal finished seventh and Colin Addison, Bob McNab and George Graham had been signed. Mee impressed Arsenal's directors who did not look further afield for a new manager. Successive League Cup finals followed – both lost – and in 1968-69 Arsenal finished fourth. In August 1969, Ian Ure, the Scottish international centre-half signed by Billy Wright and restored to the team by Mee, left for Manchester United.

In April 1970 Arsenal lifted their first major trophy for 17 years, winning the Fairs Cup 4-3 on aggregate against Anderlecht after losing the away leg 3-1. In May 1971 the Gunners confirmed themselves as League champions by winning 1-0 at White Hart Lane with a Ray Kennedy goal on the final day of the season. Five days later Charlie George – one of the youngsters brought on by Mee – scored in extra-time to secure a 2-1 win over Liverpool in the FA Cup final, completing the Double that not even the great Herbert Chapman could achieve.

At that evening's Cup final banquet, Denis Hill-Wood omitted to mention the contribution of Mee's assistant, Don Howe, who that summer left to manage his former club, West Bromwich Albion. Mee spent another 5 years as Arsenal's manager but further success eluded him. In December 1971, he signed Alan Ball from Everton for £220,000 but his critics felt that the Double-winning team had been allowed to break up too soon, as Kennedy, George and skipper Frank McLintock departed. There was a narrow FA Cup final defeat against Leeds United in 1972, and in 1972-73 Arsenal finished runners-up in the First Division and reached the FA Cup semi-finals where they lost to Sunderland at Hillsborough.

Thereafter Arsenal were on the decline. Tenth in 1973-74, they sank to sixteenth the following season, and to seventeenth in 1975-76. In March 1976 Mee announced his retirement at the end of the season. His last home game in charge was a 2-1 defeat by Ipswich Town – Keith Bertschin, a 19-year-old Ipswich substitute, scored with his first kick in League football – but at the final whistle, grateful Arsenal fans applauded Mee, hugged him and gave him their scarves.

After a break from football, in 1986 he became general manager of Watford and remained at Vicarage Road as a director until 1991. He was awarded the OBE in 1984. Bertie Mee died on 21 October 2001, aged 82.

Sammy Nelson

In the 77th minute of Arsenal's match against Coventry City at Highbury on Wednesday, 3 April 1979, the Gunners' Northern Ireland international left-back Sammy Nelson scored a stunning goal. It wiped out a 35th-minute Coventry goal that appeared to go in off Nelson after David O'Leary had lost the ball.

With 13 minutes remaining Graham Rix had robbed Barry Powell and sent Nelson in on the left to score with a fierce low shot that earned Arsenal a 1-1 draw in front of a crowd of 30,091.

Nelson's wonderful equaliser should have been the headline in the following morning's daily newspapers. But it was what happened next that blazed from the sports pages. Nelson ran behind the goal and lowered his shorts in front of the North Bank fans. As goal celebrations go, it was one of the more unusual – and it greatly displeased Arsenal chairman Denis Hill-Wood, who was 'very angry' about it.

Manager Terry Neill, perhaps unwittingly starting a tradition, said that he had not seen the incident but would 'go and explore it'. He said, 'Really, I don't know what the club policy would be on this. It's not in the rules.' Coventry manager Gordon Milne was less concerned: 'It seems a pity to bother about someone's backside when he has scored a hell of a good goal.' In the end Arsenal fined Nelson 2 weeks' wages – about £400, it was reported – and suspended him for 2 matches. Neill said, 'The feeling of myself and the club on the matter can be gauged by the speed with which we have acted and the severity of our action.'

Sammy Nelson was born in Belfast on 1 April 1949 and joined Arsenal on his 17th birthday in 1966. He was originally an outside-left and was in the Arsenal side that beat Sunderland 5-3 on aggregate in the 1966 FA Youth Cup final when Pat Rice was one of his teammates. Nelson switched to full-back and gained a regular place in the reserve team for a couple of seasons, and won under-23 caps, before making his

League debut at home to Ipswich Town on 25 October 1969. Bertie Mee told reporters that he was confident that Nelson would 'make a big name for himself', but the player had to wait as he understudied Bob McNab.

When McNab was injured in 1971-72, Nelson had a good run in the team, making 24 League appearances that season. However, whenever McNab was fit again, Nelson had to stand down and it was only after McNab left on a free transfer to Wolves in the summer of 1975 that Nelson became first choice. For the next 5 seasons he was almost an ever-present and played in 3 consecutive FA Cup finals, with a winners' medal against Manchester United in 1979, and in the 1980 Cup-winners' Cup final defeat by Valencia on penalties.

When Kenny Sansom arrived at Highbury in August 1980, Nelson again found himself on the sidelines and in 1980-81 managed only 1 League appearance, as a substitute in the last match of the season. It was his final appearance. He had played in 339 League and Cup matches for Arsenal, and scored 12 goals.

In May, he moved to Brighton for £35,000 and made 45 first-team appearances for them before retiring as a player in 1983. During his time at the Goldstone Ground the Seagulls were relegated from the First Division, and he was not selected for either the 1983 FA Cup final or the replay against Manchester United. Nelson, who won 51 full caps including 2 in the 1982 World Cup finals, spent a year coaching at Brighton before leaving football altogether for the insurance industry. In July 2018, Brighton magistrates found Nelson not guilty of sexually assaulting a 75-year-old woman on a bus the previous October when he was returning home after watching Arsenal's 2-1 win over Swansea City at the Emirates. He pleaded guilty to a separate charge of assault, and was given an unconditional discharge and ordered to pay £85 in costs.

Bob Wilson

Billy Wright had a goalkeeping problem when he selected his team to play Nottingham Forest at Highbury on 26 October 1963. Regular goalkeeper John McClelland had been out with a shoulder injury after colliding with Leicester's Ken Keyworth at Filbert Street on the last day of August. Now McClelland's replacement, 21-year-old 14 stone Ian McKechnie, was overweight.

The *Daily Mirror* reported the affair. 'I'm not a hard man, said Wright. 'In fact, I think I'm very fair, but, with the wages they get today, we are entitled to expect players to do as they are told.' McKechnie was repentant:

> I'm out because I'm having weight trouble … . Mr Wright warned me that I had to get some off and see the club's medical officer about a diet … . But I shan't like it. I enjoy eating. Still, as my livelihood is at stake I'll just have to do something about it.

Wright turned to a 20-year-old Paddington schoolteacher, and Bob Wilson, the first amateur to play in a League match for the Gunners since Irish soccer and rugby international Dr Kevin O'Flanagan in 1949, did well. Arsenal won 4-2 and, according to Bill Meredith in *The People*, 'made two thrilling saves in as many minutes … and had the crowd cheering his fearless display … after all that worry over the weights Arsenal played a cruiserweight in goal – and won by a knockout.'

The People summed it all up. 'I feel tired,' said Wilson as he sat in the dressing room afterwards. 'He must stay in the team after this display,' said Wright.

The former England schoolboy international from Chesterfield had been on Wolves' books as an amateur, after his father would not let him sign for Manchester United because he wanted his son to get a 'proper' profession. Wilson trained as a teacher at Loughborough College and played for Wolves reserve team before becoming the first amateur footballer to be transferred for a fee – £5,500, to Arsenal – in July 1963. He signed professional forms in March 1964 but had to play second fiddle to Jim Furnell and Tony Burns.

Wilson finally won a regular place in March 1968. He was Arsenal's goalkeeper for the rest of that season, and in 1968-69 did not miss a game, ending up with a League Cup runners-up medal.

Despite breaking an arm at Turf Moor in September 1969, Wilson ended the season with another winners' medal, in the Fairs Cup. In the Double-winning season that followed, he was ever-present. A leg injury sustained in the semi-final meant that he missed the 1972 FA Cup final defeat by Leeds – Geoff Barnett took over at Wembley – and the first 19 games of the following season. When he returned on 25 November 1972 Arsenal lost 5-0 at the Baseball Ground but Derby manager Brian Clough said, 'I don't think Wilson was to blame ... he's entitled to some protection from his defence.'

Nobody was blaming Bob Wilson. Again he kept his place for the remainder of the season, and missed only 1 match in 1973-74. The last game of that season, at home to QPR, also proved to be Wilson's final appearance for Arsenal's first team. He had made 308 League and Cup appearances including European games. At the age of 32 he announced his retirement, although he did re-sign during an injury crisis in 1977-78 and made 4 appearances in the Football Combination. Through his parentage he was qualified to play for Scotland and won 2 full caps.

Wilson was Arsenal's goalkeeping coach for 28 years before retiring in 2003. In 2018 he voiced concern at the growing trend for 'sweeper-keepers' who, he said, were being put at risk by being asked to play out from the back.

After he finished playing, he enjoyed a prominent broadcasting career with both the BBC and ITV, and in memory of his daughter, Anna, who died of the disease in December 1998, he set up the Willow Foundation to help sufferers of malignant schwannoma, a cancer of the nerve sheath. In 2007 Bob Wilson was awarded the OBE in recognition of his work.

John Radford

Billy Wright was over the moon. He told *The People*, 'Two years and pounds and pounds of steak from now, Radford could turn out to be one of our greatest discoveries.' The Arsenal manager was spot on. The 17-year-old who had just scored a hat-trick against Wolves at Highbury would go on to become the Gunners' fourth-highest goalscorer of all time.

Writing in *The People*, pre-war Arsenal star Joe Hulme was in full agreement:

> What a wonderful headache for Arsenal manager Billy Wright ... John Radford blasted three against Wolves ... so how can Billy drop him – even when Jon Sammels has recovered from that cracked bone in his foot? Radford, a six-footer from Pontefract, found Wolves a piece of cake and had the Highbury crowd chanting his name as he ripped through the Midlanders' defence. On this form Billy couldn't dream of dropping him. He realises that he has a star in the making.

Radford, who was born in Hemsworth on 22 February 1947, had joined Arsenal as an apprentice in October 1962 and turned full-time professional in February 1964. A prolific scorer in the youth and reserves teams, he made his League debut at Upton Park on 21 March 1964, standing in for the suspended Joe Baker. The result was a 1-1 draw and although Radford had little chance to show off his shooting skills: 'He used the ball intelligently and was always in the thick of the fight', according to Bill Meredith in *The People*. Radford's hat-trick against Wolves came in a 4-1 win, 2 in the first half and the other a few minutes from the final whistle.

By 1965-66 he was an Arsenal regular, and when Bertie Mee took over the following season Radford's career really began to blossom.

He played mostly at centre-forward or inside-right but in 1967-68, Mee put him on the right wing and he scored 10 goals in 39 League games and played in that season's League Cup final defeat by Leeds. In 1968-69 he was still in the number 7 shirt and scored 19 goals in 41 full League and Cup appearances (he also came on as a substitute 3 times) and played at Wembley again, in the League Cup final defeat by Third Division promotion-chasers Swindon Town. The following season he matched his goals tally of the previous campaign and scored the second goal in Arsenal's 3-0 win in the second leg of the Fairs Cup final. It came in the 75th minute, to be quickly followed by Sammels's aggregate winner.

By now Radford was up front again and in 1970-71 he and Ray Kennedy formed a brilliant partnership as Arsenal won the Double. Between them they scored 47 goals with Radford getting 21 of them. It was his best-ever season's haul and included a hat-trick against Manchester United at Highbury.

He continued to play regularly for the next few seasons but the goals slowly dried up and in 1975-76, injury restricted him to only 15 League appearances and 3 goals. His final appearance for Arsenal came as a substitute when he replaced Frank Stapleton at home to Stoke on 16 October 1976. By now Stapleton and Malcolm Macdonald were the first-choice attack, and on 13 December that year Radford was transferred to West Ham for £80,000. He had scored 149 goals in 481 games for the Gunners and won 2 full England caps to add to his youth and under-23 honours. He also played in goal for the last 20 minutes of the 1972 FA Cup semi-final against Stoke at Villa Park after Bob Wilson limped off with a leg injury.

After a year with the Hammers, Radford moved to Second Division Blackburn Rovers and then won the FA Trophy and Isthmian League with Bishop's Stortford in 1980-81. He also managed the Blues and was youth coach at QPR, ran the Greyhound pub at Thaxted in Essex, appeared on Arsenal TV and was one of several players conducting 'legends' tours of the Emirates Stadium.

Pat Rice

You will read almost everywhere that Pat Rice made his first-team debut for Arsenal in December 1967 against Burnley in a Football League Cup fifth-round replay at Highbury. Almost all of that is correct. He did play in that game. But his debut had come 3 days earlier, in a First Division match against Burnley at Turf Moor when he substituted for George Graham.

Rice had come close a month earlier when he stood ready to replace skipper Frank McLintock against Leeds United. However, McLintock recovered from injury to score in Arsenal's 3-1 defeat at Elland Road. Rice's chance finally arrived on 2 December, when he came on for Graham. Three days later he made his first start as Arsenal progressed to the League Cup semi-finals.

Although born in Belfast, on 17 March 1949, Rice was on Arsenal's doorstep almost from the start. He grew up in north London and worked at a greengrocer's shop on Gillespie Road, in the shadow of Highbury. He joined Arsenal as an apprentice on 21 December 1964 and signed as a full-time professional on 25 May 1966. He made his way through the South-East Counties and Football Combination teams until Bertie Mee decided that he was ready for the First Division.

For his first 3 seasons as a senior player, Rice, a full-back, was something of a bit-part performer. In 1967-68 he made 2 full League appearances and 4 as a substitute. He did not play at all in 1968-69, and although starting the 1969-70 season as first-choice right-back – when Peter Storey was suspended, and holding on for a few matches as Storey was used as a midfield provocateur – when Storey returned to right-back Rice was out of the side once more, ending up with only 7 League appearances.

It was in 1970-71, when Storey switched back to central midfield, that Rice finally won a regular place. And what a season it was to establish oneself. Arsenal won the League and FA Cup Double, and Rice missed only 1 game all season. He was now also a Northern Ireland international, having made his debut against Israel in Jaffa in September 1968 when he was still largely a reserve player at Highbury.

After the Double-winning season Rice remained a first choice. He was ever-present in 1971-72 and played in that season's FA Cup final defeat by Leeds. He now hardly ever missed a game and was ever-present in 1975-76 and 1976-77. He became Arsenal's captain in 1977, helped check a decline, lifted the FA Cup in 1979, and also played in the 1978 and 1980 finals, and in the 1980 European Cup-winners' Cup final when Arsenal lost on penalties to Valencia.

When he moved to Watford, for £8,000 in November 1980, he looked back on an Arsenal career that had seen him make 527 appearances, score 13 goals and win 49 full international caps. He was 31.

Graham Taylor made Rice captain of Watford and he helped them to promotion to the First Division in 1981-82 and to reach the 1984 FA Cup final, although he did not play at Wembley. That year Rice rejoined Arsenal as youth team coach and steered the Gunners to 2 FA Youth Cup final wins, in 1987-88 and 1993-94. He was caretaker manager of the club between the resignation of Stewart Houston (caretaker after Bruce Rioch before himself leaving to manage QPR) and the arrival of Arsene Wenger, whose assistant Rice became. Along with the Double-winning season in which he played, as a coach, Rice was also involved with those of 1997-98 and 2001-02. In May 2012, he finally retired from the club he had joined 48 years earlier and served for all but 4 of those. Arsene Wenger said, 'Arsenal was privileged to have him as a player, as a captain, as a coach, and personally I'm very grateful and privileged to have had him at my side for such a long time.'

Ray Kennedy

Ray Kennedy had a memorable 1969-70 season. On 29 September he made his first-team debut for Arsenal, against Glentoran in a first-round second-leg Fairs Cup match at The Oval, coming on as a substitute for John Radford. He made his first League appearance on 18 October, again as a substitute, this time replacing Bob McNab at Roker Park. Nine days later he was sent off, along with West Ham's Stuart Morgan, after a 73rd-minute goalmouth scuffle in the London Challenge Cup final at Upton Park. In the return fixture against Sunderland, on 28 February, he scored his first senior goal for the Gunners in a 3-1 win at Highbury. And on 22 April he came on as a late substitute for Charlie George in the first leg of the Fairs Cup final against RSC Anderlecht in Brussels and scored 7 minutes from time.

In the *Daily Mirror*, Harry Miller called Kennedy's strike 'surely the most vital goal Arsenal have collected in their European crusade this season.' Bertie Mee explained, 'I brought Kennedy on because George had a leg knock. He has ensured that it will be a tremendous second leg.' It most certainly was. Arsenal won 3-0 to lift their first trophy for 17 years, 4-3 on aggregate. Kennedy did not feature in the second game but his contribution to the first had proved vital.

Born in Seaton Delaval, Northumberland, on 28 July 1951, Kennedy was released by Port Vale whose manager, Stanley Matthews, apparently considered the 16-year-old to be too slow to be a footballer. He went home, started work as a trainee sugar boiler in a sweet factory and began scoring goals for New Hartley Juniors. He played alongside former England schoolboy international Ian Watts, as New Hartley swept all before them in local football. In 1966-67 they lost only 1 of their 38 games. Kennedy scored 53 goals but Watts scored 83 and it was he who Arsenal went to watch. It was Kennedy they signed, though. He joined the Gunners as an apprentice in May 1968 and became a full-time professional in November that year.

On the opening day of the 1970-71 season, Charlie George broke his right ankle at Goodison Park. Kennedy replaced him and played in every remaining game of the Double-winning season, scoring 19 goals in 41 League matches, including his first hat-trick in senior football, against Nottingham Forest. On the final day of the season it was Kennedy's 88th-minute goal – a header that went in off the underside of the crossbar – at White Hart Lane that confirmed Arsenal as champions.

The following season Kennedy was again the Gunners' top scorer as they finished fifth and lost the FA Cup final to Leeds, a game in which he came on as a 73rd-minute substitute for Radford. When Arsenal finished First Division runners-up in 1972-73, Kennedy managed only 9 League goals in 34 games. He played in every First Division game in 1973-74 and scored 12 goals, but there was a long barren spell, from early October to mid-January, and in July 1974, after a career total of 71 goals in 212 games for Arsenal, he was transferred to Liverpool for £200,000, a Liverpool club record.

Bill Shankly signed him but then the legendary Liverpool manager retired. Bob Paisley converted Kennedy to a powerhouse midfielder and with Liverpool he won 3 European Cup winners' medals, 3 other European winners' medals, 4 League Championship medals, an FA Cup winners' medal and a Football League Cup winners' medal, as well as 17 full England caps to add to the 6 under-23 caps he had won while with Arsenal. In January 1982, after 72 goals in 382 games for Liverpool, he was transferred to Swansea City for £160,000 and later played for Hartlepool United. He coached at various clubs including Sunderland, in Cyprus, and with non-League Ashington, and he also ran a public house. In January 1987, it was revealed that Ray Kennedy had been diagnosed with Parkinson's Disease.

Charlie George

Making the first League appearance of his career was 'the Cockney boy with a name like an aircraft recognition sign'. So said the *Liverpool Echo* on the opening day of the 1969-70 season when Arsenal travelled to Goodison Park. It is doubtful whether Bow Bells have ever been heard in Islington, and so Charlie George hardly qualifies as a Cockney. According to Dick Milford in *The People*, 'The expected new skill in midfield from George Graham and 18-year-old debutant Charlie George did not materialise.' Arsenal lost 1-0.

By the end of the season, however, George had made 28 First Division appearances and helped Arsenal win the Fairs Cup. In the opening game of the following season, after scoring the first equaliser in a 2-2 draw, he broke his right ankle in a collision with Everton goalkeeper Gordon West at Goodison. Out for 5 months, he played in the last 16 League matches as Arsenal won the title, and he scored the spectacular extra-time winner against Liverpool at Wembley that gave Arsenal the Double. George celebrated by lying flat on his back with his arms raised, a picture that gained almost iconic status.

His penalty equaliser against Stoke City in the 1972 FA Cup semi-final replay at Goodison Park helped Arsenal to another Wembley appearance but, the following August, George was among pay rebels that refused to sign new contracts because of a dispute over the Arsenal system of loyalty bonuses. The Gunners' secretary, Bob Wall, said, 'If they feel they are being treated unfairly they may take the matter to the League management committee … in the meantime they will have to play under the terms of their old contracts.' Only hours before the start of the new season, George, Eddie Kelly and John Roberts were each transfer-listed at their own request. Two other malcontents, Ray Kennedy and Sammy Nelson, signed the options on their contracts.

George made his first appearance of the season at Old Trafford on 26 August, missed an easy chance in the 26th minute of a goalless draw and afterwards told the *Daily Mirror*, 'After playing in the reserves it took me till half-time to become accustomed to the pace.'

George, who in 1971-72 had twice been fined by Arsenal for his behaviour on the pitch, was booked that day. *Thomson Newspapers'* Basil Easterbrook wrote, 'The behaviour and general demeanour of Charlie George is entirely foreign to Arsenal's earlier history, and coming from someone who has been on the football scene hardly as long as a dog watch in the Navy, it is intolerable.'

A few days later Bertie Mee announced that George had finally signed the contract offered to him during the summer but remained on the transfer list. Said George: 'I'm glad the money disagreement is settled but I'm not happy about playing in the reserves.' On 26 September he returned to the first team, at home to Birmingham City and, according to the *Daily Mirror*, 'George scored the sort of goal that makes it seem inevitable that his future lies only at Highbury ... and his impeccable conduct must have had Arsenal officials purring.'

In July 1975 George finally left Arsenal. Derby County snatched him away from Spurs who expected to sign him. He had scored 49 goals in 179 games for the Gunners, and for Derby, who paid £100,000, he scored 56 in 147 appearances. He was a great favourite at the Baseball Ground and until he dislocated a shoulder in March 1976, the Rams had a realistic shot at the Double. He also had a knee problem, and in December 1978 Tommy Docherty sold him to Southampton for £350,000. He returned to Derby in March 1982 and helped them avoid relegation to the Third Division, but the club could not meet his demands for a longer stay. The single England cap he won while at Derby was a poor return for his talent. After football he ran a pub, had joint ownership of a garage business, and worked for Arsenal in a corporate hospitality role.

George Armstrong

When George Armstrong made his debut for Arsenal, George Swindin managed the Gunners. When the little winger from Hebburn made his final appearance before being transferred to Leicester City, Terry Neill was the Arsenal boss. That meant a first-team career spanning 15 years, 621 appearances and 68 goals as well as the League and FA Cup Double and a Fairs Cup final win, not to mention successive League Cup finals and another FA Cup final.

Born on 9 August 1944, Armstrong was working as an apprentice electrician and playing local football when Arsenal spotted him. He would have been delighted – and surprised. Grimsby Town had turned him down after a trial, and although Newcastle United took him on as an amateur, that appeared to be leading nowhere. Then, in August 1961, the Gunners came calling.

Armstrong went to Highbury as an inside-forward but Swindin saw a winger in him, and when he made his debut as a 17-year-old outside-right, against Blackpool in February 1962, it was his cross that enabled Geoff Strong to give Arsenal a 14th-minute lead at Bloomfield Road. The Seasiders' goalkeeper, Tony Waiters, later had to go full stretch to save a shot from Armstrong whose first game ended in a 1-0 win.

Armstrong, who stood just 5ft 6in tall, made 3 more appearances that season, all on the left wing, and it was Billy Wright who gave him more opportunities in 1962-63. By 1964-65 he was a regular, missing only 2 matches. His ability to play on either flank, his accurate crosses and seemingly inexhaustible running made him one of the first names on the team sheet each week. He was on the losing side in 2 successive League Cup finals before gaining a winners' medal in the 1970 Fairs Cup. In the Double-winning season that followed he played in every match, laying on dozens of goals including Ray Kennedy's late header at White Hart Lane in the last League match of the season that clinched the First Division title.

Throughout the rest of the 1970s, further honours eluded both Armstrong and Arsenal, and after falling out with manager Terry Neill, a former teammate, in September 1977 the player moved to Leicester City for £15,000. Another former Arsenal teammate, Frank McLintock, had recruited him to help in a relegation battle at Filbert Street. But Armstrong, now in his mid-30s, looked jaded, and being handed a midfield role in an ever-changing line-up did nothing to enhance his reputation beyond a match-winning goal in an FA Cup game at Hull. After 3 Second Division appearances at the start of 1978-79, and an early exit from the League Cup, Leicester manager Jock Wallace allowed him to leave. After 34 games for Stockport County and a player-managership in Norway with FK Mjølner, he retired as a player. He managed non-league Enderby Town, returned to Mjølner as manager, and managed the Kuwait national team before returning to England. Armstrong, who also had coaching jobs at Middlesbrough, Fulham, QPR and Aston Villa, spent the last 10 years of his life as reserve-team coach at Arsenal.

On 31 October 2000, he collapsed while taking a session at Arsenal's training ground. He had suffered a brain haemorrhage and was placed on a life support machine at Hemel Hempstead Hospital but passed away in the early hours of the following morning.

George Graham, who was Arsenal's manager when 'Geordie' Armstrong returned to Highbury, said, 'He was such a thorough professional and a great help to me at Arsenal. As soon as I knew he was available when he was out in the Middle East I jumped at the chance to bring him back,'

Frank McLintock, the captain of the Double-winning team, said, 'The world has lost a diamond of a fellow.'

Alan Ball

'I'll be better next time,' promised Alan Ball after his Arsenal debut. Britain's most expensive footballer had made a stuttering start with his new club. In the 1-1 draw at Nottingham Forest on 27 December 1971, as he struggled to adjust to an unfamiliar style, Ball looked more like a young debutant rather than the World Cup winner he was. Writing in the *Daily Mirror*, he asked supporters to give him time: 'I know for certain that I've done the best thing in joining Arsenal'.

Bertie Mee broke the British transfer record when he paid £220,00 to sign Ball from Everton. Born in Farnworth, Lancashire, on 12 May 1945, the tireless midfielder had trials with Wolves and Bolton before joining Blackpool in 1962. He was the Seasiders' top scorer in 1963-64 and 1965-66 as they battled against relegation from the First Division. He made his England debut in 1965, and following the glorious World Cup summer, in August 1966 joined Everton for £112,000, a record between British clubs. At Goodison he won a League championship medal, forming a famous midfield with Howard Kendall and Colin Harvey. It was a surprise when Harry Catterick sold Ball to Arsenal.

Ball, though, could not help the Gunners defend either the League title or the FA Cup. In his first season, they finished fifth and were Cup runners-up. After that Arsenal never finished higher than eighth and never reached Wembley again while he was at Highbury.

He became Arsenal's captain, but when Don Revie made Ball England's skipper, Walter Johnson, MP for Derby South, wrote to the Minister of Sport, Denis Howell, a former Football League referee, urging him to ask Revie to change his mind: 'Here is a man who has set a thoroughly bad example. He has been sent off four times. Mr Revie is saying, in effect, that the way to become England captain is to behave in a bad-tempered, truculent manner.' The appointment stood.

In April 1975 Ball asked for a transfer. He said, 'I am not enjoying my football … . We've had two bad seasons and I can't see it getting any better. We need three or four new players … I'm 30 now and I don't want to go on struggling every season.' By September, Ball appeared more settled but Bertie Mee said, 'If he wants to come off the transfer list he must ask. The problem is Ball's, not mine. He asked for a transfer in the first place.' In November, Ball came off the list and was restored to the captaincy he had lost to Eddie Kelly. He said, 'I am a perfectionist … . When I asked to come off the list I asked Bertie Mee if he was prepared to take me as I am. He said "Yes" because he knows I train hard, do the job, run the side, and will never knuckle down to anybody.'

At the end of that season, however, Mee retired, to be replaced by Terry Neill. In December 1976 Ball was transferred to Southampton for £60,000. He had scored 52 goals in 217 games for Arsenal, and won 33 of his 72 England caps while with the Gunners. He said, 'I'm not leaving Arsenal because there is anything wrong with my game. Terry Neill thought it was about time he had some new faces. Only time will tell.'

Ball helped Southampton win promotion to the top flight. He later played in the North American Soccer League (NASL) and in Hong Kong, and returned to both Blackpool (as player-manager) and Southampton before ending his playing days with Bristol Rovers. He managed 7 Football League clubs including 2 spells at Portsmouth and worked as an England coach under Graham Taylor. In 2000, he was awarded the MBE for his services to football.

Alan Ball died at his home in Hampshire on 25 April 2007, from a heart attack after he attempted to extinguish a garden bonfire that had reignited and spread to a fence. His former teammate Liam Brady said, 'In my opinion he was one of Arsenal's greatest players of all time.'

Liam Brady

When 17-year-old Liam Brady was named as substitute against bottom-of-the-table Birmingham City on 6 October 1973, he probably hoped that if Arsenal were comfortably placed against a relegation-haunted team, Bertie Mee might give him his first taste of League football. In fact Brady found himself in the thick of the action after only 15 minutes. Jeff Blockley went off with a knee ligament injury, Brady came on – and how he impressed.

The Highbury faithful needed a boost after the Gunners' midweek tumble at the hands of Third Division Tranmere Rovers. Brady soon had them purring at his skill, particularly his accurate left-foot passing. Sixteen minutes after he took the field, he set up Ray Kennedy for the only goal of the game. A week later, at White Hart Lane, the youngster made his first start. He showed some neat touches but Spurs won 1-0, and Brady was out of the team until mid-January, after which he was used sparingly by Bertie Mee, making a further 8 full appearances and another 3 as a sub.

Liam Brady was born on 13 February 1956, in Dublin. He was playing for St Kevin's Boys' Club when the Gunners signed him, in 1971, and he became a full-time professional 2 years later. After his debut season he was a regular. In 1974-75 he made 30 full appearances. He was ever-present (sub once) in 1975-76, as Arsenal hovered just above the relegation pack, and made 37 starts in 1976-77 as the Gunners finished eighth. For the next 3 seasons Brady was hardly missing at all, and played in 3 consecutive FA Cup finals with a winners' medal against Manchester United in 1979. In the 1978 final against Ipswich, Brady had been carrying an injury, and on the eve of the 1979 Wembley game he said, 'That last defeat hurt dreadfully and I cannot say how grateful I am to have the chance to put it right.'

There was a minute of normal time remaining in the final – Arsenal had led 2-0 after 86 minutes but the game was now locked at 2-2 – when

Brady, who had already laid on a goal for Frank Stapleton and been involved in Brian Talbot's, conjured up another piece of brilliance. From the restart he kept position, got deep into United's half and then released a perfect pass to Graham Rix on the left. Rix crossed to United's far post where Alan Sunderland connected with his right boot for the winner. It was the most dramatic of ends.

On the Monday after the final, Arsenal chairman Denis Hill-Wood revealed that he had concerns over the futures of three Irish stars: Stapleton's and David O'Leary's contracts ended in July; Brady's had a year to run. The *Daily Mirror*'s Harry Miller had the story. Hill-Wood said, 'If foreign clubs come for these players there is no way we can compete. There is no club in this country that could. Foreign teams can pay the sort of money that just isn't legal over here.'

Brady said, 'The ball is in Arsenal's court. If they can make it right for me I will stay. I fancy playing in European football.' In the summer of 1980, having impressed them in the previous season's Cup-winners' Cup semi-final (Arsenal lost the final on penalties to Valencia), he moved to Juventus for £514,000. He had made 306 appearances for Arsenal and scored 59 goals.

With Juventus he won two Serie A championship medals before playing for Sampdoria, Inter and Ascoli. In March 1987, he was transferred to West Ham with whom he was relegated. After a season in the Second Division he retired. Liam Brady played 72 times for the Republic of Ireland, 26 caps coming when he was an Arsenal player. He managed Celtic and Brighton & Hove Albion, was the Republic of Ireland's assistant manager, and a highly successful head of youth development and academy director for Arsenal. He also forged a successful career as a media pundit and took a senior role in a UK sports management company.

Frank Stapleton

At the end of March 1975 Luton Town and Carlisle United sat at the foot of the First Division. With respect to those clubs this was no surprise. But just above them were Spurs, Leicester City, Chelsea – and Arsenal. Along with London's other elite the Gunners were battling against relegation. That day they faced Stoke City at Highbury knowing that the points were vital, especially as Alan Ball and Bob McNab were each about to start a 3-match suspension. The result was a disappointing 1-1 draw, and an equally disappointing debut for young Irish centre-forward Frank Stapleton, who was substituted. Stapleton did not appear in Arsenal's first team again that season, at the end of which Arsenal missed the drop by 4 points.

His next appearance was 6 games into the following season, in a 1-1 Highbury draw with Leicester. It was Stapleton, 1 of 6 Irishmen in Arsenal's team that day, who scored the Gunners' goal, a stunner after only 4 minutes. 'I was delighted with the way it went in,' he said. 'When Chippy Brady crossed I could see the goalkeeper off his line, and I just dipped my header over him and into the net.' Former Arsenal man Jon Sammels equalised 13 minutes from the end, but Stapleton might have snatched the winner with another header that Mark Wallington did well to save. A few days later it was Stapleton's spectacular goal at Goodison Park that earned Arsenal a League Cup replay. He came on 10 minutes from the end, in place of Terry Mancini, and lashed the ball home in the dying seconds.

Frank Stapleton, born in Dublin on 10 July 1956 and on Arsenal's books since June 1972, was making his mark, although if the Gunners had been involved in Europe at the time, then he would have been unable to play. In June 1975, UEFA banned him from club and international football for 2 years after it was discovered that the date of birth in his passport had been altered to make him eligible to play for the Republic of Ireland in a European youth tournament in Switzerland. The FA of Ireland fined him £50.

Domestically, though, he was still free, and he went from strength to strength, benefiting particularly from the exquisite passing of Liam Brady, although in August 1976 Terry Neill included Stapleton in a package of players and cash when he tried to sign Crystal Palace's England winger, Peter Taylor. The same month Stapleton was one of several young players in a pay dispute with Arsenal.

That all sorted, he went on to form a formidable strike partnership with Malcolm Macdonald, and in 1977-78 between them they scored 45 League and Cup goals, with Stapleton contributing 19. A tall, powerful centre-forward, Stapleton was Arsenal's leading scorer in 3 successive seasons from 1978-79, played in 3 successive FA Cup finals, and scored in the win over Manchester United in 1979.

He would become the first player to score FA Cup final goals for 2 different clubs. After 108 goals in 299 appearances for Arsenal, in August 1981 he joined Manchester United for £900,000, a fee set by a tribunal when the clubs could not agree. They could have had him for nothing; he was on their books as a schoolboy but they allowed him to leave.

With United he gained 2 more FA Cup winners' medals, in 1983 and 1985, scoring in the drawn first game in 1983, against Brighton, before United comfortably won the replay. Stapleton left United in 1987 – he scored 78 goals for them in 286 matches – and played for Ajax, Derby County, Aldershot, Huddersfield Town, Le Havre and Bradford City. After being sacked as Bradford's player-manager in 1994 he played twice for Brighton, who were then managed by Liam Brady, before announcing his retirement. He managed in the NASL, coached at Bolton Wanderers and was the Jordan national team's assistant manager. He then became a speaker at football events. Twenty-four of his 71 Republic of Ireland full caps came when he was with Arsenal.

David O'Leary

On the opening day of the 1975-76 season, Bertie Mee sprang a surprise by leaving out Alan Ball for the trip to Burnley. Ball, who was on the transfer list at his own request, played for the reserves that day, and Mee said that he was not fully fit. That may have come as a surprise to England manager Don Revie who, 4 days earlier, had named Ball in his team soon to face Switzerland.

Arsenal drew 0-0 at Turf Moor, and making his debut for the Gunners was centre-half David O'Leary. He may have been only 17 but O'Leary was also looking forward to international football. Along with Liam Brady and Terry Mancini, he had been named in the Republic of Ireland squad to face Turkey in a European Championship match in Dublin in October. O'Leary would have to wait a little while for his Ireland debut – which came against England at Wembley in September 1976 when Charlie George was in the opposing team – but his Arsenal career was already on its way. He made 30 League and Cup appearances that season, and for the next 10 years he was a fixture in the team, missing games only when he was injured, which, apart from 1980-81 when a damaged heel bothered him for weeks, was rarely.

For O'Leary records tumbled. In all he made 719 appearances for the Gunners, and if one adds 3 FA Charity Shield matches then the figure most often quoted is a remarkable 722, far more than any other Arsenal player has ever achieved. He was the youngest player to reach 100 and 200 appearances, was only 26 when he played in his 400th game, and sailed past George Armstrong's appearances record in November 1989. He played in 2 League championship-winning sides, in 1988-89 and 1990-91; 2 FA Cup-winning teams, in 1979 and 1993; in winning League Cup final teams in 1987 and 1993 (he missed the 1988 final because of injury); and in a Cup-winners' Cup runners-up side in 1980. There were also 2 losing FA Cup finals, in 1978 and 1980.

His international career was impressive, too. Although born in Stoke Newington, on 2 May 1958, he moved with his family to Dublin and grew up there, qualifying to play for the Republic of Ireland because of his parentage. Despite 2 years out of the side following a disagreement with manager Jack Charlton, O'Leary won 68 caps, captaining his country on his final appearance – a friendly match against Wales at Tolka Park in Dublin in September 1993 – but was carried off injured after only 2 minutes. In 1990, he had scored the winner in the penalty shootout against Romania that put Ireland through to the quarter-finals of the World Cup in Italy.

Towards his latter days at Highbury, Tony Adams and Steve Bould were the preferred central defence, and O'Leary made his last appearance for the Gunners as an 81st-minute substitute in the 1993 FA Cup final replay win against Sheffield Wednesday.

O'Leary joined Leeds United on a free transfer but an Achilles tendon injury ruled him out for much of his time at Elland Road. In September 1995, after only a handful of League games for Leeds, he announced his retirement as a player. He was George Graham's assistant at Leeds for 2 years before becoming manager. He took Leeds to the semi-finals of the Champions League and the UEFA Cup before being sacked in the summer of 2002. 'I went in to clear a few things up before I went on holiday and I got the sack,' he said. He managed Aston Villa from June 2003 until July 2006, and in 2010-11 spent 10 months as manager of the United Arab Emirates club Al-Ahli before that ended in acrimony.

Graham Rix

Before he had even made his Arsenal debut, 19-year-old midfielder Graham Rix feared that he would never play football again. In a pre-season game in 1976 he broke 2 vertebrae and was in a plaster cast for 12 weeks. But Rice did recover, and in late March 1977 he played in a friendly game against Chelsea. Then Bertie Mee told him that he was to make his League debut against Leicester City at Highbury on 2 April. On the eve of the game Rix said:

> I was told the injury was a dodgy one, and I wondered if I'd ever play again. In fact, I couldn't even put my socks on. But I worked hard and I'm delighted to get the chance of first-team football. It doesn't worry me that the team is going through a sticky patch. They are the same players who were doing so well earlier in the season.

Arsenal had been as high as fourth in the table, but by the time Leicester visited, thanks to a run of 7 consecutive defeats that was ended only by a 1-1 draw at Stoke, they had dropped to eleventh. Their most recent win had been as long ago as 15 January.

It took Rix, in for the suspended Liam Brady, only 3 minutes to score his first goal for Arsenal. Put through by Richie Powling he coolly beat Mark Wallington from the edge of the penalty area. Before half-time Arsenal led 3-0 with further goals from David O'Leary, and that was how the scoreline remained. By the end of the season Rix had played 7 times, 3 as a substitute, and Arsenal had climbed to eighth.

For the next 3 seasons Rix and Brady formed a wonderful attacking midfield as the Gunners recovered much of their poise to finish fifth, seventh and fourth, and reach consecutive FA Cup finals. In the Wembley game that Arsenal won – the sensational 1979 final against Manchester

United – it was Rix's cross from Brady's pass that provided Alan Sunderland's last-gasp winner. In the following season's Cup-winners' Cup final against Valencia, Rix missed his kick in the penalty shootout that Arsenal lost.

After Brady left for Juventus that summer, Terry Neill appointed Rix as the Gunners' captain, but he never lifted any trophies. Most of the 1980s proved to be a fallow period for Arsenal, and when they did win some silverware, the 1987 League Cup, Rix was in and out of the team that season and was not in the squad for Wembley. He made only 7 starts in 1987-88 – he went on loan to Brentford for a while – and his final appearance in an Arsenal shirt came in the last match of the season, as a substitute at Goodison Park. His final seasons had been plagued by a recurring Achilles tendon injury. Rix had made 463 appearances for Arsenal and scored 51 goals. He won 17 full England caps with Arsenal.

Born at Askern, Doncaster, on 23 October 1957, Rix had joined the Gunners as an apprentice in 1974. Now he went on a free transfer to the French club Stade Malherbe Caen, where he spent 3 years before moving to Le Havre and then Dundee. In 1993 Rix joined Chelsea as youth-team coach and on the final day of the 1994-95 season made his very last League appearance – against Arsenal, coming on as a substitute at Stamford Bridge. He was a successful coach of the England under-21 team, and first-team coach at Chelsea. In March 1999 Rix was sentenced to 12 months in prison – he served 6 – for unlawful sex with a 15-year-old girl, and indecent assault.

He managed Portsmouth from February 2001 until March 2002, then Oxford United, and was first-team coach at Hearts. He managed Central FC, a Trinidad and Tobago club, for 5 months in 2012, and Wessex League club AFC Porchester who he left in 2017. In 2018 former Chelsea youth team players made allegations of racism against Rix and Gwyn Williams, another former member of the Chelsea staff.

Malcolm Macdonald

Still buzzing from their last-minute FA Cup final victory over Manchester United 48 hours earlier, as Arsenal prepared to meet already-relegated Chelsea on the Monday evening of 14 May 1979, they welcomed back a familiar face. Centre-forward Malcolm Macdonald's last First Division appearance had been in the third match of the season, and his most recent first-team game when he came on as a 70th-minute substitute in a UEFA Cup-tie against Red Star Belgrade in November.

Injured in a League Cup defeat at Rotherham on 29 August, Macdonald recovered from a cartilage operation, but immediately after the Red Star game he was back in hospital for further treatment on his left knee. Now, on the last day of the season, Terry Neill said, 'He is fully fit again. He's had several games in the reserves and looked really sharp. It will make a very good finish to a smashing weekend.' Macdonald scored Arsenal's equaliser in a 1-1 draw on a bumpy Stamford Bridge pitch, but it was his final appearance. After a summer with Djurgården IF in Sweden he announced his retirement. He was 29.

Born in Fulham on 7 January 1950, Macdonald played for Fulham and Luton Town before Newcastle United signed him for £180,000 in the 1971 close season. Newcastle supporters idolised him. A home debut hat-trick against Liverpool was just the beginning. He was the Magpies' top scorer for 4 successive seasons, won 15 England caps, scored 5 goals in 1 game against Cyprus, and altogether for Newcastle scored 121 goals in 228 appearances.

He fell out with manager Gordon Lee, and after joining Arsenal for a British record fee of £333,333 in July 1976 he promised that he would definitely score on his debut, against First Division newcomers Bristol City at Highbury. The game ended 1-0 to Bristol, whose captain Geoff Merrick, said:

Malcolm made us determined to ensure that it didn't happen. None of us had played against him before, but from watching him on TV we knew that we'd be in trouble if we allowed him to run on to passes hit over the top of defenders. We made sure that didn't happen.

Most other defenders did not work him out so easily. Macdonald scored 29 League and Cup goals that season, ending it as the Gunners' top scorer. In 1977-78 he top-scored again with 26 goals. When injury called time on his playing career, he had scored 57 goals in 108 League and Cup matches for Arsenal. With Newcastle he had gained runners-up medals in the 1974 FA Cup final and the 1976 League Cup final, and he won a runners-up medal with Arsenal in the 1978 FA Cup final.

Despite standing only 5ft 8in tall, he was dangerous in the air. In December 1976, his hat-trick in a 5-3 win over Newcastle on an icy Highbury pitch included 2 towering headers. Afterwards he said, 'It was most gratifying and has given Gordon Lee something to reflect on.' He also fell out with Terry Neill. Along with Alan Hudson he was sent home from Arsenal's tour to Australia in the summer of 1977. Macdonald said, 'The manager told us we were a bad influence on the younger players.'

After his playing days ended Macdonald joined Fulham as marketing executive. He managed the Cottagers from 1980 to 1984. He steered them clear of relegation to the Fourth Division and put together a promotion-winning team for 1981-82 that so nearly got into the First Division the following season. In 1983-84 the team struggled, though, and in April, when publicity surrounded his private life, he left to run what had been the Wigmore Arms in Worthing but was now renamed the Far Post. He returned to management in October 1987, with Huddersfield Town, but after only 206 days in charge, and Huddersfield doomed to Third Division football, his contract was mutually terminated on 4 May 1988. He was later involved in a football agency and works in the media as a public speaker.

Pat Jennings

Monday, 3 May 1971. The final day of the First Division season. Early in the first half at White Hart Lane, Charlie George turned and drove the ball towards Spurs' goal. Pat Jennings was surprised by both the speed and power of the shot, but in a split-second reflex he somehow turned the ball round the post for a corner. Two minutes from time the game was still goalless. Jennings cleared a shot from Radford but the ball was returned to the goalmouth and the 20-year-old whom the newspapers liked to call a 'Port Vale reject' connected with his forehead and the ball crashed against the underside of the crossbar and into the net. Even Pat Jennings could do nothing to stop it. Ray Kennedy had won the game for Arsenal, the Gunners were champions, and, 5 days later, winners of a League and FA Cup double.

Monday, 8 August 1977. Arsenal goalkeeper Jimmy Rimmer, who has missed only 3 League games in the past 3 seasons, says he is shocked at the Gunners' interest in Pat Jennings. The 28-year-old Rimmer says, 'I'm not happy. Who would be? Pat wouldn't join Arsenal expecting to be number-two. I love Arsenal. All I know about it is what I've read.' Rimmer will soon be on his way to Aston Villa. Jennings is about to start a new career with Arsenal.

Born in Newry on 12 January 1945, Jennings joined Watford from Newry Town, for £6,000 in May 1963. Just over a year later he was transferred to Spurs for £27,000. It was the start of a remarkable career at White Hart Lane. Statistics alone tell the tale: 591 appearances, 75 Northern Ireland caps to add to the 2 he won while with Watford, winners' medals in the FA Cup, League Cup (2) and UEFA Cup, Footballer of the Year, PFA Player of the Year – and an MBE. He even managed a goal, from a huge clearance in the 1967 FA Charity Shield match.

By August 1977, though, Spurs were a Second Division club. Tottenham manager Keith Burkinshaw decided that Jennings, now 32 and recently recovered from a broken ankle, could leave. He was obviously nearing the end of his career. He was wrong. Jennings was transferred to Arsenal for £30,000, to rejoin Terry Neill who had managed him at Spurs. Far from being over the hill, Jennings would spend the next 8 seasons at Highbury, win another 42 caps to take him to a record of 119 for Northern Ireland, play in 3 FA Cup finals with a winners' medal in 1979, and a European Cup-winners' Cup final, become the first player in English football to make 1,000 senior appearances when he kept a clean sheet at the Hawthorns on 26 February 1983, and altogether made 326 appearances for the Gunners before he retired from League football in 1985.

His style was demonstrably that of a goalkeeper whose seemingly uncanny positional sense made spectacular saves largely unnecessary. Crosses always seemed to find their way into his hands, and oncoming forwards rarely got the better of a one-on-one confrontation with one of the best goalkeepers in the world.

He returned to Tottenham in 1985, to play reserve-team football in preparation for the following year's World Cup in Mexico, and his final game was on the biggest stage of all, against Brazil in Guadalajara. He was 41.

Jennings, who was also awarded the OBE, became a goalkeeping coach at Spurs, and also works as a corporate hospitality host for them. There are lounges named after him at White Hart Lane and Windsor Park in Belfast, and he also has a park in his hometown of Newry named for him.

Speaking at the launch of the McDonald's Fun Football initiative in April 2019 he said, 'Yes, I got sold, believe it or not, to Arsenal and went to Highbury ... and enjoyed some great days ... . They were brilliant to me. They gave me two four-year contracts and I always had a good relationship with the supporters.'

Alan Sunderland

Arsenal's sensational last-minute goal that won the FA Cup in 1979 quite naturally features in the stories of several Arsenal players. But the man whose name will always be recalled the most is the one who arrived at the far post just in time to put the ball in the net and send Arsenal supporters into ecstasy, and Manchester United fans into misery.

A Yorkshireman, born at Conisbrough, near Doncaster, on 1 July 1953, Alan Sunderland had already been to Wembley, not just the previous year with Arsenal when the Gunners lost to Ipswich Town, but with Wolves in the 1974 League Cup final when they beat Manchester City. He began his career as an apprentice at Molineux, and as well as the League Cup he helped Wolves win the Second Division title, 2 points ahead of Chelsea, in 1977. The following November, after scoring 30 goals for Wolves in 158 League games, he was transferred to Arsenal for £220,000. A goalscoring midfielder at Molineux, he became a goalscoring striker for Arsenal.

He made his League debut in a 2-1 win at Old Trafford on 5 November 1977, and his home debut a week later against Coventry City. Sunderland had unhappy memories of his previous appearance at Highbury, 'It was for Wolves, 13 April 1976, and we were fighting relegation. I was playing right-back because we had injury problems. I was substituted at half-time and we lost 2-1. We went down with Burnley and Sheffield United.'

So with Arsenal, Sunderland was stepping back up to the top flight. He remained in the team until being injured against West Brom on Easter Monday 1978. An X-ray of his left leg revealed a stress fracture that kept him out for 3 weeks, which meant that he would miss the FA Cup semi-final against Orient at Stamford Bridge. Terry Neill said, 'It's a great disappointment for Alan, and for the club. It's a blow to miss the semi-final but he'll be fit for the final.' Sunderland returned for the last

2 League games of a season in which Arsenal finished fifth, and he then played against Ipswich Town at Wembley.

The following season he made 37 appearances but his return of only 9 goals was disappointing. He more than made up for that in the FA Cup, though, and netted 6 times including, of course, his most famous goal of all. In January 2019, he told the *Daily Mail*:

> My childhood dream was to score the winning goal in the FA Cup final. I'd done it a thousand times in the garden. Sir Bobby Charlton was my childhood hero. I had his picture on my bedroom wall. After I scored, I sprained my ankle so I hopped along for the lap of honour. We went to a hotel near Marble Arch. We had comedy from Mike and Bernie Winters. It was a great and late night.

Sunderland remained at Highbury for another 4 full seasons, at first forming a good striking partnership with Frank Stapleton. In May 1980, after playing in the FA Cup final against West Ham United, he won an England cap when Ron Greenwood selected him to play against Australia in Sydney.

He made his final appearance for Arsenal in a home League Cup defeat by Walsall in November 1983. Injuries had hampered him, and also Tony Woodcock and Charlie Nicholas had arrived on the scene. In the summer of 1984, after scoring 91 goals in 280 games for Arsenal, Sunderland was allowed to leave on a free transfer. He had been on loan to Ipswich Town, helping them avoid relegation from the First Division, including scoring a vital late winner against Manchester United, and the move was made permanent. He stayed at Portman Road until 1986, scoring 12 goals in 50 games for Ipswich before a brief spell with Derry City in the League of Ireland. He ran a pub, the Halberd Inn, at Ipswich before emigrating to Malta where he coached Birkirkara FC.

Brian Talbot

Brian Talbot had always wanted to play in London. Born in Ipswich on 21 July 1953, and on Ipswich Town's books since he was a schoolboy, the powerful midfielder had given yeoman service – 227 appearances and 31 goals – to his hometown club before moving to Arsenal in January 1979 for Gunners' record fee of £450,000. In March 2008 he told the *Ipswich Star*:

> I wanted to move for two reasons – one was personal [his marriage had broken up] and the other was that I had always wanted to play in London.
>
> I'd been at Ipswich since I was 13 and in those days there was no freedom of contract and no Bosman Ruling. Manchester City offered a lot of money for me, but I told Bobby Robson that I would only go to Arsenal or Manchester United, and United didn't want me. Arsenal got me for less than Manchester City were prepared to pay. No disrespect to Ipswich, but I thought before at the time, and still do today, that Arsenal are a bigger club.

There was, though, one small problem before Talbot's debut, against Nottingham Forest. He arrived in the Highbury dressing room to find a long-sleeved shirt hanging on his peg. He told Terry Neill that he always played short-sleeved, but the manager explained that Arsenal liked every player to wear exactly the same kit. A compromise was reached: Talbot would be allowed to roll up his sleeves, which, in a way, was symbolic. He made an impressive start to his new club career as Arsenal, who won 2-1, became only the second team to defeat Brian Clough's Forest in the past 14 months. On television the previous evening, Clough had been critical of southern managers. After the game, Arsenal's assistant Don

Howe caught up with the outspoken Clough in the tunnel and challenged him about his remarks. Neill stepped in to act as peacemaker.

Talbot, meanwhile, had to miss Arsenal's next match because he was signed too late to be eligible to play in the FA Cup third-round second replay against Sheffield Wednesday. He was, though, back for the next League game, and for most of Arsenal's matches for the next 6½ seasons. He was a First Division ever-present in 1979-80 (when, including the FA Charity Shield, he played in an astonishing 70 matches as Arsenal reached the finals of both the FA Cup and the European Cup-winners' Cup), 1981-82 and 1982-83 (when he was a substitute 4 times). The only full season in which he missed a significant number of games was 1983-84 when he was injured.

Altogether for Arsenal, Talbot made 326 appearances and scored 49 goals including Arsenal's first in that epic 1979 FA Cup final. Talbot put the Gunners in front after only 12 minutes. He told the *Ipswich Star*, 'Sundy kicked my boot as I connected with the ball. I don't know if he would have been quite so keen to give the goal to me if he hadn't scored the winner.' Ipswich had won the Cup in 1978 – against Arsenal – and so Talbot was the first player in 100 years to win it consecutively with different clubs.

Talbot might have been the midfield powerhouse that complemented the artistry of Brady and Rix, but he was also a fine footballer in his own right. He won 5 England caps with Ipswich, and 1 with Arsenal, in Sydney in May 1980 when Alan Sunderland also played for Ron Greenwood's England against Australia.

In June 1985, aged 31, Talbot moved to Watford for £150,000, then played for Stoke City and West Brom (for a time as player-manager) and had a handful of games for Fulham and Aldershot (player-manager) to take his career League appearances to 643. He had 2 highly successful spells managing in Malta, with Hibernians and Marsaxlokk FC, took Rushden and Diamonds into the Football League and then into Division Three, and also managed Oldham Athletic and Oxford United before being appointed Fulham's chief scout and assistant director of football operations.

Kenny Sansom

After the 70-match slog of the 1979-80 season – with nothing to show for it – it was clear that Arsenal needed fresh legs and new blood. In June the Gunners' manager, Terry Neill, signed 19-year-old England under-21 forward Clive Allen from QPR for £1.25 million, a sum that obliterated the previous highest Arsenal club record, the £450,000 they paid for Brian Talbot. Allen made his debut in a friendly at Ibrox on 1 August when Arsenal lost 2-0 and the new boy hardly had a kick. Less than 2 weeks later, there were reports that Allen was on his way out of Highbury without ever making a First Division appearance for the Gunners.

Chairman Denis Hill-Wood said:

> I've not seen Terry Neill since he returned from Yugoslavia [where Arsenal had taken part in an international tournament] but we believe in allowing a manager to manage the side. It is up to Terry to fashion the team and I would have no objection if he wanted to sell Clive Allen.

On 13 August, the player was on his way to Crystal Palace in an exchange deal that saw England full-back Kenny Sansom travelling in the opposite direction, in exchange for Allen and goalkeeper Paul Barron who was valued at £400,000. Clive Allen, too, would eventually play for England at full level. Kenny Sansom would continue his international career and go on to captain Arsenal.

Sansom was born in Camberwell on 26 September 1958 and attracted the attentions of scouts from Arsenal, Spurs and QPR before signing for Palace. He captained their victorious 1977 FA Youth Cup final team against Everton, skippered England Youth, won 9 full caps, helped Palace's young side rise from the Third Division to the First, and made 197 League and Cup appearances before, it was reported at the time, realising a boyhood ambition to play for Arsenal, although he later admitted that as a youngster he was a Chelsea fan.

Sansom made his debut against West Brom on 16 August 1980 and helped lay on Frank Stapleton's winner. That season he was ever-present, and again in 1981-82, playing in every First Division, FA Cup and League Cup match. In the entire 1982-83 season he missed only 2 matches, both through injury, and that was pretty much the picture of his Arsenal career for the next 5 seasons. He captained the Gunners to victory in the 1987 League Cup final when they came from a goal down to beat Liverpool 2-1 after Ronnie Whelan deflected Charlie Nicholas's 83rd-minute shot into the net to give Arsenal their first major honour for 8 years.

The following year Arsenal lost the League Cup final to Luton Town, but this time it was 21-year-old Tony Adams, not Sansom, who led out the team. Sansom's relationship with manager George Graham had become strained but he was still the regular left-back. As the season wore on, however, a new signing from Wimbledon, Nigel Winterburn, seemed the logical successor to Sansom who was approaching 30. In December 1988, Jim Smith rescued the fast-fading Arsenal career of Kenny Sansom who had not appeared in the senior side all season. Sansom moved to Newcastle United for £300,000. He looked back on 394 games and 6 goals for the Gunners in which time he added 77 full caps. His spell at Newcastle was short as his playing days wound down slowly with QPR and Coventry City, and then a handful of games for Everton, Brentford and Watford, for whom he made just 1 League appearance to take his overall tally to 637 with his 8 clubs. There followed some non-League football with Croydon, Chertsey Town and Slough Town but, unlike many of his contemporaries, there was to be no managerial career. Sansom fell on hard times with business failures, gambling problems and alcohol addiction, while his personal life made the news pages. His life apparently back on track, he became a guide for the legends' tours at the Emirates, made media appearances, writes a football blog, and makes personal appearances at dinners, golf days and other events.

Tony Adams

Tony Adams had an unfortunate start to his first-team career. An error by the central defender who had only just celebrated his 17th birthday allowed Sunderland's Colin West to give the visitors to Highbury a third-minute lead on 5 November 1983. There were no fireworks from the Gunners that day. They lost 2-1, and Adams played only twice more that season. No one could have imagined what he would go on to achieve.

By the time his Arsenal career came to an end, 22 years had passed and Adams had won almost everything available to a top-class footballer, some of them more than once or even twice. There were 4 top-flight championships as the First Division became the FA Premiership and he captained title winners in 3 different decades; 3 FA Cup final victories; 2 Football League Cup final wins and a Cup-winners' Cup final success. Add to that 66 England caps and the captaincy of both club and country and one can see why, to many supporters, Tony Adams is simply 'Mr Arsenal'. Arsene Wenger said that Adams was 'a doctor of defence'. George Graham regarded him as 'my colossus'.

Adams was born in Romford on 10 October 1966 and grew up in Dagenham. He signed for Arsenal as a schoolboy in 1980, became an apprentice in 1983, and his first League game came 2 months before he signed full-time professional forms on 30 January 1984.

Slowly but surely he grew into the role: 16 League games in 1984-85, 10 in 1985-86, and then an ever-present 42 in 1986-87, after which only injury kept him out of the side until a battle with alcoholism needed to be fought.

Along with Steve Bould, Lee Dixon and Nigel Winterburn, Adams formed the most famous back 4 in football, renowned under George Graham's managership for its finely tuned use of the offside trap. Their raised arms became almost iconic, a part of Britain's sporting pop culture. Wenger said, 'When I first came to Arsenal, I realised the back four were all university graduates in the art of defending.'

In January 1988 Adams took over the Arsenal captaincy from Kenny Sansom and remained club captain until his retirement 14 years later. In 1992-93 he skippered Arsenal to the first-ever FA Cup and League Cup double, beating Sheffield Wednesday in both finals. The following season he was lifting the Cup-winners' Cup after Arsenal beat Parma in the final in Copenhagen. The First Division championship was won twice, in 1988-89 with a nail-biting win over Liverpool in the last game of the season, and in 1990-91 when all season Arsenal lost only 1 League game, at Chelsea in February. A player brawl at Old Trafford in October 1990 saw Arsenal have 2 points deducted (Manchester United were docked 1 point) and in December Adams was given a 4-month prison sentence for drink-driving. He served six weeks and missed 8 League games in that time.

Adams repaid Wenger's understanding. In 1997-98 and 2001-02 he captained Arsenal in Premiership and FA Cup double-winning seasons, albeit by the time of the second, due to injury he made only 10 League appearances. In 2002 he announced his retirement from playing, so his last Arsenal appearance was at home to Everton in the final match of the 2001-2 Premiership season, which was played after the FA Cup final win over Chelsea at the Millennium Stadium, Cardiff. Adams had made 666 appearances for Arsenal and scored 48 goals.

He managed Wycombe Wanderers, Portsmouth, Gabala (Azerbaijan) and the Spanish club Granada, and coached at Feyenoord in the Netherlands. In September 2000 he founded the Sporting Chance Clinic, a charitable foundation aimed at providing treatment, counselling and support for sportsmen and sportswomen suffering from drink, drug or gambling addictions. Adams, who was awarded the MBE, was elected as the new president of the Rugby Football League in 2019. In May 1998, his autobiography *Addicted* was published to great critical acclaim. A statue of Tony Adams stands outside the Emirates Stadium.

Charlie Nicholas

When Charlie Nicholas made his debut for Arsenal on 27 August 1983, he faced a team that altogether cost less than the £750,000 the Gunners had paid Celtic for the Scottish striker 8 weeks earlier. Nicholas had a relatively quiet debut against Luton Town at Highbury as Tony Woodcock and Brian McDermott scored the goals that gave Arsenal a 2-1 win.

Two days later, however, Nicholas gave a scintillating performance at Molineux, scoring both goals as again Arsenal won 2-1. He did not score again until Boxing Day but his 2 goals that day were special – they came in a 4-2 win at White Hart Lane.

Nicholas was born at Cowcaddens, Glasgow, on 30 December 1961. He was only 17 when he scored on his debut for Celtic, against Queen's Park in a Glasgow Cup match. He was on his way to being acclaimed as the most exciting young player in Scotland since the emergence of Kenny Dalglish. By the time he moved to Highbury, Nicholas had scored 84 goals in 117 appearances for Celtic, including 48 in 53 games in 1 season alone, 1982-83. With Celtic he won the Scottish Premier Division twice, and the Scottish League Cup when he scored the opening goal against Rangers in the 1982 final. In 1983, he was both the Scottish Football Writers' Player of the Year and the Scottish PFA Player of the Year. His first full cap had come in March that year, when he scored in a 2-2 draw against Switzerland at Hampden Park. He would add another 13 caps as a Gunner, and win 20 in all.

After he signed for Arsenal in June 1983 he told the Aberdeen *Press and Journal*:

> It's a big relief to get it all settled. It was a difficult choice because of the respect I have for Liverpool and Manchester United ... [but] I believe that Arsenal is the right selection because I'm not following in the shadow of players like Dalglish and Keegan at Liverpool.

He said he was also impressed with the management partnership of Terry Neill and Don Howe and that 'I don't want to be tied as an individual. I want to be known as a team player and I believe that the boss [Neill] and Don Howe can coach one into me'. He said that, in some ways, signing for Arsenal was like winning a trophy:

> Anybody can say that I'm just interested in the money but I could have gone to Italy and been a millionaire in two years ... . The Football League is going to be a lot tougher than playing in Scotland. A lot of players have come south and failed. But a lot of Scots have succeeded – and I aim to be one of them.

With Arsenal, Nicholas won only 1 major honour, the Football League Cup in 1986-87 when he scored both goals in the 2-1 win over Liverpool at Wembley. But if the Gunners lacked silverware in his time at Highbury, Nicholas entertained with his flamboyant style and his 'Champagne Charlie' reputation. It was a lack of consistency that troubled some supporters, though, and in his first 2 seasons he scored only 11 and then 9 League goals respectively. Of course, as he said, the English First Division was stronger than its Scottish equivalent, and he also played a slightly different role to the one he had enjoyed at Parkhead.

George Graham's arrival as manager signalled the beginning of the end for Nicholas at Highbury, and in January 1988, after being in reserves since August, he was transferred to Aberdeen for £400,000. He said, 'I'm a different person to the one who went to London ... . I don't rate the bright lights that highly ... . I've returned to Scotland for football rather than for money.' He had scored 54 goals in 184 senior appearances for Arsenal.

With Aberdeen, he rediscovered his scoring form and with the Dons won the Scottish Cup and the Scottish League Cup, returning to Celtic for 5 seasons before ending his career with Clyde in 1995-96. He now works in the media with a newspaper column and as a Sky Sports pundit.

David Rocastle

There were many highlights in Arsenal's season in 1988-89 as the Gunners won the Football League championship for the ninth time. For many supporters, however, the sight of David Rocastle dribbling past defenders, sending inch-prefect passes to colleagues, even scoring the occasional spectacular goal, will remain the standout memory of that glorious campaign. It was perhaps fitting that 'Rocky' Rocastle wore Liam Brady's number 7 shirt, although he was more in the mould of Arsenal outside-rights such as Joe Hulme than that of the traditional midfielder.

Rocastle was born in Lewisham on 2 May 1967. Millwall gave him a trial but rejected him. Arsenal had no such reservations. He joined the Gunners on schoolboy forms in 1982, became an apprentice in August 1983, and a full-time professional in December 1984. There was a problem with his eyesight but contact lenses sorted that out and he made his League debut in a goalless draw against Newcastle United at Highbury on 28 September 1985. He played in 16 League games that season, 3 of them after coming on as a substitute, and scored once as Arsenal finished seventh.

He was ever-present in the FA Cup, although 5 matches did not take Arsenal far in the competition. After 2 replays against Luton Town they went out 3-0 at Kenilworth Road in the fifth round. Rocastle had scored his first goal for the Gunners – a 27th-minute header from a Tony Woodcock cross – in the first game, a 2-2 draw also at Kenilworth Road. From 1986-87 Rocastle was a first-team regular and made 36 League appearances that season. It would have been more but in a stormy game at Old Trafford in which 7 players were booked, Rocastle was sent off by referee George Tyson and subsequently suspended. By the end of the season, though, after scoring the winner in the semi-final replay over Spurs at White Hart Lane, he had a League Cup winners' medal against

Liverpool. The following season he was back at Wembley in another League Cup final but this time Arsenal surrendered a 2-1 lead with 7 minutes remaining to lose 3-2 to Luton. Arsenal would have taken a 3-1 lead after Rocastle was fouled in the penalty area, but Andy Dibble saved Nigel Winterburn's penalty.

Rocastle was ever-present that season, and again in 1988-89 as Arsenal won their first League championship for 18 years. By then he was an England player, against Denmark at Wembley in September 1988, the first of his 14 full caps. But there would be no European Cup football. English clubs had been banned after the Heysel Stadium deaths and so Arsenal also missed out on a UEFA Cup place after finishing fourth in 1989-90. When the Gunners won the League again, in 1990-91, a knee injury and then being inexplicably 'surplus to tactical requirements' restricted Rocastle to 13 League games, 3 as a substitute, although he did play in 4 European Cup matches in 1991-92. The ban was over and Arsenal went out in the second round, on aggregate to Benfica.

In July 1992 Arsenal supporters were shocked when George Graham sold the man whom Arsene Wenger would later describe as having 'an exceptional dimension as a footballer' to Leeds United for £2 million. Rocastle, who was distraught at leaving Arsenal, had scored 34 goals in 275 games for the Gunners but within 16 months of arriving at Elland Road, he was off to Manchester City with Leeds recouping the club record fee they had paid for him. In August 1994, he signed for Chelsea for £1.25 million but injuries now hampered him. In 1996 he was on the move again, had trials with Hertha Berlin, Aberdeen and Southampton and was loaned to Norwich City then Hull City, and played for Sabah FC in Malaysia before retiring in December 1999.

David Rocastle died from non-Hodgkin's lymphoma on 31 March 2001, aged 33. When the 38,121 crowd at Highbury before a north London derby match with Spurs observed a minute's silence, there was not the faintest interruption.

Viv Anderson

Viv Anderson spent only 3 seasons with Arsenal but during that time he rarely missed a match. It also did much to revive an England career that had stalled after the Nottingham Forest side with which he had won 2 European Cups began to age. Brian Clough tried to tie him to a new contract but the player said, 'I've been with Forest my entire career. Now I have a chance to make a change. I think the time is right.'

As Arsenal signed the 21-year-old in July 1984, for £250,000, Gunners' manager Don Howe said, 'He is a good attacking full-back and that is what I have bought him for. He can't help but do a good job for us because he's such a quality player.' Right-back had become a problem position for Arsenal but Anderson ended that particular headache for Howe. Born in Nottingham on 29 July 1956, he was on Manchester United's books as a schoolboy but they released him and Forest picked up the rising talent on their doorstep. With Forest he won promotion to the First Division, then the Football League championship, 2 League Cups and, of course, those 2 European Cups. He had made 430 appearances and scored 22 goals for Forest before moving to Highbury. He was also an international, the first black player to win a full England cap. He had 11 by the time he joined Arsenal and would add 16 more with the Gunners.

The man that Forest fans had nicknamed 'Spider' because of his long legs and galloping strides missed only 3 First Division games for Arsenal in 1984-85, 3 the next, and just 2 in 1986-87. That season he helped Arsenal end a barren spell by winning the League Cup. Anderson's arrival had meant that Howe could use Robson in his more effective role in midfield, while Anderson and his left-back partner Kenny Sansom delighted supporters with their marauding style.

However, the arrival of George Graham curtailed that approach and in 1986-87 a more disciplined Anderson – he was now 30 – was organising a defence in which 20-year-old Tony Adams was an ever-present. Arsenal fans didn't know it but the final game of that season, a 2-1 defeat at home to Norwich City, was Anderson's final game for their club. He had enjoyed a brilliant spell as Arsenal went to the top of the table and for some time looked as though they would win the title. But they fell away to finish fourth, and Anderson was at the end of his contract. After 150 games and 15 goals for the Gunners, in the summer of 1987 he moved to Manchester United for £250,000. However, the deal rumbled on for weeks as Graham described United's initial offer of £100,000 – Arsenal wanted £450,000 – as 'insulting to us as a club and to the ability of the player. He is a current international. I'm amazed that such a great club as United could come up with such an offer.' When a tribunal eventually set the fee, Graham said, 'Something is wrong when big clubs have to come down to this sort of haggling.'

Anderson was Alex Ferguson's first major signing for United but injuries hampered his time at Old Trafford. In January 1991, he joined Sheffield Wednesday on a free transfer and helped the Owls win promotion to the First Division and then finish third in the top flight. He did not play in either Wembley final against Arsenal in 1993 and that summer became player-manager of Barnsley, leaving after a year to go to Middlesbrough as assistant manager. He played twice for Boro during an injury crisis. He left them, and football altogether, in June 2001. In the Millennium Honours list Anderson was awarded the MBE for services to football. The man who played a groundbreaking role in the progress of black footballers within the game now works as global ambassador for several companies and sits on FA judicial panels. He is also a patron for Youth Against Racism.

Paul Merson

On 22 November 1986 Arsenal topped the First Division. The Gunners had dropped only 2 points from their last 7 matches and in that time had fielded an unchanged line-up. However, for the visit of relegation-bound Manchester City, Perry Groves – new manager George Graham's only signing so far – was suffering from an ankle injury and was replaced by Ian Allinson. Eighteen-year-old Paul Merson was named as substitute. Merson came on for his debut, replacing the injured Niall Quinn, and Arsenal won 3-0.

It was a quiet but solid start for Merson who went on loan to Brentford for 7 games before being recalled to bolster the squad for the match at Stamford Bridge in March. By now Arsenal had slipped from the top of the table. They eventually finished fourth and Merson was thrust into the team for the final few games. Undaunted by the experience, he scored 3 goals in his first 5 starts. The following season he made 15 League appearances, 8 of them as substitute, but in 1988-89 he was in from the start and missed only 1 game as Arsenal won their first League title in 18 years. The player who had been on Arsenal books since he was 14 – he was born at Harlesden on 20 March 1968 – had become one of English football's hottest prospects.

Originally a striker, Merson began to play a deeper role, his hard work and skill behind Alan Smith made him a vital member of the side. When the Gunners won the title again, in 1990-91, he missed only 1 game and weighed in with 13 goals. In September 1991, he won the first of his 15 full England caps while with Arsenal, coming on as a 67th-minute substitute against Germany at Wembley. He would win 21 overall.

There were dark clouds on the horizon, however. Merson underwent therapy for now well-publicised addictions to cocaine, alcohol and gambling, but he returned to the Arsenal team and impressed so much that he earned an England recall. It was a surprise when in July 1997

Arsene Wenger, after his first season at Highbury, decided that Merson could go to newly relegated Middlesbrough for £4.5 million, the most a club outside the top flight had ever paid for a player.

There have been suggestions that, despite being offered a new contract, Merson was joining Boro because they were doubling his salary, but at the time he told the *Sunday Life*:

> I thought I would end my career at Arsenal. When they said I could leave I felt terrible ... Arsene Wenger came to me and said, 'We've been offered £4.5 million for you.' I asked if he was going to try to keep me and he just said, 'No'. He kept saying that it was a lot of money for a 29-year-old and he had to take it. So my 15 years at Arsenal were over in 15 minutes .... They didn't make any effort to keep me.

Supporters were shocked but fan Ian Harvey had particular reason to feel mortified. Hours before the transfer went through, Harvey had named his new baby boy after Paul Merson. He said, 'I'm gutted. Not only is my favourite player leaving, my son is named after a Middlesbrough player.'

Merson had made 422 appearances for Arsenal, scored 99 goals and helped the Gunners win 2 League championships, the FA Cup, the League Cup and the European Cup-winners' Cup.

He helped Boro back into the Premiership before moving to Aston Villa FC for £6.75 million in September 1998. He went to Portsmouth on a free transfer in August 2002 and a year later joined Walsall, eventually becoming the Saddlers' manager before being sacked in February 2006. There were a tiny handful of non-League games before he retired from playing.

Merson embarked on a career in the media, most notably with Sky Sports, but sometimes he did not endear himself to Arsenal supporters with criticism of his former club. Nonetheless, warm memories of the flair and imagination he brought to the Gunners remain.

George Graham

In May 1986, Arsenal ended weeks of speculation about who would replace Don Howe as manager – in March, Howe had been asked to be released from his contract – when the Gunners' chairman, Peter Hill-Wood, paraded former Arsenal player 41-year-old George Graham as the new man. Watford's Graham Taylor, Terry Venables at Barcelona, and Aberdeen and Scotland manager Alex Ferguson had been among several names mentioned. But, in the end, the Gunners went into the Second Division and elected to go for potential rather than proven managerial ability.

The appointment brought a mixed reaction from Arsenal supporters, many of whom were hoping that their club would go for one of the game's big names but Hill-Wood had long been an admirer of Graham, a talented left-side midfielder versatile enough to also play as a striker, who had been a key figure in the 1970-71 Double-winning team. He was born at Bargeddie, Lanark, on 30 November 1944 and joined Arsenal from Chelsea, for £6,000 in September 1966. Man of the Match in the 1971 FA Cup final, he made 308 appearances for the Gunners, scoring 77 goals and winning 8 Scotland caps while at Arsenal before being transferred to Manchester United for £120,000 in December 1972. He played for Portsmouth and Crystal Palace, and coached at Palace and QPR before managing Millwall, taking them from near relegation to the Fourth Division and into the Second before rejoining Arsenal.

Graham discarded some of the old guard, brought on younger players, and introduced a new discipline both on and off the field, the latter never more evident than when his back 4 of Dixon, Adams, Bould and Winterburn were in their pomp. In 2015 Dixon told *The Independent*:

> George was chipping away at us five days a week, saying, 'Be in this position when the ball is here.' He would put us in our positions with nobody else around. He would have a

ball in his hand and jog around from the wings to the edge of the box and then the halfway line. All we had to do was react to where the ball was, keeping our positions and our spaces.

In his first season in charge at Highbury, Graham took the team to the top of the First Division before they dropped away to finish fourth, and with the League Cup he delivered the Gunners' first major silverware since the 1979 FA Cup final victory.

In 1988-89 he became only the fifth Arsenal manager to lead the club to a League championship, a feat they repeated in 1990-91. There followed the unique double of the FA Cup and the League Cup in 1992-93, and then the European Cup-winners' Cup, meaning that 6 major trophies had been won in 8 seasons under his managership.

Alas, it was not to last. In February 1995 Arsenal were forced to sack arguably the most successful manager – in terms of the number of major honours won – in their history. It turned out that in 1992 he had accepted illegal payments of more than £400,000 from Norwegian agent Rune Hauge during Arsenal's acquisition of John Jensen and Pål Lydersen, both of whom were Hauge's clients. The FA subsequently banned Graham, whose Arsenal salary was reported as £300,000 per annum, for a year after he confirmed that he had received an 'unsolicited gift' from the agent. He left a fine legacy at Highbury. Besides giving youth its chance, he also signed players such as Ian Wright, David Seaman, Perry Groves, Anders Limpar, Martin Keown, Lee Dixon, Steve Bould and Nigel Winterburn.

In September 1996 Graham replaced Howard Wilkinson as manager of Leeds United. He signed David O'Leary from Arsenal and guided Leeds to UEFA Cup qualification before, in October 1998, replacing David Pleat as Tottenham's manager. Five months later Spurs won the Football League Cup and a place in the UEFA Cup. However, in March 2001, new owners of the leisure group ENIC sacked Graham for an alleged breach of contract. Since then, although touted for several top-flight managerial jobs, he has worked as a media pundit.

Nigel Winterburn

At the start of the 1987-88 season George Graham had a problem at right-back. Viv Anderson had gone to Manchester United and although Michael Thomas wore the shirt for half the season, it was clear that his best role was in midfield. In May 1987 Graham had signed Nigel Winterburn from Wimbledon for £350,000 (the fee was also reported as £250,000 and £407,000). Winterburn made his debut as a substitute against Southampton in November, and in January 1988 made his first start, in his accustomed position of left-back. But Graham wanted Thomas in midfield and so the primarily left-footed Winterburn then filled in on the right. At the end of the season he was playing at Wembley in the League Cup final against Luton Town.

Arsenal were favourites against mid-table Luton, but that did not take into account the Gunners' apparent vulnerability against underdogs in cup finals. Swindon Town (1969), Ipswich Town (1978), West Ham United (1980) and Valencia (1980) had all upset the form book. Yet 'all the pointers suggest that the game might be as one-sided as a bout between the Christians and the lions,' wrote Steve Curry in the *Daily Express*.

Sure enough, with 9 minutes remaining, Arsenal, who for long periods had been utterly brilliant, led 2-1 through Martin Hayes and Alan Smith. Then the Gunners were awarded a penalty. They had missed 4 that season, including 2 by the regular taker, Thomas, and so Winterburn stepped up to take his first spot-kick for Arsenal. ITV's Brian Moore thought it 'a curious decision'. Winterburn drove the ball hard to Andy Dibble's left but the goalkeeper guessed correctly and made a brilliant save. Thus inspired, Luton scored twice in the dying stages to win 3-2. It was one of the very few low points in Nigel Winterburn's Arsenal career.

Born at Arley in Warwickshire on 11 December 1963, Winterburn was on the books of both Birmingham City and Oxford United without playing a senior game before Dave Bassett signed him for Wimbledon in 1983. Already an England youth international, he won under-21 caps as he helped Wimbledon win promotion to the top flight and was the supporters' player of the year in each of his 4 seasons at Plough Lane.

At Arsenal, Winterburn was always going to be the successor to Kenny Sansom. In 1988-89 he was in his familiar position, and there he stayed, with another new signing, Lee Dixon, at right-back, and superb central defenders in first Tony Adams and David O'Leary and then Adams and Steve Bould. He made his full England debut coming on as a substitute against Italy at Wembley in November 1989, and won a second cap, also as a substitute, against Germany at the Pontiac Silverdome in Michigan in June 1993. There were also 3 appearances for the England B team.

With Arsenal, Winterburn won 2 Football League championships and also the Premiership title, 2 FA Cups, a League Cup and the European Cup-winners' Cup. Altogether he made 584 senior appearances for the Gunners and scored 12 goals, 1 of them a superb 25-yard drive with his weaker right foot in a 2-2 draw against Wimbledon at Highbury in the penultimate match of the frantic championship race of 1988-89. In the last match, at Anfield, Winterburn's perfect free-kick provided the ball for Alan Smith's header that put the Gunners ahead on one of the most famous nights in Arsenal's history.

In June 2000 he joined West Ham for £250,000 on a 2-year contract. Arsene Wenger said, 'Nigel is the consummate professional and to lose a player who has dedicated thirteen years of outstanding service to this club is a great loss.' Winterburn made 94 senior appearances for the Hammers before retiring at the end of the 2002-03 season. He spent a few months as Paul Ince's part-time defensive coach at Blackburn Rovers before new manager Sam Allardyce felt that, 'I can look after that area myself now.' Like many of his former colleagues, Winterburn was also working as a football pundit on television and continues in a media role today.

Alan Smith

Alan Smith signed for Arsenal from Leicester City for £750,000 in March 1987, but it was the end of August before he scored his first goal for the Gunners. There was a good reason: George Graham had flown back from Portugal in a bid to complete the signing before transfer deadline day, but Arsenal loaned the tall centre-forward back to Leicester for the remainder of the season. Told that his new signing spoke German, French and Spanish, Graham said, 'Very useful in Europe, then.'

Smith's debut for the Gunners came on the opening day of 1987-88, a 2-1 home defeat at the hands of Liverpool, but when his first goal came, it was quickly followed by 2 more. On 29 August, Arsenal hammered Portsmouth – Pompey would be relegated that season – 6-0 at Highbury, and Smith scored a hat-trick. The Gunners, who had dropped Charlie Nicholas, went ahead through Smith after 15 minutes. A minute before half-time he scored again, and netted a third goal in the 65th minute. He was, of course, voted man of the match. Over Christmas and New Year he lost his place briefly to Niall Quinn, but at the end of the season he had made 36 full appearances, come on as a substitute 3 times and scored 11 goals in the First Division. There was 1 FA Cup goal, in the final against Luton when Arsenal fans were shocked by a late defeat.

In 1988-89 Smith began with a hat-trick against Wimbledon, and as Arsenal won the title he scored 23 goals in 36 appearances, the last 1 coming in the thriller at Anfield. When the First Division was won again, in 1990-91, Smith scored 22 goals in 37 matches. In the following seasons age began to catch up on him – he was born in Birmingham on 21 November 1962 and was now in his 30s – but when leading scorer Ian Wright was suspended for the 1994 Cup-winners' Cup final against Parma in Copenhagen, it was Smith's 21st-minute goal that decided the game. Arsenal were hanging on when a misjudged clearance fell to Smith whose left-foot shot rebounded off a goalpost and found the back of the net. The Gunners hung on again, not least 19-year-old Ian Selley who said afterwards, 'The fans were brilliant. I don't think we caused Parma too many problems after Alan's goal. It was a question of keeping our shape.' Alas, young Selley's highly promising career would be cut short by injuries.

Smith, meanwhile, was drawing to the end of his career. A target man who could collect the ball, hold it and supply it to others, as well as almost always being available for a pass from a colleague, he was Arsenal's leading overall scorer in 4 consecutive seasons. Besides 2 League championships and the Cup-winners' Cup, he was part of the team that did the unique double of FA Cup and League Cup in 1992-93.

In the summer of 1995 Smith announced his retirement as a player, on a specialist's advice because of knee trouble. He said, 'Everyone wants to carry on playing football until they are 35, but I'm not able to. I can't complain, though. I've had a good career.' He had scored 115 goals in 349 appearances for Arsenal.

In his Leicester days, Smith, who started his career with non-League Alvechurch, had struck up an attacking partnership with Gary Lineker, and after he moved to Arsenal they resumed it with England, Smith winning 13 full caps during his time at Highbury.

Alan Smith has become a familiar figure on Sky Sports as one of the channel's main commentators and pundits. He also put his weight behind a scheme, the idea of David Dein, to twin every UK professional football club with a jail. The aim is for offenders to gain experience and qualifications in sports coaching and refereeing so they can obtain jobs when they are released. In November 2018 Smith told 100 inmates at Rochester Prison, 'Hard work, vision and courage – you're going to need those three to be successful.'

Steve Bould

In June 1988, Second Division Stoke City's centre-half Steve Bould had a decision to make – Arsenal or Everton? Toffees' manager Colin Harvey wanted a replacement for Derek Mountfield who had moved to Aston Villa. After recovering from a series of injuries Mountfield had been covering for Dave Watson. At Highbury, meanwhile, David O'Leary had undergone an operation during the close season. Bould chose the Gunners where it seemed there was a greater chance of immediate first-team football. His former Stoke teammate Lee Dixon had joined the Gunners 6 months earlier.

Bould, who cost Arsenal £350,000, the fee set by a tribunal, made his debut in the first match of the season, against FA Cup holders Wimbledon, leaving O'Leary to express his feelings at being left out: 'Bitterly disappointed … since my operation I have worked extremely hard at regaining fitness and quite honestly have never felt better in my life … my job now is to prove to the manager that I am match fit.'

Arsenal beat Wimbledon 5-1 but Bould was injured and was out for the next 4 League matches. Thereafter he missed only 4 more matches in a season in which Arsenal once more lifted the First Division title. He missed the first half of the 1989-90 season after injuring a groin before the first game. There was also the matter of the rumpus outside the Holiday Inn hotel in Swiss Cottage at a dinner to celebrate the club's title success the previous season. Police were called in the early hours, and, according to newspaper reports, Bould and Paul Merson were disciplined. Club secretary Ken Friar said, 'Footballers are engaged in a high profile profession and must expect therefore to conduct themselves in an appropriate manner. It is the policy of the club that any punishments imposed are an internal matter and will remain confidential.'

Bould played in the last 19 games of the season, and was an ever-present in 1990-91 when Arsenal reclaimed the title. The following season saw the Gunners finish fourth, make an early exit from the European Cup and an even earlier one from the FA Cup – knocked out by Wrexham, the club that had finished bottom of the entire Football League the previous season. Bould missed that game.

This was the era of the Dixon-Adams-Bould-Winterburn defensive grip, but that did not stop Bould scoring against Norwich City at Highbury on the first day of the 1992-93 season. A crisp header from one of those classic Winterburn free-kicks gave the Gunners their first goal in the new Premiership, although they went on to lose 4-2. Injury ruled Bould out of both the FA Cup final and the League Cup final that season. He was, though, in the team that won the Cup-winners' Cup in 1994, and when Arsenal won another League and FA Cup double in 1997-98 it was Bould's wonderful through ball that set up Tony Adams' late goal in a 4-0 Highbury win over Everton that gave them the title. Two weeks later Arsenal beat Newcastle United 2-0 at Wembley.

In July 1999, now aged 36 – he was born in Stoke on 16 November 1962 – Bould moved to Sunderland for £500,000. He had made 372 appearances for Arsenal and scored 8 goals. He won 2 full caps for England, the first when he was 31. Peter Reid appointed Bould club captain at the Stadium of Light but he made only 21 Premiership appearances for Sunderland before retiring in September 2000, partly due to the fact that he was suffering from arthritis. He returned to Arsenal on the coaching staff, guiding the Gunners to 2 Premier Academy League titles and the FA Youth Cup before, in 2012, replacing Pat Rice as assistant manager. In June 2019 Arsenal announced that Bould would take charge of the Gunners' under-23 team with Freddie Ljungberg becoming assistant first-team coach. Bould said, 'I've always had a deep commitment to developing young players and am delighted to be back working in an area which is so important to the future of our club.'

Lee Dixon

With the departure of Viv Anderson to Manchester United in the summer of 1987, George Graham was on the lookout for a replacement right-back. A specialist was needed and in January 1988, Graham dipped into the Second Division to sign Stoke City's Lee Dixon. It took Dixon time to adjust to the top flight and he made only 5 First Division appearances before the end of the season. For the next 12 years, however, he was rarely out of the team.

Dixon was a schoolboy Manchester City fan – he was born in the city on 17 March 1964 – but his first club was Burnley who he joined in 1980. He played twice in the Second Division and once in the Third for the Clarets before dropping into the Fourth with Chester City (63 appearances). Then it was Third Division Bury (58 games) before Stoke City took him back up a level. After 88 appearances in 1½ seasons for the Potters, Dixon was on his way to Highbury and the top flight. The fee was £350,000.

He was a member of that famous back 4 but could also get forward and supply telling passes, none more so than in the dying seconds of the last match of 1988-89. Arsenal needed to win by 2 clear goals at Anfield to win their first top-flight title for 18 years and end Merseyside's 7-year dominance of the First Division. They could not have left it any later that evening of 26 May 1989.

Liverpool had not lost at home by 2 clear goals for more than 3 years and were unbeaten in their previous 24 games. At the end of February, they had been 19 points behind Arsenal, but after beating Everton in the FA Cup final the Double was now within their grasp. Alan Smith put the Gunners ahead in the 52nd-minute but it seemed that the title would remain on Merseyside. Then goalkeeper John Lukic released the ball to Dixon. He sent a superb long ball on to Smith, and Thomas took Smith's pass, drove forward and hit the second goal past Bruce Grobbelaar. There were 91 minutes and 26 seconds on the clock.

For Dixon there were 2 more First Division titles, a Premiership championship, 2 FA Cup final victories on the pitch – and he was also an unused substitute in the 2002 final – and a Cup-winners' Cup winners' medal. He missed the 1993 League Cup final after being suspended following his sending-off in the 84th minute of Arsenal's FA Cup semi-final win over Spurs. Ironically, Dixon had almost missed that match after injuring a shin while playing for England against Turkey in a World Cup qualifier a few days earlier.

Dixon won 22 full England caps, and for Arsenal he played in 618 matches, scoring 25 goals. He was a clean hitter of the ball, especially at set pieces, and when it came to penalties he was calmness personified.

Dixon retired in 2002, the same year that Tony Adams called it a day. In April he told Kevin Palmer of the Dublin *Sunday World*:

> I always said that I'd finish my career with Arsenal and that won't change. I went into this season knowing that I was no longer first choice for right-back. Arsene Wenger told me in the summer that I couldn't play every week any more, which is fair enough when you're pushing 38. I'm lucky a club as massive as Arsenal still wants me at my age. Then I got a knee injury and it looked as though I wouldn't make it back for the end of the season. But there is a Double to be won. What a way that would be to go out.

The Double was won, of course, and Lee Dixon's final appearance for Arsenal was in the last match of another memorable season, at home to Everton. After football, he pursued business interests and worked as a pundit on several channels including the BBC, ITV and NBC Sports.

David Seaman

On 16 May 1990 David Seaman became Britain's most expensive goalkeeper when he was transferred from QPR to Arsenal for £1.3 million. The 26-year-old England international had almost moved to Highbury in March but the deal fell through when Arsenal goalkeeper John Lukic refused to go to QPR. Eight years earlier Seaman had left his first club, Leeds United, because he could not dislodge Lukic from the first team.

Seaman not only became the most expensive goalkeeper in Britain, he was also Arsenal's record signing, beating the £800,000 that brought Alan Smith from Leicester City 2 years earlier.

Born in Rotherham on 19 September 1963, Seaman left Leeds for Peterborough United in August 1982. The Posh paid £4,000 for him and just over 2 years later Birmingham City were shelling out £100,000. Seaman helped the Blues win promotion from the Second Division but the following season, with Seaman an ever-present, they were relegated. He did not return to the second tier, however. In August 1986 QPR paid £225,000 for the England under-21. Full England honours followed and after 175 senior games for QPR he signed for Arsenal. That month, 7 years after he arrived at Arsenal for £75,000, Lukic returned to Leeds, for £1 million.

In Seaman's first season, 1990-91 under George Graham, despite having 2 points deducted following a player brawl at Old Trafford, Arsenal won the League championship. Seaman played in every game and conceded only 18 goals. It was 4 May 1993 before he missed a game, against his former club, QPR, but he played in the teams that won the FA Cup and the League Cup – Seaman saved 3 Millwall penalties in the shootout at the end of the second-round replay – before undergoing a double hernia operation that meant he would miss England's summer tour to the USA. He played in the victorious 1994 Cup-winners' Cup side, and saved another 3 penalties in the 1995 Cup-winners' Cup semi-final shootout against Sampdoria.

Under Arsene Wenger in 1997-98 Seaman won Premiership and FA Cup winners' medals. The following season, as the Gunners finished runners-up, a point behind Manchester United who also knocked Arsenal out of the FA Cup semi-finals, he missed 6 games, 1 with a rib injury and 5 due to a shoulder problem that gave a chance to Alex Manninger who kept 4 clean sheets; Arsenal conceded only 17 Premiership goals that season. In 2001-02 there was another Premiership and FA Cup double, although Seaman missed half the League season because of a recurrence of the shoulder injury that had first sidelined him in 1998-99.

After Seaman captained Arsenal to their 2003 FA Cup final win over Southampton – and in a match-winning performance made a brilliant late save from Brett Ormerod – Arsene Wenger said, 'I'm very proud of him.' It was his last game for Arsenal. In all he had played in 562 games for the Gunners and won 72 caps while with them, playing for his country in 15 consecutive years.

Seaman, now 39, moved to Manchester City, but after only 26 games for City – 5 of them in the UEFA Cup – in January 2004, out of action again through injury, this time a suspected broken collarbone, he announced his retirement. Minutes earlier Manchester City's under-pressure manager, Kevin Keegan, had revealed that he had signed England goalkeeper David James.

Some may remember David Seaman for Ronaldinho's lob for Brazil that knocked England out of the 2002 World Cup quarter-finals, or for Nayim's lob that lost Arsenal the European Cup-winners' Cup to Real Zaragoza in May 1995. Others for his brilliant save, on his 1,000th senior appearance, from Sheffield United's Paul Peschisolido in the 2003 FA Cup semi-final. Maybe the last word should go to Arsene Wenger: 'He has shown the calm, the authority, the responsibility on the pitch, and that's what you want from a super professional.'

Seaman, who was awarded the MBE, went on to forge a media career in a number of diverse programmes, his on-screen persona making him a popular choice with producers.

Anders Limpar

In August 1990, Arsenal supporters looked forward to seeing the club's 3 summer signings – David Seaman, Andy Linighan and Swedish international Anders Limpar. Seaman would enjoy a great career with the Gunners. Defender Linighan was generally waiting for his chance. In 6 years at Highbury he made only 118 League appearances and is perhaps best remembered for his header – he had just had his nose broken – that won the 1993 FA Cup final replay and gave Arsenal the FA Cup and League Cup double.

Limpar, meanwhile, will be remembered for his incisiveness and speed on Arsenal's left. It was George Graham who signed him, for £1 million from Cremonese in July 1990, and it was Graham who sold him less than 4 years later, so the Swede was not part of the squad that prospered under Arsene Wenger. He won just 1 major honour with Arsenal, and that came in his first season when he made 34 appearances and scored 11 goals as Arsenal won the First Division. At times Limpar was quite stunning.

Born in Solna, north of Stockholm, on 24 September 1965, after beginning his career with IF Brommapojkarna he joined Örgryte IS just after their surprise 1985 Swedish championship play-off win against IFK Göteborg. One of Swedish football's most sought-after young players, Limpar moved to BSC Young Boys in Bern and then spent 1 season with US Cremonese as they were relegated from Italy's Serie A.

His move to Arsenal was thus a huge one but Limpar was far from overawed. In that first season he scored some important goals as the Gunners took the title – their second in 3 seasons – 7 points ahead of runners-up Liverpool. They included 2 in a draw at Leeds in late September; 2 at Coventry in early November; and a hat-trick at home to Coventry on the final day of the season, although by then Arsenal had already been confirmed as champions. In the following seasons Graham seemed unsure about the mercurial Swede who had won the hearts of Arsenal fans. Whenever he was left out of the team some of those fans booed the manager. In 1993 Limpar missed both the FA Cup final and the League Cup final, although he was injured for the former.

On the eve of the 1993-94 season it was reported that Graham had 'successfully negotiated clear-the-air talks' with Limpar, and having sufficiently recovered from a groin injury the Swede was restored to the team for the opening game, at home to Coventry. Arsenal lost 3-0 whereupon Graham dropped Limpar and Paul Merson and was immediately rewarded with away wins at Spurs and Sheffield Wednesday. Merson was soon back in favour and went on to make 33 Premiership appearances that season, but Limpar, out with a foot injury and also a groin injury for some of the time, managed only 10. In late October, after not even making the bench for a League Cup game against Norwich, he said that he believed he was finished at Arsenal.

In March 1994 his time was indeed over. Although he remained a cult figure with the fans, Limpar's relationship with Graham had been irreparably soured by a club versus country tug-of-war and a lack of first-team football. After 95 games and 23 goals for the Gunners he moved to Everton for £1.6 million. He helped the Toffees narrowly avoid relegation that season, and in 1995 to lift the FA Cup, running from his own half to set up Paul Rideout's winning goal against Manchester United. But he fell out of favour at Goodison too and in January 1987, made what turned out to be an unsuccessful move to Birmingham City for whom he played only 4 times before returning to Swedish football and AIK Stockholm with whom he won the championship in 1998. There followed spells in the MLS with Colorado Rapids and back to Sweden with Djurgården IF, Brommapojkarna again, and a newly formed club Sollentuna United FF whose reserve team he managed. After football Limpar went into business.

Ray Parlour

Eighteen-year-old Ray Parlour had an outstanding debut for Arsenal – except for one dreadful moment. A minute before half-time at Anfield on 29 January 1992, when Ronnie Rosenthal evaded challenges by Nigel Winterburn and substitute Steve Bould, Parlour's rash challenge was punished by a penalty that Jan Molby sent high into the roof of David Seaman's net. Up to then Arsenal had controlled the game but the spot-kick changed everything. In the second half it was Liverpool's show and Ray Houghton scored a brilliant second when he chipped a Steve Nicol pass over Seaman. Parlour's was a momentary lapse. Over the next 14 years he would make 466 appearances in the Gunners' midfield, score 32 goals and win 10 England caps.

Born in Romford on 7 March 1973, Parlour joined Arsenal as a schoolboy in January 1988, became an apprentice in June 1989 and a full-time professional in March 1991. After his debut, he made 1 more start that season and came on as a substitute 4 times, but in 1992-93 he came more into the reckoning, playing in about half the League programme and winning a League Cup winners' medal. He also played in the first FA Cup final match that year but was dropped for the replay. More significantly, in August 1992, 7 months after his penalty upset at Anfield, he returned there and was outstanding in Arsenal's 2-0 win.

It was following Arsene Wenger's arrival as Arsenal manager that Parlour's career really took off. Either in central midfield or on the right, Parlour was a regular. He was the unsung star in a team of stars as the Gunners won the Double in 1997-98, although he was voted man of the match in that season's FA Cup final win over Newcastle United. Another Double followed in 2001-02 when Parlour scored with a 30-yard shot in the FA Cup final win against Chelsea, his 70th-minute screamer going over a diving Cudicini and into the top right-hand corner. 'A vintage FA Cup goal for Arsenal,' said commentator Martin Tyler. Ten minutes later

Freddie Ljungberg put the result beyond doubt. Parlour also played in the 2003 FA Cup final win over Southampton.

The ironically nicknamed 'Romford Pelé' specialised in special goals, especially in Europe. In March 2000, he scored a hat-trick against Werder Bremen in a UEFA Cup quarter-final tie. In April 2001, his 25-yarder was the winner against Valencia in the Champions League quarter-final first leg at Highbury. In December 2000, there was a hat-trick in a 5-0 thrashing of Newcastle United at Highbury.

In the summer of 2004 details of Parlour's private life were splashed over the nation's newspapers during a court case involving a divorce settlement between Parlour and his wife. In July that year it was announced that Parlour, whose last season at Highbury had been dogged by a knee injury as the Gunners won another Premiership title, would be leaving Arsenal. His agent, Steve Kutner, said, 'Middlesbrough and Arsenal have agreed a deal. It pays Arsenal a substantial amount subject to appearances, and Ray is taking a substantial pay cut in return for signing a three-year contract.' The fee was reported to be £1.7 million for Parlour, who was now 31. In 2½ years with Boro, Parlour made 60 appearances before being released in January 2007. He then helped Hull City avoid relegation from the Championship in 2006-07, after which his playing days ended, except for an appearance for non-League Wembley FC in 2012. Parlour, then 39, said, 'I've always believed grassroots football is essential to the lifeblood of the game, so I jumped at the chance.' The idea was for the battle to get Wembley FC to Wembley Stadium in the FA Cup final to be filmed for a television documentary, but they went out to Uxbridge in a preliminary round. In 2017 Parlour became an ambassador for Playon Pro, a company founded by Viv Anderson to provide former players with an opportunity to keep earning in retirement, and assist with issues such as depression and anxiety.

Ian Wright

According to some commentators, striker Ian Wright faced only one possible snag after his move from Crystal Palace to Arsenal – how was he going to get into the team? In September 1991, the Gunners may have paid a club record £2.5 million when George Graham finally moved after being inactive in the transfer market as elsewhere more than £70 million changed hands in the close season, but Alan Smith, Paul Merson and Kevin Campbell were already busy scoring goals. It was claimed that Graham faced a dilemma of where to fit in Wright who had been on target 5 times for Palace that season.

In fact, Graham put Wright straight into the team for a League Cup tie at Leicester – Alan Smith was out with an ankle injury – and the new man scored in a 1-1 draw. Three days later Wright started at The Dell and stole the show with a second-half hat-trick. Graham did now have a dilemma. As Niall Quinn wrote in the Dublin *Sunday World*, 'You have got to feel sorry for whoever will lose out to Wright.'

Born in Brockley, south London, on 3 November 1963, Wright had a difficult early life with a bullying stepfather. In 1982, when he was 19, he spent 2 weeks in Chelmsford Prison for non-payment of fines imposed for motoring offences. Brighton had already rejected him and he worked in the building trade and played non-League football for Greenwich Borough. He was 22 when Palace signed him, and in 6 and a bit seasons at Selhurst Park he scored 118 goals in 277 appearances, helping Palace into the top flight in 1989.

In the final match of his debut season for Arsenal, Wright scored another hat-trick against Southampton. It took his season's tally of First Division goals for the Gunners to 24. With those scored for Palace earlier in the season, that saw him edge out Gary Lineker as the First Division's leading scorer for 1991-92. After watching Wright score 3 times in the last 20 minutes, Graham said, 'He's got a lovely appetite for the game, he's dangerous, and he scores goals.'

Wright's last goal against the Saints was also the last to be scored in the old First Division, which gave way to the FA Premiership. The game also marked the end of Highbury's famous North Bank, which was being replaced by a £16.4 million 12,000 capacity all-seater stand, much to the anger of Arsenal's fans.

Wright was Arsenal's leading scorer for 6 consecutive seasons. He played in the 1993 FA Cup and League Cup winning teams, scoring in the first FA Cup final game and also the replay, and saw the Gunners through to the 1994 Cup-winners' Cup final, although he was suspended for that game.

After George Graham's departure, under Bruce Rioch, Wright handed in a transfer request that was refused, but after the arrival of Arsene Wenger he scored 10 goals in 24 games as the Gunners won the Premiership in 1997-98. On 13 September 1997, he broke Cliff Bastin's record of 178 goals for Arsenal to become the Gunners' all-time leading scorer. Wright, who scored a hat-trick that day, celebrated by lifting his shirt to reveal another that read, '179 Just done it'. He was an unused substitute in the 1998 FA Cup final as Arsenal completed another Double.

In July 1998 Wright signed for West Ham United for £500,000. He had scored 185 goals in 288 games for the Gunners, and won 27 of his 33 full England caps as an Arsenal player. He spent 15 months at Upton Park and had short spells with Nottingham Forest, Celtic and Burnley whom he helped promote to the second tier before retiring in 2000. He was awarded the MBE and has since carved out a major career in television and radio.

Thierry Henry, who broke Wright's Arsenal goalscoring record in 2005, said, 'I fell in love with Arsenal because of Ian Wright. I loved the way he played, and his commitment.'

Martin Keown

'I think he's going to be a hell of a player. In his first three first-team games he's been up against Mark Hughes, Paul Walsh and Garth Crookes and he's played all three of them out of the game.' So said Arsenal manager Don Howe about Martin Keown, the young defender who had been recalled from a loan spell at Brighton and displaced Tommy Caton. Howe was speaking after Keown had been 1 of 3 raw 19-year-olds – Gus Caesar and Niall Quinn were the others – in the Gunners' team that won 1-0 at Old Trafford in December 1985.

Sure enough Keown, who had made his debut against West Brom at The Hawthorns a month earlier, missed only 2 games to the end of the season. He would go on to have a wonderful career with Arsenal, but first he would have to leave. In May 1986 George Graham was appointed manager, and a fortnight later the out-of-contract Keown was on his way to Aston Villa for £125,000.

Keown, who was born in Oxford on 24 July 1966, had been with Arsenal since he was a schoolboy. In his first season at Villa Park he could not help save Villa from relegation only 5 years after being European champions, but in 1987-88 he missed only 2 games as they regained their First Division status. In August 1989 he was on the move again, this time to Everton for £750,000.

A bright start at Goodison faded, although he won his first England caps there, and in February 1993 Keown was on his way back to Highbury. Toffees' manager Howard Kendall said, 'Keown is a good defender and it will be difficult to replace him. But a player can move at the end of his contract, and that is what Martin has done twice before.'

Cup-tied, Keown played no part in the Gunners' 1993 FA Cup and League Cup double but his presence gave Arsenal's now famed central defence of Adams and Bould new depth. He missed the 1994 Cup-winners' Cup final defeat of Parma but was a regular until the Double-winning season of

1997-98 when, aged 31, he made only 18 Premiership appearances but did play in the FA Cup final win over Newcastle.

He received some criticism for not staying on his feet when Ryan Giggs scored his solo goal that won the 1998-99 FA Cup semi-final replay for Manchester United, but Giggs had rounded several defenders without anyone putting in a serious challenge. In the first game Keown had given one of the displays of career, dominating the air and thwarting United on the ground with his uncanny anticipation. Arsene Wenger said afterwards, 'Keown was outstanding. He was sharp and physically determined.'

In September 2000 Keown proved an unlikely saviour when he scored twice in the last 6 minutes of a Champions League tie against FC Shakhtar Donetsk to help Arsenal win 3-2 after being 2-0 down inside the first half-hour. In 2001-02, when Arsenal won the title, he made 22 Premiership appearances and came on as a substitute in the FA Cup final as Arsenal beat Chelsea 2-0 to set up another Double. He also played in the 2003 FA Cup final win over Southampton and made 24 Premiership appearances as Arsenal finished runners-up, missing another Double after a late-season dip. There was 1 more Premiership title, though, in 2003-04 when Keown made 10 appearances, the last a 4-minute cameo role on the right wing against Leicester City to give him enough games to qualify him for another medal.

In July 2004 Keown, now 38 and at the end of yet another contract, signed for Leicester. He had made 449 senior appearances for Arsenal and scored 8 goals. He won 34 of his 43 England caps as a Gunner. After a few Championship games for Leicester and Reading, in the summer of 2005 he retired. He returned to Arsenal as a coach and then forged a career as a television football pundit and newspaper columnist.

Dennis Bergkamp

In June 1995 the nation's sportswriters speculated – where would striker Dennis Bergkamp end up? One reported that Chelsea were prepared to pay £5.5 million for the Inter Milan star. Newcastle United would go as high as £7 million, said another. Yet another had Bergkamp going to Everton in an exchange deal involving Daniel Amokachi plus money. Then it was claimed that Aston Villa were favourites to get him for £6.5 million. After all that an Inter spokesman told the *Liverpool Echo*, 'Dennis Bergkamp is happy here and will be staying.' However, by the end of the month – on the same day that the Belgian Jean-Marc Bosman attempted to bring the inflated transfer market crashing down through the European Court of Justice – it was all sorted: Bergkamp signed for Arsenal who paid a club record £7.5 million and wages of £25,000 a week to smash the Highbury pay scale.

The Gunners' chairman, Peter Hill-Wood, admitted that the fee for Bergkamp was 'absolutely mad'. He said:

> The transfer market has been crazy for twenty years and getting crazier all the time. But if you want to compete for the best players you either compete or opt out. We have a responsibility to stay in the game. I know this is a lot of money but we're getting better value than some buys – he's world-class and he's only just 26.

Bergkamp made his Arsenal debut at home to Middlesbrough on the opening day of the 1995-96 season. At first he struggled to adapt to the Premiership. It was 23 September before he scored his first goal, 2 in fact, in a 4-2 home win over Southampton, but by the end of the season from 33 appearances he had 11 goals, 4 behind leading scorer Ian Wright. Bergkamp's last goal of the season was the winner against

Bolton Wanderers that ensured Arsenal fourth place and UEFA Cup qualification.

Born in Amsterdam on 10 May 1969, Bergkamp began his career with Ajax before moving to Inter in 1993. With Ajax he won domestic honours and the Cup-winners' Cup and UEFA Cup, and with Inter the UEFA Cup when he was the competition's joint leading scorer.

By the time Bruce Rioch signed him for Arsenal, Bergkamp was a regular in the Netherlands national team. The following year Arsene Wenger took over at Highbury and the fitness and health regime that he introduced found great favour with Bergkamp whose Arsenal career was now in full bloom: Premiership titles in 1997-98, 2001-02 and 2003-04; FA Cup wins in 1997-98; 2001-02, 2002-03 and 2004-05.

He never started more games for Arsenal than he did in his debut season, but by the time he retired in May 2006 – following Arsenal's penalty shootout win over Manchester United in the 2005 FA Cup final Bergkamp signed a 1-year extension to his contract – he had made 423 senior appearances and scored 120 goals for the Gunners. His goals tally included 3 at Filbert Street in August 1997 which Leicester City manager Martin O'Neill described as 'the best hat-trick that I've ever seen'. More than 40 of Bergkamp's 79 caps were won while he was an Arsenal player.

As the last season at Highbury drew to a close, Arsenal designated 15 April 2006 'Dennis Bergkamp Day'. The crowd was decorated with orange shirts in his honour and when he came on as a second-half substitute he received a thunderous reception. He laid on a goal for Robert Pires that restored Arsenal's lead before himself making it 3-1 with a stunning last-minute goal. Afterwards Wenger said that he had asked the man who Arsenal fans had nicknamed 'the non-flying Dutchman' because of his fear of flying, about joining the Highbury coaching staff but that the player wanted to take a year off. Wenger said, 'I'm sure that after that he'll want to stay in the game. It's important that these kind of people stay in football.' Bergkamp did return to the game as assistant coach to the Netherlands B team, and as assistant manager at Ajax until December 2017.

David Platt

On 1 July 1995, David Platt was apparently heading for Manchester United. Disillusioned with the break-up of Sampdoria's star-studded team, Platt had recently bought a £1 million mansion in Cheshire, close to United's training ground, and Sampdoria's asking price of £3 million together with Platt's £15,000-a-week wages were well within Alex Ferguson's budget. Already a millionaire from his time in Italy, and with commercial deals with Mizuno boots, Tic Tac and McDonalds, money was no longer a deciding factor for the free-scoring midfielder who began his career as a Manchester United apprentice before moving to Crewe Alexandra on a free transfer in February 1985.

Premiership champions Blackburn Rovers were also said to be in the hunt, but on 10 July Platt signed for Arsenal. New manager Bruce Rioch interrupted his holiday in Portugal and flew to Italy to complete the deal for the 29-year-old. Three weeks after paying £7.5 million for Dennis Bergkamp, Arsenal had found another £4.75 million for Platt who would spend 3 seasons at Highbury.

Born in Chadderton, near Oldham, on 10 June 1966, Platt's first big move was to Aston Villa in 1987-88. Villa paid Crewe £200,000 and Platt rewarded them by helping them back to the First Division from where they had been relegated the previous season. In 1989-90 Platt's goals were a factor in Villa finishing First Division runners-up behind Liverpool. In April 1991, he went in goal against Arsenal when Nigel Spink was injured. Arsenal were leading 4-0, Platt kept goal for the final 17 minutes and did well to concede only 1 more.

In July 1991 Villa sold Platt to Bari for £5.5 million. One year later he was off to Juventus for £6.5 million and after winning a UEFA Cup medal in 1993 – although he was not part of the squad for the final, he still qualified from earlier rounds – he moved to Sampdoria for £5.2 million and with them, won the Coppa Italia under Sven-Goran Eriksson's managership. But after the departure of Attilio Lombardo to Juventus, the loss of Ruud Gullit to Chelsea, and the sale of some of the club's top youngsters, Platt was concerned that a season with a struggling team might harm his form for the 1996 European Championships in England.

Platt took to Rioch straight away. 'My talks with him were exceptional,' he said, 'and we hit it off immediately. He has some exciting ideas on tactics and a definite view on how he sees me fitting in.' Rioch said, 'I've admired him for a long time and I'm very impressed by his knowledge and his ambition.' Ian Wright was also a fan: 'With David Platt and Dennis Bergkamp at the club, things are so exciting,' he said.

Rioch would only last 1 season as Arsenal manager. He was replaced by Arsene Wenger who, in his first season in charge, played Platt mostly in the centre of midfield alongside 20-year-old Patrick Vieira. In the Double-winning season of 1997-98, however, Platt made only 11 starts, coming on as a substitute 20 times as Wenger preferred Emmanuel Petit, who had played under Wenger at Monaco. There was at least 1 memorable moment for Platt, though, a soaring header 7 minutes from time to cap a tireless display and win the game against Manchester United at Highbury in November 1997.

That season Arsenal accepted a £1.5 million offer for Platt from Middlesbrough who were trying to get back to the Premiership at the first attempt (they managed it as runners-up to Nottingham Forest who had also just been relegated), but the deal did not proceed. Neither did a move to struggling J-League club Urawa Red Diamonds as Platt decided to concentrate on gaining coaching qualifications. He had made 108 appearances for Arsenal and scored 15 goals. Seven of his 62 England caps had come while he was at Highbury.

On 1 July 1999 he was appointed manager of relegated-again Nottingham Forest. Despite spending some £12 million on players in 2 seasons, Forest could get no higher than mid-table and in July 2001 Platt left to manage the England U-21 side.

Patrick Vieira

In August 1996, 5 days before the start of the new season, Bruce Rioch became the second Gunners manager to be sacked inside 18 months. As Bolton's manager, Rioch had been the boss. At Highbury, everything had to be done through chairman David Dein. Despite submitting a list of almost 30 potential targets, after buying Dennis Bergkamp and David Platt, Rioch had gone a whole season without being allowed to sign another player – unless you count goalkeeper John Lukic, back from Leeds United on a free transfer. Yet his replacement, Arsene Wenger, had already lined up 2: Patrick Vieira, a 20-year-old French under-21 midfielder who had been playing in AC Milan's reserve team, and 30-year-old French international Remi Garde from Strasbourg, a free agent under the new 'Bosman rule'. Wenger, meanwhile, was trying to extricate himself from Japanese club Nagoya Grampus Eight and would not be available until October. It was a rum state of affairs.

Patrick Vieira was born in Senegal on 23 June 1976. When he was 8 he moved with his family to France. He was eligible for French nationality at birth because his grandfather had served in the French Army. Vieira made his debut for AS Cannes in 1993-94. He impressed in the French top division and in 1995 was transferred to AC Milan but, partly due to injury, made only 2 appearances in Serie A before Wenger decided that he wanted Vieira at Highbury when he took over.

Vieira, who joined the Gunners for £3.5 million, made his debut against Sheffield Wednesday on 16 September. It was a strange game. Kick-off was delayed after a power failure in Highbury's East Stand prevented turnstiles opening. Andy Booth gave the Owls a 25th-minute lead. Caretaker manager Pat Rice sent on Vieira in place of Ray Parlour. David Platt equalised just before Wednesday centre-back Des Walker was sent off for a second yellow card, giving away a penalty from which Ian Wright put Arsenal ahead. Wright scored 2 more to complete

100 League goals and become the Gunners' leading post-war scorer; Arsenal won 4-1 – and everyone agreed that it was Vieira's elegant touches and boundless energy that had transformed the game. By the season's end he had made 31 League appearances in an Arsenal side that finished third and missed a Champions League place on goal-difference.

In 1997-98 Vieira's midfield partnership with France teammate Emmanuel Petit was a key factor in Arsenal winning the Double. By the time he left Arsenal, for Juventus in 2005, Vieira had 3 Premiership titles and 4 FA Cup winners' medals to show for his 9 seasons in English football. There had been some on-field disciplinary problems, and reports that he had become unsettled at Arsenal after Petit and Marc Overmars left for Barcelona in the summer of 2000. There were rumours that both Manchester United and Real Madrid wanted to sign Vieira but he remained at Highbury and in 2002 replaced Tony Adams as club captain. Altogether he made 407 senior appearances and scored 34 goals for the Gunners.

A year after he joined Juventus, they were relegated in a match-fixing scandal and so Vieira moved to Inter Milan. He helped them win 4 consecutive Serie A titles before ending his playing career with a season and a half at Manchester City. He came on as a 90th-minute substitute to win an FA Cup winners' medal in 2011 final before becoming a football development executive at the Etihad, then head coach to City's under-21s. In November 2015, he signed a 3-year contract with MLS club New York City. Under him they reached the play-offs in each of his first 2 seasons. In June 2018 Vieira, now 42, was appointed manager of French Ligue 1 club OGC Nice. The 6ft 4in box-to-box midfielder who played 107 times for France, winning the 1998 World Cup and Euro 2000, was tipped to succeed Arsene Wenger but said, 'I spent nine years at Arsenal, which makes the club really special for me. But that is not enough to coach the team.'

Emmanuel Petit

According to the nation's tabloid sports pages, transfer frenzy was developing in the close season of 1997. Manchester United, Newcastle United, West Ham United and Liverpool were all said to be lining up big signings. It was Arsenal, though, who took the headlines in early June when Arsene Wenger completed the signings of left-sided midfielder Emmanuel Petit and central defender Gilles Grimandi for a combined fee of £5 million from his former club AS Monaco. There were rumours that Marc Overmars from Barcelona, Graham Le Saux from Blackburn Rovers, and Derby County's Dean Sturridge were also Highbury-bound. Only one of them turned out to be true.

Wenger said, 'I needed to bring in younger players. We have the best players in the country in the 28 to 35 age group, but between 20 and 28 they are all at Manchester United, Newcastle or Liverpool.' Petit and Grimandi were both 26; Remi Garde, signed before Wenger took over but on his recommendation, was 30. Patrick Vieira, also signed as the Gunners were awaiting Wenger's arrival, was a fresh-faced 20. In February 1998 Wenger would sign 18-year-old Nicolas Anelka from Paris Saint-Germain.

Petit was born in Dieppe on 22 September 1970. He signed for Monaco when he was 18 and played for them in the 1992 European Cup-winners' Cup final, which they lost to Werder Bremen, and captained their 1996-97 Ligue 1 title-winning team. When he moved to Arsenal, Petit was valued at £3.5 million. It was a snip. His midfield partnership with Vieira brought instant success as the Gunners won the Double. There was one particularly memorable moment, against Derby County at Highbury in April 1998. A few days earlier Derby had collapsed spectacularly at Pride Park, losing 4-0 to Leicester City, but for half an hour on this Wednesday evening a physical Rams were holding their own. Then Petit scored what turned out to be the only goal of the game, a scorching left-foot drive that took Arsenal 4 points clear of Manchester United and gave the Gunners their ninth consecutive win, a Premiership record and 1 short of their club record set in 1986. Four days later, against a petulant Everton side, they made it 10 out of 10, winning 4-0 to confirm their eleventh top-flight title. In the Gunners' midfield, Petit and Vieira had grown in stature with every passing game, their central midfield partnership binding the side together. The FA Cup was won against Newcastle United, and that summer Petit and Vieira won the World Cup with France. Petit played the whole of the final and scored against Brazil, while Vieira came on as a 74th-minute substitute for Inter Milan's Youri Djorkaeff. After the final, a fan approached Petit and told him that while he did not like him at Monaco, now he was the fan's hero. 'I told him to get lost,' Petit recalled. Altogether he would win 63 full caps for his country.

For Petit in particular, it had been an incredible winning streak – in little over a year he had won the World Cup, Premiership, FA Cup and Ligue 1 medals. Because of a fever, he missed France's Euro 2000 final win and later that month, together with Overmars, arrived at Arsenal's training camp in Germany both determined to make big-money moves to Barcelona. Wenger apparently made a last-ditch attempt to persuade the pair that their futures lay with Arsenal but it was in vain. David Dein, who brokered the £28 million joint deal, said that it had been done with Wenger's blessing although admitting 'it's sad to see world-class players go, especially when they are under contract'. The offer from the Spanish giants had simply been too much to resist. For Petit, who had made 118 appearances and scored 11 goals for Arsenal, the move was not a happy one, however, and in 2001 he returned to the Premiership with Chelsea in a £7.5 million transfer. He made 76 appearances for Chelsea before being released in 2004. In January 2005, he announced his retirement after not fully recovering from knee surgery.

Marc Overmars

In June 1997 Arsenal signed 24-year-old Dutch winger Marc Overmars for £7 million. Overmars said, 'I like what I have seen of the Premier League. I think that there will be more freedom for me and with my speed I can make use of the spaces.' Arsene Wenger said, 'I want players who are used to winning things and are familiar with the pressures of a big club.'

Overmars certainly fitted that description. He was already an established international and with Ajax had won the Champions League, as well as a host of domestic trophies. Born in Emst, a small town in the Gelderland province, on 29 March 1973, at the age of 14 he joined the Deventer club Go Ahead Eagles. In 1991, he was transferred to Willem II and a year later signed for Ajax, whose manager Louis van Gaal described him as a 'multi-functional player'.

Compared to Arsenal's other foreign signings that summer, Overmars was expected to make the most impact. Yet there was a question mark. After suffering a knee injury on an icy pitch in December 1995, Overmars had had the joint rebuilt with tendons from his own leg. After long months spent at the Dutch national fitness centre near Utrecht, he returned to the Ajax team for 1996-97 and was voted player of the year. Thus heartened, the Gunners hoped that he was still the fast, 2-footed winger that had impressed the likes of Alex Ferguson, and so it tuned out.

Overmars made his Arsenal debut at Elland Road on 9 August 1997. Two weeks later, at The Dell, he scored his first goal for the Gunners. Receiving the ball wide on the left he appeared to be short of options, but somehow jinked his way into the penalty area before slipping the ball under Saints' goalkeeper Paul Jones to give Arsenal a 19th-minute lead. A second goal should have come only 3 minutes later but Overmars spooned the ball over the crossbar when finding the back of the net seemed the easier option. No matter. Dennis Bergkamp scored twice, Arsenal won 3-1 and by the end of the season Overmars had 15 goals – he was the Gunners' second highest scorer behind Bergkamp – and Premiership and FA Cup winners' medals. When Arsenal won the title with a 4-0 win against Everton, Overmars scored twice, and he scored the opening goal in the FA Cup final against Newcastle.

The following August in the FA Charity Shield game against Manchester United, he opened the scoring and was voted man of the match. He was also on target on the first day of the Premiership season when Arsenal beat Nottingham Forest 2-1 at Highbury. The Gunners' Champions League campaign was brief. Through injury Overmars missed the decisive group match against Dynamo Kiev, which Arsenal lost 3-1. In February 1999 Overmars scored that infamous goal in the FA Cup game against Sheffield United, when Arsenal's new Nigerian star Nwankwo Kanu intercepted the usual sporting throw-in back to an opposition that had kicked the ball into touch so that an injured player could receive treatment. He passed to Overmars who scored virtually unchallenged. The FA accepted Wenger's offer to replay the match. Arsenal won both games 2-1. It was Overmars who opened the scoring in the second, this time with a goal of utter perfection that no one could dispute.

The Dutchman's final game for the Gunners was the 2000 UEFA Cup final against Galatasaray, which Arsenal lost on penalties in Copenhagen. Overmars had scored 41 goals in 142 games for Arsenal. In July 2000 he moved to Barcelona for £14 million but, like Emmanuel Petit, he enjoyed no success there. He was injured and was also the subject of transfer rumours. In 2004 he announced his retirement. In 2008 he came back for 1 season with Go Ahead Eagles again. In 2012 Overmars was appointed Ajax's director of football. In 2019 he signed a new contract that bound him to Ajax until 2024.

Freddie Ljungberg

On 5 September 1998, an England team that included David Seaman and Tony Adams collapsed to a 2-1 defeat in an incident-packed European championship match in Stockholm. Star of the show for Sweden was 21-year-old Fredrik Ljungberg. Six days later Arsene Wenger had beaten off competition from Chelsea to sign Ljungberg for £3 million. Rumour had it that Barcelona and Parma were also keen but Wenger was anxious to add fresh blood to his ageing Double-winning squad.

Freddie Ljungberg, who was born in Vittsjö on 16 April 1977, scored 16 goals in 139 appearances for Halmstads BK before moving to Highbury a few weeks after Ian Wright had left for West Ham and the collapse of an Arsenal bid to sign Patrick Kluivert from AC Milan. He said that the only similarity between himself and Wright was a tendency to get into bother with referees: 'When I was younger I was too aggressive and got angry with referees ... . But I thought I should concentrate more on my game. You have to use your brain or you don't play well.'

Wenger did not see Ljungberg as a natural replacement for Wright: 'He could do more in place of David Platt. I see him as a support player for the front two, or wide on either flank. He is a player of intelligence and technique with pace and a fighting desire – and, of course, he is young.' Ljungberg scored 5 minutes into his Arsenal career, coming on as a substitute against Manchester United at Highbury on 20 September 1998. Wenger said, 'His positioning for the goal to avoid being offside was good.' That season he made 18 appearances, 10 of them as a substitute, as Arsenal finished runners-up to Manchester United. In 2001-02 he was in great form as the Gunners won their second Premiership and FA Cup double. He was especially needed after Robert Pires was injured and he scored some vital goals throughout the season – 17 in all competitions – including the second in the FA Cup final defeat of

Chelsea when he curled the ball past Carlo Cudicini from the edge of the penalty area. Ljungberg was named man of the match. A few days later he was involved in a training ground fight with teammate Olof Mellberg as Sweden prepared for the World Cup finals.

His later career with both Arsenal and Sweden was dogged by health scares and injuries, although he did overcome an ankle problem to play in the 2-1 defeat by Barcelona in the 2006 Champions League final in Paris. There was also an ongoing hip problem that resulted in tests for AIDS and cancer before it transpired that he was suffering from blood poisoning due to his ornate tattoos.

Supporters still loved him but although Wenger stressed that Ljungberg would see out his contract to the end of 2009, in July 2007 he was transferred to West Ham. Ljungberg, who had scored 72 goals in 328 appearances for the Gunners, winning 2 Premiership titles and 3 FA Cup winners' medals, said, 'When I spoke to Arsene Wenger, he wanted me to stay … . For me it is about why I wanted to join West Ham, not why I wanted to leave Arsenal.'

A year later, however, Sandy Macaskill in the *Daily Telegraph* reported Ljungberg as saying:

> I went to West Ham in order to play against Arsenal as often as possible. I wanted to prove that Freddie Ljungberg hadn't had his last word as a player. And at West Ham no one gives you a puzzled look if you get called up for your national team and players are never asked to play on injections.

He made only 25 Premiership appearances for the Hammers, suffering broken ribs against Newcastle United, and in June 2008 agreed to terminate his contract. After winning 75 caps he also retired from international football. Thereafter Ljungberg did the rounds with Celtic and in the USA, Japan and India. He coached at the Gunners' academy and with VfL Wolfsburg before returning to Arsenal where in June 2019, he was promoted to first-team assistant coach. In November that year he took over as caretaker manager after Emery was sacked.

Thierry Henry

On 1 August 1999, the deal that took Nicholas Anelka to Real Madrid for £22 million was finally going through. Having complained that Real had made an illegal approach to Anelka, Arsene Wenger said that Arsenal had now received an explanation that satisfied them. The Gunners could focus on signing a replacement. Top of their list was the unsettled Juventus forward Thierry Henry. Wenger said, 'Now we will try to buy two strikers. Thierry Henry is one of them and he is keen to play for us.'

Two days later – and 24 hours after Arsenal signed the 31-year-old Croatia striker Davor Suker, top scorer in the 1998 World Cup finals, from Real Madrid for £3.5 million – Henry stepped off a plane from Turin. The fee was £11 million, an Arsenal club record.

Henry was born on 17 August 1977, in Les Ulis, 14 miles southwest of Paris. He joined Monaco as a youth player. When he left for Juventus in January 1999, for £10.5 million, he had helped them win the Ligue 1 title, and France win the 1998 World Cup, although he watched the final against Brazil from the bench. He said, 'We had to change our plans after Marcel Desailly was sent off. I was frustrated at first but I was only 20. It was not like it was the end of my career.' He was still France's top scorer of the tournament with 3 goals.

One of Wenger's last acts as Monaco's manager was to give Henry his debut in 1994. Four years later Wenger had hoped to bring him to Highbury, but after Henry's World Cup exploits Monaco doubled the asking price. A year later Wenger said, 'I have had to be patient but now I am pleased to have him.' The number of forwards at the Stadio delle Alpi had limited Henry's opportunities and Juventus played him on the wing. Wenger, though, saw him as his main goalscorer. He would not be disappointed. While Suker was on his way to West Ham United, within 12 months Henry's Arsenal career would glitter with achievements.

It was 8 games before he scored his first goal but by the end of the season he was Arsenal's leading Premiership scorer with 17 goals.

After winning Euro 2000 with France, Henry was again Arsenal's leading Premiership scorer with another 17 goals in 2000-01. His first silverware with the Gunners came in the Double-winning season of 2001-02 when he was the Premiership's leading scorer with 24 goals. And on he went until he was Arsenal's all-time record goalscorer in all competitions with 228 goals from 376 appearances. When he left in June 2007 he looked back on an 8-year career that saw the Gunners win 2 Premiership titles, 2 FA Cups, and reach the Champions League final in 2006. In his last 2 seasons with Arsenal he was their captain.

Bookmakers William Hill cut the odds from 10/1 to 3/1 that Henry would join Liverpool but it was to Barcelona he went for £24 million, telling Gunners' fans that he could not face life at the Emirates without David Dein, who had already left, and Wenger, who had not committed himself beyond the end of his contract that expired at the end of the forthcoming season. 'I will be 31 then and I cannot take the chance to be there without Arsene Wenger and David Dein,' he said. 'But I will miss the fans at Arsenal dearly. They have stuck with me through thick and thin.'

With Barcelona, Henry won an unprecedented haul of trophies before joining MLS club New York Red Bulls in 2010. He returned to Arsenal for a brief loan spell in 2012 before retiring. Henry, who won 123 caps and scored a record 51 goals for France, coached Arsenal's youth players, was Belgium's assistant coach and head coach at Monaco from October 2018 to January 2019 when he was dismissed. He is one of the most marketable of football personalities, both as a pundit and in advertising.

Kanu

Within 11 minutes of entering English football, Arsenal's £4.5 million signing from Inter Milan unwittingly ensured that his name would be forever linked with one of the most controversial episodes in the history of the FA Cup. On 13 February 1999 Arsenal were leading Sheffield United in a fifth-round tie at Highbury when Arsene Wenger brought on Olympic gold medal winner Nwankwo Kanu. After a player was injured, Kanu intercepted a throw-in from Ray Parlour meant for the Blades' goalkeeper and crossed for Marc Overmars to restore Arsenal's lead. The game was held up for 8 minutes and United threatened to walk off. The final minutes were eventually played out in a simmering atmosphere and Wenger asked for the game to be replayed. The FA agreed and Arsenal won the second match by the same 2-1 scoreline. It was a shame that Kanu's name should be tarnished so early in his career in England. Whether he knew about the unwritten convention or not, it was, as Overmars said, a mistake.

Wenger signed Kanu in January 1999. All summer the Arsenal manager had pursued the Nigerian international who led his country to the 1996 Olympic football title a year after he and Overmars had won the Champions League with Ajax. Shortly after the Olympics, the 20-year-old Kanu joined Roy Hodgson's Inter Milan but a medical examination revealed a serious heart defect. In November 1996 Kanu underwent an operation to replace an aortic valve. He returned to Inter the following April but after only 12 appearances in Serie A, and following months of negotiation and medicals to ensure that the operation had been a complete success, Arsenal decided to bring him to Highbury.

It was always going to be a battle to overcome the events surrounding his debut but after spending what was left of his first season at Highbury mostly on the bench, Kanu set about it by scoring goals. On 24 October 1999, there were only 16 minutes remaining of Arsenal's match at

Stamford Bridge. The Gunners were trailing 2-0 and never looked like scoring. Cue Kanu. Weaving his magic on a waterlogged pitch, he scored a hat-trick against a team that had hitherto not conceded a Premiership goal at home that season. The winner came in injury time when Kanu found himself unmarked. From the byline he curled the ball past 2 defenders and into the net. Chelsea manager Gianluca Vialli said, 'That is the sort of thing that happens once in a lifetime.' Arsene Wenger said, 'We needed a bit of luck and we took a risk up front. The huge talent of Kanu did the rest. His second and third goals were amazing.'

Kanu's place in Arsenal's rich story was confirmed, and for the right reason. In 2001-02 he won Premiership and FA Cup winners' medals but now the likes of Henry, Pires and Ljungberg were in their pomp. Kanu was an unused substitute for the 2003 FA Cup final win and made only 3 starts in 2003-04 when the Gunners went through the season unbeaten to win the Premiership again. That summer, his contract ended and Kanu left Arsenal. He had made 199 appearances for the Gunners and scored 44 goals. He signed for newly promoted West Brom but when they were relegated again in 2006, now a free agent, he left for Portsmouth. He scored for Pompey in their 2008 FA Cup final 1-0 win against Cardiff City and was voted man of the match. He came on as an 81st-minute substitute in the 2010 FA Cup final defeat by Chelsea and his time at Fratton Park ended in bitterness as Pompey tumbled down the league and were put into administration. Kanu eventually dropped a legal case against Portsmouth for unpaid wages of £3 million. He made 87 appearances for Nigeria, scoring 12 goals. He is a UN ambassador for UNICEF and opened his own internet sports channel. The Kanu Heart Foundation was set up to help underprivileged children and young people from Africa receive life-saving heart operations.

Robert Pires

It seemed that France midfielder Robert Pires was going to sign for Real Madrid and not Arsenal. Speaking minutes after setting up the golden goal that won his country the Euro 2000 final he said, 'Madrid is the best club for me. We'll see what Madrid want.' One month earlier it looked like the Gunners had sealed their protracted £6 million move to bring Pires from Olympique de Marseille. The clubs had agreed. All that remained was for personal terms to be sorted. But Euro 2000 came and went and still nothing was settled. And then suddenly it was. Pires travelled from Rotterdam to London to sign for Arsenal, and then went on to Paris to enjoy France's Euro celebrations.

Arsene Wenger was thrilled to have Pires as part of his French foreign legion. The *Irish Independent* reported him as saying:

> We will again be challenging for the Premiership title and hoping to make further progress in the Champions League. So we are very pleased to have signed both Peres and Edu [the Brazilian's signing from Corinthians would be put on hold until 2001 when it was discovered that his Portuguese passport was a fake; in 2019 he became Arsenal's technical director]. Both players are very talented, versatile midfielders with fantastic ability who will give us an extra dimension in facing the demands of the forthcoming season.

The Gunners, who were now without Petit and Overmars, both gone to Barcelona, put Pires and the Cameroonian Lauren, a close-season £7 million from Real Mallorca, on the bench for Arsenal's opening game of 2000-01, at Sunderland. At 1-0 down Wenger sent on both of them, together with Dennis Bergkamp, in a bid to get back in the game, but to no avail. Arsenal's bad start to the season was compounded when Vieira was sent off in the final minute.

Pires, who started his career with Metz and who was now 26, initially complained that the Premiership was too physical in comparison to Ligue 1 but he settled down and the loss of Overmars was forgotten as Pires, a member of France's 1998 World Cup-winning squad, scored goals and made them for others.

When Arsenal won the Double in 2001-02, Pires was named Footballer of the Year by the Football Writers' Association, despite suffering medial knee ligament damage after 25 minutes of Arsenal's 3-0 FA Cup sixth-round replay win over Newcastle in March. The injury would keep him out for 7 months. Just before the Newcastle tie, Pires had scored a wonder goal at Villa Park, controlling a long pass from Ljungberg, turning George Boateng and lobbing the ball over Peter Schmeichel's head. Earlier, Edu's goal had seen Arsenal equal a 72-year-old record of scoring in 31 consecutive matches. They would extend it considerably.

In 2002-03, back in the fray from late October, Pires scored 14 Premiership goals including a hat-trick against Southampton in the penultimate game and he also netted the winner in the FA Cup final against Southampton. In 2003-04, as Arsenal won the Premiership again, he scored another 14 goals, and there were yet another 14 in 2004-05, this time as the Gunners finished runners-up. In 2006 Pires was coming to the end of his contract and Villarreal were interested. It was sad that his final appearance for Arsenal should end only 18 minutes into the Champions League final against Barcelona in the Stade de France when Gunners' goalkeeper Jens Lehmann brought down Samuel Eto'o and was sent off. Pires had to be sacrificed, replaced by reserve keeper Manuel Almunia, and watched the rest of the game from the bench as 10-man Arsenal were beaten 2-1. A few weeks later the move to Villarreal on a free transfer was completed. Pires had made 283 appearances for Arsenal and scored 84 goals, leaving Gunners' fans with a host of warm memories.

In November 2010, his Villarreal contract ended, Pires became Gerard Houllier's first signing for Aston Villa. Villa released him in May 2011. Pires, who won 79 caps for France, was 40 when he ended his career with Goa in the Indian Premier League.

Cesc Fabregas

On 29 October 2003, Francesc Fabregas Soler became the youngest player to appear for Arsenal in a senior competitive game when he started a League Cup match against Rotherham United at Highbury. He was 16 years and 177 days old. Rotherham, struggling near the foot of the First Division, surprised an experimental Arsenal team that evening. Arsene Wenger rested everyone who had started the Premiership match at Charlton 3 days earlier and gave debuts to 4 players. It was one of the debutants, former Republic of Ireland under-21 goalkeeper Graham Stack, who was the hero of the tie, pulling off a string of fine saves, scoring Arsenal's penultimate penalty of the shootout that followed a 1-1 draw, then saving the Rotherham penalty that set up Sylvain Wiltord's match-winning spot-kick.

Arsenal had signed Fabregas – his friends called him Cesc – a few weeks earlier after his first club, Barcelona, failed to tie him to a long-term contract. It was reported that the Gunners paid the Spanish club £1 million in compensation. In early December, Fabregas set another record as Arsenal's youngest-ever scorer in a top-class match. The Gunners hammered Wolves 5-1 in a League Cup fourth-round match at Highbury and Fabregas completed the rout with a simple tap-in 2 minutes from time.

His Premiership debut had to wait until the first game of the following season as Arsenal set off to defend their title at Goodison Park. The Gunners won their first 5 matches, scoring 19 goals. Fabregas, who was replacing the injured Vieira in midfield, started the first 4, and in the 3-0 win over Blackburn Rovers he became Arsenal's youngest-ever scorer in a League game. It was quite a start for the Academy player who that September signed a full-time professional contract. In late October, after Manchester United had ended Arsenal's 49-match unbeaten Premiership run, it was Fabregas who was suspected – it was later confirmed by the player himself – of throwing a slice of pizza at Sir Alex Ferguson.

That incident aside, Fabregas was proving a sensation on the field. Wenger said, 'In the centre of midfield he is responsible for the quality of the team play. To have the maturity to do that so early makes him very special.' In December, at 17 years and 217 days old, Fabregas became Arsenal's youngest European scorer, and the second-youngest scorer in Champions League history, when he first juggled the ball and then sent it left-footed into the Rosenberg net for the Gunners' fifth and final goal of the evening.

After Vieira left for Juventus, Arsenal needed to look no further to replace him, although it had to be said that the Gunners perhaps missed the additional aggression that Vieira had brought them. In 2006, Fabregas played against his former club in the Champions League final that Barcelona won to leave Arsenal without a trophy that season.

With Spain he won Euro 2008 – that year he was named as Arsenal's captain – and Euro 2012 and the 2010 World Cup. In August 2011, much to the disappointment of Arsenal supporters, Fabregas rejoined the club that had let him go as a teenager. He said he was moving back home to take up 'the greatest challenge of my life'. He added, 'I have waited a long time for this moment … . I hope to leave you all with many great memories.'

Fabregas had made 290 appearances for the Gunners and scored 50 goals but apart from the 2005 FA Cup final when Arsenal beat Manchester United on penalties, the Gunners won no major trophies during Fabregas's 8 years with them. With Barcelona, who paid £35 million for him, he fared better; in 3 years at the Nou Camp, he won La Liga and the Copa del Rey. In June 2014, he signed for Chelsea for £30 million and with them won 2 Premier League titles, the FA Cup and the League Cup. In January 2019, he signed a 3½-year contract for Thierry Henry at AS Monaco, only to see Henry sacked 2 weeks later.

Lauren

Laureano Bisan Etame-Mayer led an early life that few professional footballers could ever imagine. Born in Cameroon after his parents fled Equatorial Guinea because of political persecution, he grew up in Seville to where the family moved again. In Equatorial Guinea his father had been a civil servant but in Spain, life was very different. In April 2019, he told BBC Sport:

> For my mum, it was very hard. She had everything and now she was in Spain and having to take care of all the kids [his father sired fifteen, six of them with Lauren's mother]. For her it was very, very tough. You'd get one tortilla and some rice and then cut it into pieces to feed everyone. It was difficult. What could I do? My mum was suffering, so from then on I was very concentrated about what I wanted to do. I wanted to be a footballer.

His ambition was realised. In May 2000, after Real Mallorca's final match of the season, Arsenal signed their 23-year-old Cameroon international midfielder for £7 million. In August, Arsene Wenger said:

> Call me crazy but I believe we can go on to new horizons even without Marc [Overmars] and Manu [Petit]. We have brought Robert Pires from Marseilles and Lauren from Real Mallorca to replace them and I still aim to sign one or two more players before the start of the Premiership season.

Lauren made his Gunners debut on the opening day of the 2000-01 season, coming as a substitute in a 1-0 defeat at Sunderland. Two days later he scored his first goal for Arsenal in a 2-0 win over Liverpool at Highbury. It came in the 7th minute of a strange game where both sets of supporters shouted abuse at referee Graham Poll, who sent off Liverpool's Gary McAllister and Dietmar Hamann as well as Arsenal's Patrick Vieira. It was Vieira's second red card of a season that was only 48 hours old.

Lauren must have wondered what he was stepping into. As well as this, his first season at Highbury was dogged by injury but he eventually replaced Lee Dixon as the Gunners' regular right-back. In the Double-winning season of 2001-02 he was a key member of Arsenal's defence. In 2002-03 he recovered from injury to play in the FA Cup final defeat of Southampton. However, in 2003-04, when Arsenal went through the Premiership season unbeaten, there was a large blot on the Gunners' copybook. Lauren was suspended for 4 matches and fined £40,000 for verbally abusing and pushing Manchester United's Ruud van Nistelrooy at Old Trafford. It was a fiery game. Vieira had been sent off for the eighth time, this one for retaliating to a challenge by van Nistelrooy who made a real meal of the incident. Van Nistelrooy then thundered a penalty against the crossbar and at the final whistle, Lauren was one of several Arsenal players who surrounded the United player. Lauren paid a hefty price. But it was quite a charge sheet: Arsenal were fined £175,000; Keown £20,000 and a 3-match ban; Parlour £10,000 and a 1-match ban; Cole was reprimanded and fined £10,000; Vieira, guilty of improper conduct for failing to leave the field after being sent off, received a 1-match suspension and a £20,000 fine.

In 2005 Lauren scored the first of Arsenal's penalties as they beat Manchester United in the FA Cup final shootout, but a knee injury sustained in January 2006, against Wigan Athletic in the League Cup semi-final, sidelined him for the rest of that year. In January 2007 the 30-year-old moved to Portsmouth for an undisclosed fee thought to be around £500,000. He had made 242 appearances for Arsenal and scored 11 goals. He played 28 times for Pompey before ending his career with 5 games for Cordoba in the Spanish second tier. He won 24 caps for Cameroon, winning the 2000 Olympic football tournament and the 2000 and 2002 Africa Cup of Nations. Remaining a well-respected figure at Arsenal he became a club ambassador and also an authoritative TV football pundit.

Sol Campbell

In May 2001, Barcelona reportedly accepted Tottenham Hotspur's £9 million offer for Emmanuel Petit. It was up to Petit to decide if he wanted to join his former club's most bitter rivals. Spurs, meanwhile, wanted to demonstrate their ambition and convince their captain and 26-year-old England defender Sol Campbell to sign a new contract. The situation rumbled on. Barcelona themselves were said to be interested in Campbell, as were Inter Milan, Bayern Munich, Manchester United and Liverpool. But in June, Arsenal, who had just bought striker Francis Jeffers from Everton for £8 million and paid Rangers a similar figure for Dutch international Giovanni van Bronckhorst to play alongside Vieira in midfield, now needed a centre-half. On 2 July, Campbell joined the Gunners on a free transfer. He said, 'I was keen to stay in the Premiership and continue playing for England. I could have earned more abroad, but this is the place to be.'

Campbell, who was born in Plaistow on 18 September 1974, the youngest of 12 children, could look back on a 9-year Spurs career of 315 appearances and 15 goals and a League Cup final win. With Arsenal he was about to win the Double, then another Premiership title followed by another FA Cup win. His debut came on the opening day of 2001-02, in a 4-0 win at Middlesbrough. Together with Lauren, Tony Adams and Ashley Cole he was part of an unfamiliar back 4 in a game that was dominated by the brilliance of Patrick Vieira whose summer-long on-off transfer saga had been a constant worry for Gunners' fans. Campbell returned to White Hart Lane in November when the sides drew 1-1 thanks to a 92nd-minute goal from Spurs' Gus Poyet. Inevitably Campbell was subjected to a barrage of abuse from home supporters. But he had the final say. On 4 May, he played in the FA Cup final win over Chelsea and 4 days later the Gunners took the Premiership title with victory at Old Trafford.

When Arsenal retained the FA Cup in 2003 Campbell missed the final, suspended after elbowing Manchester United's Ole Gunnar Solskjaer at Highbury. It was Campbell's second red card of the season. In the 2003-04 'Invincibles' season, as Campbell formed a new defensive partnership with Kolo Toure, it was a sweet moment when the Premiership title was regained at, of all places, White Hart Lane on 25 April. Campbell diplomatically left the pitch without joining in the victory celebrations. The previous September, on the eve of Campbell's 29th birthday, his father had died after a series of strokes and heart attacks. It was one of a number of painful incidents in the player's personal life.

A knee injury kept Campbell out of the opening games of the 2004-05 season and he was an unused substitute in the FA Cup final penalty shootout defeat of Manchester United. Beset by injuries, loss of form and personal problems, the following season was a struggle for him. Yet it might have ended in glory. In the Champions League final against Barcelona in Paris, Campbell opened the scoring with a majestic 37th-minute header but the Gunners, already down to 10 men after goalkeeper Jens Lehmann was sent off – Arsenal's 63rd red card of Wenger's reign – lost 2-1.

Two months later Campbell left Arsenal by mutual consent. He had made 197 appearances and scored 11 goals for the Gunners with whom he won 29 of his 73 full England caps. At 21 he was England's youngest captain since Bobby Moore.

He signed for Portsmouth whom he captained to FA Cup final success in 2008 before leaving when Pompey were relegated and went into administration. A 5-year contract with cash-strapped League Two Notts County, then managed by Sven-Goran Eriksson, ended after 1 game after which Campbell made another 11 appearances for Arsenal before a brief spell with Newcastle United. In May 2012, he retired as a player and later helped League Two Macclesfield Town narrowly escape from relegation before they sacked him 2 games into the 2019-20 season after 8 months in charge.

Jens Lehmann

Jens Lehmann kept goal in every one of Arsenal's Premiership matches of the 'Invincibles' 2003-04 season. The former Schalke 04, AC Milan and Borussia Dortmund player's only problem when he signed for the Gunners in July 2003 was a poor disciplinary record. However, Arsene Wenger, who had been searching for a replacement ever since David Seaman left for Manchester City, showed no reluctance in taking the 33-year-old German international on a 3-year contract. Wenger announced that he had finalised the deal after the Gunners' 2-0 pre-season friendly win over Austria Vienna. A few days later Lehmann made his debut, keeping a clean sheet in another friendly, against the Turkish club Besiktas.

In the opening game of the season Lehmann made an immediate impact on the Premiership with a superb close-range reflex save from Everton's Nick Chadwick at Highbury. Arsenal won 2-1 despite playing for three-quarters of the game with only 10 men after Sol Campbell was sent off for a professional foul on Thomas Gravesen. Campbell had been banned for 4 games at the end of the previous season after being sent off by the same referee, Mark Halsey. The Gunners' disciplinary record under Wenger was beginning to read like a crime sheet. It seemed that Lehmann would feel at home.

Lehmann's somewhat eccentric style could produce anxious moments, though. When Arsenal won the title at White Hart Lane in April he gave away a silly 90th-minute penalty, pushing Robbie Keane who equalised from the spot. 'That tarnished the moment,' said Wenger at the final whistle.

The goalkeeper's future at Highbury had already looked in doubt. In the home leg of Arsenal's Champions League semi-final against Chelsea, he had come racing out to kick clear but the ball ran loose and Eidur Gudjohnsen scored a priceless away goal. Lehmann said, 'I am to blame for most of the goals I concede and this was no different. But I've come out of goal hundreds of times before and this time, unfortunately, it was unlucky because he touched it with both his right and left feet.' Lehmann could also plead guilty to Frank Lampard's 51st-minute equaliser in the second leg when he failed to control a cross from Claude Makelele.

Halfway through 2004-05 Lehmann lost his place to the Spaniard Manuel Almunia but he too suffered lapses and Lehmann won it back. In that season's FA Cup final win over Manchester United the German excelled himself, keeping the scoresheet blank even after 30 minutes' extra time and then brilliantly saving from Paul Scholes in the penalty shootout. In 2005-06 Lehmann had 10 consecutive clean sheets in Champions League matches to set a record. The tenth came in the semi-final when he saved an 89th-minute penalty from Villarreal's Juan Roman Riquelme. Unfortunately, Lehmann was sent off after only 18 minutes of the final against Barcelona after bringing down Samuel Eto'o. Ten-man Arsenal lost 2-1 but Lehmann was still named goalkeeper of the tournament.

In the summer of 2007 Wenger extended Lehmann's contract for another year. In the opening minute of the new season, however, he gifted Fulham a goal, screwing an attempted return pass against his own knee to give David Healy the easiest chance to score. In his second game of the season, against Blackburn, Lehmann dropped David Dunn's shot into the net. Wenger said, 'We don't want to blame him. We want to keep the positives.' An Achilles tendon injury sustained while playing for Germany against England then sidelined Lehmann for almost 4 months. He made his final appearance for Arsenal coming on as an 80th-minute substitute against Everton at Highbury in May 2008. Now 38, he received a wonderful reception from the fans. Wenger said, 'He was the best goalkeeper in the Premier League. He is not frightened of anyone and I have never known him not to be committed for a single minute.' Lehmann signed for VfB Stuttgart but returned to Arsenal to play 1 more game, in April 2011, before retiring. It took his Arsenal appearances to exactly 200.

Robin van Persie

It did not take Robin van Persie long to collect his first honour as an Arsenal player. It came in the 2004 FA Community Shield win over Manchester United. A few weeks later he marked his first competitive start with a goal in the 2-1 League Cup defeat of Manchester City. Earlier, the 21-year-old's rushed shot that flew over City's bar had raised questions about whether he would be the full deal as Dennis Bergkamp's replacement.

Fast forward to September 2006 at the Valley. After narrowly escaping a red card when his kick at Jimmy Floyd Hasselbaink was surprisingly punished with yellow, van Persie equalised Darren Bent's opener for Charlton. 'I thought about taking him off,' said Arsene Wenger. Thank goodness he did not. Just after half-time, van Persie leapt high to propel a stunning volley into the top corner of the net from just outside the penalty area. Wenger said, 'No one expected it. The technique was perfect. It was the goal of a lifetime.'

Van Persie joined the Gunners from his boyhood club, Feyenoord, for £3 million in May 2004. The forward, who was born in Rotterdam on 6 August 1983, won the UEFA Cup with Feyenoord in 2002 but 2 years later he was ready to move to the Premiership. His talent was there for all to see but there was a hot-headed side to him. In February 2005, he was sent off in a nasty-tempered march at Southampton that also saw the Saints' David Prutton dismissed. Van Persie had already been booked when he lunged at Graham Le Saux and was shown a red card. Wenger said, 'I told him at half-time that when a home player is sent off, the referee is under pressure to square up matters. So if anyone had to behave, it was him.'

The Dutchman, who was on the brink of winning the first of 102 caps for his country, was both villain and hero. Later in the season he scored 2 late goals as Arsenal beat Blackburn Rovers in the FA Cup semi-final, and in the final he came on as a substitute and scored 1 of the penalties in the shootout that beat Manchester United.

Van Persie's Arsenal career would be dogged by injury. When he fractured a bone in his right foot scoring a late equaliser against Manchester United in January 2007, it meant that the Gunners would have to manage without their leading scorer for the remainder of the season. The following season he was out for 2 months after injuring a knee while playing for the Netherlands against Slovenia. In 2008-09 he was sent off after clattering Stoke City goalkeeper Thomas Sørensen. At the end of the season van Persie was again Arsenal's leading scorer. He missed half the 2009-10 season after another injury while playing for his country, and 2010-11 also saw him absent for periods, although when he did play he scored goals, including his first Premier League hat-trick, against Wigan Athletic. He also skied a penalty that afternoon. There was a brilliant goal in the Champions League round of 16 match against Barcelona at the Emirates but in the second leg at the Nou Camp, van Persie was sent off after a second yellow card for kicking the ball away after the whistle had gone. Wenger directed his anger towards referee Massimo Busacca, saying, 'It killed the game.'

Van Persie was named Arsenal captain for 2011-12 but at the end of the season he was on his way to Manchester United. He said later that Arsenal would not offer him a new contract. The Gunners' former transfer negotiator, Dick Law, said that United's offer of £24 million for a 29-year-old whose career had been regularly interrupted by injuries was too good to turn down. Either way, his move was an acrimonious affair. Van Persie had scored 132 goals in 278 appearances for Arsenal. With United he won the Premier League before injuries dogged him again. He moved to Fenerbahce in Turkey and then rejoined Feyenoord on a free transfer.

Kolo Toure

The 2003-04 season was a triumph for Kolo Toure, as indeed it was for almost everyone connected with Arsenal. The Gunners went through an entire Premiership season unbeaten to win the title with 4 matches still to play. At the centre of the Gunners' defence, alongside Sol Campbell, was Toure, the £150,000 Ivorian who had seemingly come from nowhere to star in arguably the most competitive league in world football.

Yet it could have all ended before it began. The story is now well known. Toure was already an international with Ivorian Premier Division club ASEC Mimosas when he arrived at Highbury in 2002 for a trial with the Gunners. During a training session, despite being told not to tackle, he took out Thierry Henry and Dennis Bergkamp before turning his attention to Arsene Wenger, who ended up with an icepack on his ankle.

Nevertheless, Wenger was impressed enough to sign Toure who did not need the complication of a work permit because of his status as a full international. At first Wenger used him as a defensive midfielder and as a stand-in right-back. In his first season, he made 9 starts and came on 17 times as a substitute as Arsenal finished runners-up, 5 points adrift of retaining their title. In the FA Cup final win over Southampton he was an unused substitute. The following season Toure and Campbell were a partnership in true Arsenal mould as the Gunners swept to the title. In 2004-05 Philippe Senderos and Pascal Cygan made their cases for inclusion but, while Campbell was hampered by injury, Toure made 35 Premiership appearances and played in the FA Cup final win against Manchester United.

In 2005-06 Toure was again dominant as the Gunners went 10 straight games without conceding a goal to reach the Champions League final. Occasionally it could be said that he lacked composure with the sometimes erratic Jens Lehmann behind him, and his absence, together with that of fellow Ivorian Emmanuel Eboue, due to the Africa

Cup of Nations, hampered Wenger's selection process. In April 2006, Toure made a magnificent flying save to deny Wayne Rooney at Old Trafford. Unfortunately for Arsenal it was rewarded with a red card for Toure and a penalty for United, from which Rooney hammered them in front 9 minutes into the second half. Park Ji-sung wrapped up a ninth successive Premiership win for United.

In April 2009, following a fall-out with his defensive partner William Gallas, Toure asked for a transfer. Arsenal chairman Peter Hill-Wood turned it down and Toure appeared to have made peace with the situation until the close season at least. But in July his transfer to Manchester City for £16 million was announced. A few months later he told Daniel Taylor of *The Guardian*:

> When you play with somebody and you don't even talk to each other on the pitch it's really difficult. Me and Gallas ... we didn't talk to each other at all. One of us had to go and it was me. It was coming down to me really because I didn't want to put the team in a difficult position, so I was the one who said I wanted to go. As a player, I had great respect for Gallas because he was older than me and in Africa when someone is older you have respect for them, but I think sometimes he took advantage of that in some ways. I had six years at Arsenal but the last two were very difficult. It can happen in football that you argue with somebody in training but when you are not even talking on the pitch something has to change.

Toure had made 326 appearances and scored 14 goals for Arsenal. With Manchester City he won the Premier League in 2011-12 before moving to Liverpool on a free transfer in May 2013. In July 2016, he was reunited with Liverpool manager Brendan Rodgers at Celtic. He became a coach at Celtic in 2017 and when Rodgers left for Leicester City in February 2019, Toure joined him there.

Jack Wilshere

On 13 September 2008, Arsene Wenger gave a first-team debut to Jack Wilshere, bringing him off the bench at Ewood Park. At 16 years and 256 days old it meant that, after eye-catching performances for Arsenal's youth and reserve teams, Wilshere became the youngest player to represent the club in a League match. Ten days later, he scored his first ever senior goal as a youthful Gunners team tore Sheffield United to shreds, 6-0, in the League Cup. By November the boy had tasted Champions League football. He was not yet old enough to sign a full-time professional contract.

Arsene Wenger felt that Wilshere – 'bandy of leg but neat of touch' according to sportswriter Henry Winter – could become an Arsenal legend. He told *Arsenal TV Online*:

> I believe he will end up a central midfielder, just off the striker, in the Bergkamp role. I am convinced that he will have tremendous penetrative power and we forget that this boy is only 16 … give him four more years and he will be massively strong. He can find the final ball and can score goals. He is a passionate and committed guy, he is not afraid of tackles … But I would not like to put too much pressure on him because of the expectation level.

In August 2015, during a routine press conference at Arsenal's London Colney training ground, Wenger told reporters that Wilshere, who was under treatment for the latest of a series of injuries, would be back in 'three to four weeks'. Wenger admitted, 'Maybe when he was younger we overplayed him because he was such a good player, but now we are cautious with him.' In fact, Wilshere did not play again that season in which Arsenal finished runners-up, 10 points behind shock champions Leicester City.

It was perhaps already too late in the 23-year-old's career to recognise the damage that had been done to him after he matured so early. Setbacks had come at regular intervals since then for the lad who joined Arsenal when he was just 9. After his Arsenal first-team debut there was a loan spell with Bolton Wanderers in 2009-10 and the Trotters wanted to take him for another season, but in 2010-11 he was a regular in the Gunners' Premier League side – he was suspended for 3 games after being sent off against Birmingham City – and also became the tenth youngest player ever to win a full England cap. Then, despite encouraging bulletins from Wenger, Wilshere missed the entire 2011-12 season after suffering a stress fracture to an ankle in a pre-season Emirates Cup match against New York Red Bulls.

Wilshere won 2 major honours with Arsenal. He was an extra-time substitute in the 2014 FA Cup final win over Hull City, and he came on 13 minutes from the end of the following season's Wembley victory over Aston Villa, but his Premier League appearances became fewer and fewer each season, again due to injuries, mostly to his ankles. In August 2016, after 2 substitute appearances, Wilshere went on loan to Bournemouth for the rest of the season but injury again dogged him and in April he suffered a hairline fracture to his left fibula after a collision with Harry Kane at White Hart Lane. In December 2017, he made his first Premier League start for Arsenal in 17 months, and in January 2018, against Chelsea, he scored his first Premier League goal since May 2015.

In July 2018, at the end of his Arsenal contract, Wilshere signed for West Ham United, the club he had supported as a boy. He had made 197 senior appearances and scored 14 goals for the Gunners with whom he won 34 caps. There had been disciplinary issues, both on and off the field, but he will perhaps be best remembered for a career blighted by injury. In 2015 he told *The Telegraph's* Sam Rider: 'I made mistakes but I've learned from them and I'm a better person for it. Now if I get injured I know what it takes to come back.'

Mikel Arteta

When Arsenal bought Mikel Arteta from Everton for £10 million in August 2011, it signalled the end of a frustrating summer for Arsene Wenger who had chased the 29-year-old Spaniard for some time. He had almost become resigned to the likelihood that Chelsea's Yossi Benayoun, taken on a season-long loan, would be the only reward for his efforts to strengthen the team following the departures of Cesc Fabregas and Samir Nasri, as well as injuries to others. At the eleventh hour – well, maybe closer to a minute to midnight, figuratively speaking – Arteta changed his mind, leaving Everton manager David Moyes to explain that, while he was sorry to lose him, 'Champions League football was something that I wasn't able to offer him.'

Arsenal's original offer of £5 million had been waved away by Everton, and £10 million was still not enough until the player suddenly announced that he wanted to leave. The Gunners could well afford it. They had sold Fabregas to Barcelona for £35 million and Samir Nasri to Manchester City for £25 million. And even though Arteta had apparently taken a pay cut to ensure that he tasted European football at the highest level in the coming season, and be given a 4-year contract, his reported £75,000 a week still made him the highest paid player in Arsenal's history.

In his first season at the Emirates, Arteta made 38 appearances in all games and scored 6 goals. It would have been more but in April 2012 he sprained an ankle against Wigan Athletic that kept him out of the last few matches. The Gunners, watched by majority shareholder Stan Kroenke who had flown in from the United States to attend a board meeting the following day, lost 2-1 at home. At the end of the match, those Arsenal supporters who had bothered to remain to express disapproval of their own club gave the Wigan players a standing ovation as they left the field.

In 2012-13 Arteta helped Arsenal to their seventeenth successive top-4 finish, and although he missed the start of 2013-14 because of injury, he captained the Gunners when they won the FA Cup by beating Hull City 3-2 in an exciting extra-time Wembley final. It was Arsenal's first serious piece of silverware for 9 years. He was appointed skipper for 2014-15 but made only 11 appearances that season, and only 14 in 2015-16, as injuries to calf, thigh muscle and ankle all took their toll.

Never a natural holding midfielder, he had been moved into a deeper role by Wenger who told *The Guardian's* Amy Lawrence, 'I am hugely impressed by Arteta because he is a tactical leader and a winner.' Arteta was not doing it all on his own, however. Wenger said, 'We try to find the defensive balance collectively.'

When Arteta left to become Manchester City's assistant coach in July 2016, the former Barcelona, Paris Saint-Germain, Rangers, Real Sociedad and Everton midfielder had played 149 senior games for Arsenal and scored 16 goals. In May 2018, Arteta was strongly tipped to become manager of Arsenal in succession to Wenger, but it did not happen. There were several accounts flying around. That he was due to take over but first insisted that the Gunners sack their long-serving head of medical services, Gary Lewin, who Arteta apparently blamed for rushing him back too soon from injury. That he wanted full control over transfers and was not prepared to work within a budget of £50 million. There were also reports that he had not been popular during his time as a player at Arsenal. According to the *Daily Mirror* he had 'divided opinion'.

Wenger said that Arteta had all the qualities to succeed him. He told the global network of sports channels *beIN Sports*, 'He was a leader, has good passion for the game, knows the club and knows what is important at the club … but I don't want to influence that publicly. I believe it is important they make their choice in an objective way.' Eventually, of course, Arteta remained at Manchester City.

In December 2019, however, he did return to Arsenal, as head coach in the wake of Unai Emery's sacking.

Laurent Koscielny

It is not very often that a footballer goes on strike. George Eastham did it in 1960. In his case it was on a matter of principle and his actions revolutionised players' working conditions. It started the game on the road from so-called soccer slaves to where we are today with millionaire footballers – and their agents – calling most of the shots.

When Newcastle United finally relented, Eastham ended up at Arsenal. Fifty-nine years later, another Gunners player went on strike. This time, however, his aims were considered to be far less laudable, not least because at the time he happened to be the club captain. When, in 2019, Laurent Koscielny refused to travel on Arsenal's pre-season tour to the United States he was hardly a 'soccer slave'. The 33-year-old centre-back still had a year left on his contract at the Emirates and with no new deal on the horizon, he decided that he would try for a longer contract elsewhere, preferably in his native France. The impasse was that while the player believed that he should be given a free transfer, the club wanted a fee for such an experienced defender.

Koscielny had first signed for Arsenal in July 2010, for a reported £8 million from the Ligue 1 club Lorient. Arsene Wenger said, 'We identified him as a very strong centre-half ... he has shown he is mentally strong, he's a fighter and a very strong competitor. Koscielny is a great addition to our squad.' Koscielny said:

> I'm very excited to be joining Arsenal. They are one of the biggest clubs in Europe with many great players .... Also, in Arsene Wenger, Arsenal has one of the best managers in the world and I can't wait to work with him and do my best for the Arsenal supporters.

With Arsenal, Koscielny became regarded as one of the best central defenders in Europe. He won his first cap for France and played in Euro

2012 and in the 2014 World Cup finals, and in the team that lost the Euro 2016 final to Portugal.

He helped the Gunners win 2 FA Cup finals, in 2014 and 2015. A red card on the last day of the season, when he lunged at Everton forward Enner Valencia, meant that he missed the 2017 final against Chelsea, and then an Achilles tendon injury sustained during the Europa League semi-final against Atletico Madrid in May 2018 ruled him out for 7 months. He came back against Qarabag in a Europa League game in December. Three days later he was picked to play against Southampton and made some costly errors, but he kept being selected – another 5 times playing twice in 3 days as the Gunners attempted to qualify for the Champions League – and he skippered the side that lost to Chelsea in the 2019 Europa League final in Baku. Apparently he felt that he was being overworked and a few weeks later he told Arsenal that after 9 years, 353 games and 27 goals for the Gunners, he wanted away. The club refused and the situation came to an ugly head when the player refused to go on the pre-season tour.

Unai Emery went to Arsenal's head of football, Raul Sanllehi, who issued a statement: 'We are very disappointed by Laurent's actions, which are against our clear instructions. Laurent Koscielny has refused to travel to the US for our pre-season tour. We hope to resolve this matter and will not be providing any further comment at this time.'

The Gunners took disciplinary action and when the players reported in for training at London Colney, Koscielny was ordered to work with the under-23 squad. Emery said, 'Now it is one issue only for the club and for him. My idea is continuing with the players we are working with and the players that want to be here.'

In early August 2019 Arsenal sold Koscielny to Ligue 1 club Bordeaux for £4.6 million. He announced the transfer by taking off an Arsenal shirt to reveal the new Bordeaux home shirt.

Arsene Wenger

On 6 May 2018, Arsene Wenger, the 68-year-old almost eponymous manager of Arsenal, received a standing ovation from supporters when his team beat Burnley 5-0. It was not so much the result that brought the Emirates crowd to their feet as the fact that it was the last home game in charge for the longest-serving and most successful manager in the Gunners' history. One year earlier, an aircraft trailing a banner that read, 'Wenger – Out Means Out!!' flew over Stoke City's ground where Arsenal were playing. It was not the first time that some disgruntled supporters had taken to the skies, campaigning for the board to withdraw a new contract believed to be ready for the manager to sign.

The man who had made such a huge impact on the club and on top-flight football in England was now paying the price for declining performances. The manager who had introduced new ways of training, new tactics, and fresh ideas on nutrition, was now out of favour with fans who saw failure to qualify for the Champions League as unforgivable. The manager who had signed hitherto unknown players and helped them to become global stars was on his way out. Not everyone was of the same opinion, of course. Tens of thousands of fans were unhappy at the sky-high protests.

Against Burnley at the Emirates they acknowledged the immense contribution that he had made to their club. From aerial protests to a standing ovation – that was the story of Arsene Wenger's final few months with Arsenal.

His arrival at Highbury almost 22 seasons earlier had been a drawn-out affair. An erudite man who can speak several languages and who reportedly has a masters' degree in economics, Wenger had an undistinguished playing career in French football. He was always going to be a better coach than he was a footballer and worked at Nancy and Monaco before taking over at Japanese club Nagoya Grampus Eight for the start of the 1995 J-League season. But if his reputation was growing inside tighter football circles, his name was unknown in Britain. When the Gunners announced him as the successor to Bruce Rioch in 1996, Arsenal fans were asking, 'Arsene who?'

It took some time for him to arrive because he was still under contract to Grampus Eight, but the identity of the Gunners' new manager eventually became an open secret, not least when 2 French players, Patrick Vieira and Remi Garde, were signed on his recommendation. At his first press conference, Wenger explained, 'The main reason for coming is that I love English football, the roots of the game are here. I like the spirit round the game and at Arsenal I like the spirit of the club and its potential.'

His first game in charge was a 2-0 win at Blackburn on 12 October 1996. There were to be many more triumphs: 3 Premier League titles and a record 7 FA Cup final wins, the most recent the 2017 defeat of Chelsea. There were 2 Double-winning seasons and in 2003-04 the Gunners went through the Premiership season unbeaten. He was also influential in Arsenal moving from Highbury to the Emirates, although the move to a new stadium meant that he could not spend big money on players and so there was a period of relative austerity. There were a few disciplinary issues too. When Konstantinos Mavropanos received the 118th red card of Wenger's reign in May 2018 it was noted that he was not born when Steve Bould became the first Arsenal player to be dismissed under Wenger in November 1996.

For all the success that Arsene Wenger brought to Arsenal, there were growing concerns as the Gunners would finish outside the top 4 for the second successive season. So the manager who thought he might be pushed – and who did not want to work in a new management structure anyway – decided to walk first. 'I have some bad news,' he told the players at London Colney. His announcement was met by a stunned silence. His legacy is immense.

Ivan Gazidis

In May 2018, Arsenal's chief executive, Ivan Gazidis, introduced Unai Emery as the Gunners' new manager. It was an illuminating address, detailing how the process to select Arsene Wenger's successor had been carried out with the proverbial fine toothcomb. In the end there were 3 runners and Gazidis, together with Arsenal's head of football relations, Raul Sanllehi, and the club's head of recruitment, Sven Mislintat, agreed unanimously that Emery was the man. Gazidis said he was delighted to be working with the former Paris Saint-Germain manager.

Two months later, Arsenal's chairman, Sir Chips Keswick, acknowledged the rumours that AC Milan were keen to take Gazidis to the San Siro Stadium. In September, rumour became fact and it was announced that Gazidis would take up his new position on 1 December.

The media – and the fans – speculated as to why the club's chief executive should move at this time. He had won a power struggle with Wenger, restructured the football management side of the club to the point where, after a trebling of staff, there were now 9 department heads, and had just appointed a new head coach – manager is becoming such an outdated title in today's football – whose presence, he said, 'energised' him. So why leave now? The obvious answer, to some at least, was a reported £1 million increase in annual salary together with an equity stake in the Italian club. But Gazidis did not boast an extravagant lifestyle and accounts in the Italian press disputed the salary figure reported by the British media.

Another reason put forward was simply that, with Wenger gone, the restructuring complete, and Emery, Sanllehi and Mislintat poised to take Arsenal forward, it was a case of 'my work here is done'. After that it was simply the lure of a new challenge with even greater power and responsibilities that were propelling him to Milan, who pointed out that, under his hand, Arsenal had doubled their turnover and become more profitable.

Ivan Gazidis was born in Johannesburg on 13 September 1964 but moved to Manchester when he was 4. He won a soccer blue at Oxford University, from where he graduated with a law degree in 1986. In 1992, he moved to the United States to work for international law firm Latham & Watkins. Two years later he was one of the management team that founded Major League Soccer (MLS), becoming its deputy commissioner in 2001. He was president of MLS's marketing arm, Soccer United Marketing. On 1 January 2009, he started work as Arsenal's chief executive, taking over from the Gunners' former managing director, Keith Edelman, who had been instrumental, indeed the key figure, in the development of the Emirates Stadium.

Gazidis was not a man who courted publicity. Although he initially engaged with Arsenal's supporters at fans' forums, he became less available to the media who wanted to ask about Wenger's role and, later, to obtain a reaction to fans' complaints that, while the cost of going to watch a match at the Emirates rose sharply, there were no improvements on the pitch, at least none that during Gazidis's time brought more than three FA Cups. Champions League qualification was now a step too far for the team.

In January 2019, when Emery announced that Arsenal were unable to spend during the transfer window, many supporters harked back 6 years to when Gazidis told *The Independent*:

> My own view is we are moving into a new phase where if we make our decisions well, if we get the right chemistry, and if we do a variety of other things as well, not just the new players that come in but the right kind of things on the football side, that we can compete with any club in the world .... We've seen two clubs this year in the Champions League final [Bayern Munich and Borussia Dortmund] both of whom run responsible financial models and they're pretty fantastic teams and exciting to watch. There's no reason why we can't do that.

David Dein

When, in April 2007, David Dein resigned as Arsenal's vice-chairman, Arsene Wenger said it was 'a sad day for the club'. Ian Wright said, 'I know the players aren't happy ... we are talking about a man who goes into the dressing room at the end of every single game, shakes every player by the hand, and who knows all the youth-team players.' Wenger agreed: 'Red and white are the colours of his heart ... this guy has revolutionised this club and English football. He is top quality.'

Dein was the casualty in a boardroom battle over a takeover bid by American billionaire Stan Kroenke whom he had introduced to the club. Dein was in favour of Kroenke taking control. The rest of the board, led by chairman Peter Hill-Wood and diamond merchant Danny Fiszman, were not. Outnumbered, Dein stood down.

Hill-Wood said:

> We sincerely regret that irreconcilable differences between Mr Dein and the rest of the board have necessitated a parting of the ways. In light of recent speculation with regards to the ownership of the club, the remaining board members, who together own 45.45 per cent of the issued share capital of the company, would like to reassure the supporters, shareholders and employees of Arsenal Football Club that they remain long-term holders of their interests in the club. To this effect, they have entered into an agreement not to dispose of their shares for at least one year and have confirmed that they intend to retain their interests on the expiration of this period.

Somewhere in the not-too-distant future, that would not be the case.

Dein had been Arsenal's vice-chairman since 1983 when he bought a 16.6 per cent share – then worth £290,250 – in the club. Hill-Wood thought him 'crazy' because 'to all intents and purposes it's dead money'. By 1991, Dein owned 42 per cent of Arsenal and was very much a hands-on director, involving himself in transfers and contracts. Writing in the *Sunday Tribune* in 1996, sports journalist Peter Ball said:

> When Rioch was sacked, ... by the end of the week it appeared ... that his only mistake was to fail to get on with David Dein ... . Before he became a power figure at Highbury, Dein was a sugar importer from Colombia. He reportedly started out as a barrow boy. If so, then he has not done that profession much credit.

In *The Independent*, Paul Hayward wrote, 'When Wenger was approached behind Rioch's back, people said it wasn't the way that Arsenal used to behave.'

Despite these opinions of him, Dein made a huge contribution to Arsenal. Besides identifying Wenger, he was a major figure in turning Highbury into an all-seater stadium. He took Arsenal into the G-14 cartel of major European clubs and became the organisation's president. The Gunners became a club with some world-class players and life looked red and white for years to come. But after investing heavily in a new stadium – something that Dein was not overly keen on – huge new revenue streams were needed if Arsenal were to compete on the field. Dein had much earlier sold shares to Danny Fiszman, and in August 2007 he disposed of his remaining 14.58 per cent for £75 million to an investment vehicle of Uzbek-born Russian metal billionaire Alisher Usmanov. From the comfort of an Islington restaurant, Dein reminded the media that he had now introduced two billionaires to Arsenal:

> This marks a significant step towards realising the vision I share with thousands of fans at home and abroad of making Arsenal the world's No.1 football club ... . I believe the board should welcome non-British involvement. Without new investors, I feel very soon Arsenal might not be able to compete successfully at the very top level, despite the fantastic work of Arsene Wenger.

David Dein held a number of prominent positions with the Football League and FA. He was one of the major architects of the FA Premiership. A key figure in promoting anti-racism and diversity in football, today, he is a high-profile speaker on football and motivational matters.

Stan Kroenke

In July 2019, various Arsenal supporters' groups joined together to send a strongly worded letter to the club's owner, telling him that Gunners' fans had never 'felt more marginalised' and urging him to make 'new and dynamic appointments' into what 'feels like an investment vehicle'. They described the Emirates Stadium as a 'soulless place' on matchdays because it was 'blighted' by a 'poor' atmosphere and empty seats.

When Stan Kroenke first bought shares in the club, Arsenal had recently played in the 2006 Champions League final. In 2019 the Gunners were looking at their third successive Europa League season – and had to hark back 15 years for their most recent Premier League title.

Kroenke, who was born in Missouri on 29 July 1947, can be counted among the world's most powerful sports and real estate entrepreneurs. His Kroenke Sports & Entertainment (KSE) empire embraces Colorado Avalanche of the National Hockey League, Colorado Rapids of MLS, Los Angeles Rams of the National Football League, Denver Nuggets of the National Basketball Association, and Colorado Mammoth of the National Lacrosse League – and, of course, Arsenal.

In April 2007, KSE UK Inc bought a 9.9 per cent stake in Arsenal Holdings plc. A further purchase took Kroenke's stake to 12.9 per cent, and in September 2008 he joined the board, his shareholding now 29.9 per cent. In April 2011, following the purchase of shares held by diamond merchant Danny Fiszman and Lady Nina Bracewell-Smith, his stake had increased to 62.89 per cent. In August 2018, Alisher Usmanov announced that he would accept Kroenke's £550 million bid for his 30 per cent stake in the club to take full control. One year earlier, Usmanov had made a £1 billion bid to take control of Arsenal but Kroenke rejected it.

Arsenal were now valued at £1.8 billion, and Kroenke acquiring Usmanov's shares meant that all remaining shareholders had to sell their shares – a total of 1,779 valued at £52.3m – to the American. In a statement, the Arsenal Supporters' Trust said:

> This news marks a dreadful day for Arsenal Football Club. Stan Kroenke taking the club private will see the end of supporters owning shares in Arsenal and their role upholding custodianship values … . The most dreadful part of this announcement is the news that Kroenke plans to forcibly purchase the shares held by Arsenal fans … Kroenke's actions will neuter their voice and involvement. It is an action designed to remove shareholder scrutiny on how Arsenal is managed.

Supporter Mary Maude spoke for many when she wrote on the Arsenal Supporters' Trust website:

> I was given a share in Arsenal some twenty years ago and since then have referred to it as the best present I have ever received … . That we are now forced to sell our shares is the final act of what has, over recent years, been a gradual erosion of the pleasures that being both an Arsenal supporter and a shareholder gave me. I could weep when I realise that this proud club, with its long history that is so often held up as an example of how a football club should be managed, has been relegated to a small, insignificant, private US company registered in Delaware.

Another season came and went without Arsenal qualifying for the Champions League – to add insult to injury Tottenham took the final place, just 1 point above Arsenal – and the Gunners lost 4-1 to Chelsea in the Europa League final and were knocked out of the FA Cup and the League Cup. In July 2019, Josh Kroenke, son of Stan and himself an Arsenal director, said:

> We know we have some of the most passionate fans in any sport, anywhere in the world. It's part of what makes us such a special and unique club. And while we understand, appreciate, and agree with concerns about our club failing to achieve our goal of qualifying for the 2019-20 Champions League, we respectfully disagree about our club being at a crossroads and that things need to change because so much change has recently occurred.

Unai Emery

On 23 May 2018, Unai Emery was appointed head coach of Arsenal in succession to Arsene Wenger. Unlike Wenger, the 46-year-old Spaniard came with an already high profile. When Wenger had joined the Gunners 22 years earlier, 'foreign' football was still something of an unknown to the average British fan, and apart from some success at Monaco, Wenger had achieved nothing that made headlines in the UK. By 2018, all that had changed. Almost saturation television coverage of the game in Europe and beyond meant that football followers here were familiar with events in La Liga, Serie A, Eredivisie and Ligue 1, and it was in the latter that Emery had become a recognisable name after guiding Paris Saint-Germain to the French title, as well as 4 domestic cups. If that was not enough, previously he had steered Sevilla to 3 successive Europa League triumphs.

Arsenal's chief executive, Ivan Gazidis, said:

> Unai has an outstanding track record of success throughout his career, has developed some of the best young talent in Europe and plays an exciting, progressive style of football that fits Arsenal perfectly ... . His hard-working and passionate approach and his sense of values on and off the pitch make him the ideal person to take us forward.

Emery was equally pleased to be signing a 2-year contract at the Emirates:

> I'm very excited to be given the responsibility to start this important new chapter in Arsenal's history. I'm thrilled to be joining one of the great clubs in the game. Arsenal is known and loved throughout the world for its style of play, its commitment to young players, the fantastic stadium, the way the club is run. I'm excited about what we can do

together and I look forward to giving everyone who loves Arsenal some special moments and memories.

Like Wenger, Emery had a modest playing career. As a midfielder, his 339-game career in Spain had been spent mostly in the second tier and was ended by a knee injury while playing for Lorca Deportiva, whom he then managed and won them promotion to the Segunda Division. He then took Almeira into La Liga for the first time in the club's history. Then it was Valencia's turn. Emery saw them qualify for the Champions League before he spent a brief and unsuccessful spell with Spartak Moscow. Then it was on to Sevilla and a hat-trick of Europa League titles, and finally to Paris before Arsenal identified him as their man.

When he signed for the Gunners, French football writer Julien Laurens said on the *BBC Sport* website:

> Emery will get Arsenal more organised than they have been. He's really keen on drills and discipline, worked PSG hard at training and has got a very good idea of what he wants to do … . If the Arsenal players are on board with what he wants to do, that's how he won three straight Europa Leagues, because that Sevilla team were all on board.

After a disappointing start – Arsenal lost his first 2 games in charge, to Manchester City and Chelsea – the Gunners embarked on their best run of form since 2007, winning 11 games in a row and going 14 Premier League games undefeated. But purse strings were as tight as ever and with no money made available to Emery in the January 2019 transfer window, the only arrival was Denis Suarez on loan from Barcelona to add to summer signings Bernd Leno, Lucas Torreira, Stephan Lichtsteiner, Sokratis Papastathopoulos and Matteo Guendouzi.

Arsenal ended the season in fifth place and lost the Europa League final to Chelsea. In August 2019, Chelsea's David Luiz, who had worked with Emery at Paris Saint-Germain, joined the Gunners for £8 million. The 32-year-old Brazilian defender said, 'My goal is to win things for Arsenal.' Alas, after a mediocre start to the season, in November 2019, following a Europa League defeat by Eintracht Frankfurt, Emery was sacked.

Bibliography

Buchan, Charles, *A Lifetime in Football*, (Phoenix House, 1955)
Chapman, Herbert, *On Football*, (Garrick, 1934)
Gibson, Alfred; Pickford, William, *Association Football and the Men Who Made It*, (Caxton Publishing Company, 1905)
Hapgood, Eddie, *Football Ambassador*, (Sporting Handbooks, 1945)
Joy, Bernard, *Forward Arsenal*, (Phoenix House, 1952)
Kelsey, Jack; Glanville, Brian, *Over The Bar*, (Stanley Paul, 1958)
Knighton, Albert Leslie, *Behind the Scenes in Big Football*, (Stanley Paul, 1948)
Ollier, Fred, *Arsenal: A Complete Record*, (Breedon Books, 1995)
Risoli, Mario, *When Pelé Broke Our Hearts*, (Ashley Drake Publishing, 1998)
Storey, Peter, *True Storey: My Life and Crimes as a Football Hatchet Man*, (Mainstream Publishing, 2011)
Whittaker, Tom, *Tom Whittaker's Arsenal Story*, (Sportsmans Book Club, 1958)

Newspapers
(Aberdeen) *Press and Journal*
Athletic News
Belfast Telegraph
(Birmingham) *Sports Argus*
Burnley Express
Bystander
Coventry Evening Telegraph
Daily Express
Daily Herald

Daily Mail
Daily Mirror
Daily Telegraph
Derby Evening Telegraph
Dundee Evening Telegraph
Exeter and Plymouth Gazette
Greenock Telegraph and Clyde Shipping Gazette
Guardian
Illustrated Police News
Ipswich Star
Irish Independent
Kentish Independent
Lancashire Evening Post
Leeds Mercury
L'Étoile Belge
Liverpool Echo
London Daily News
Luton Times and Advertiser
Manchester Evening News
Nottingham Evening Post
Nottingham Journal
(Portsmouth) *Evening News*
Prager Tagblatt (Germany)
(Sheffield) *Star Green 'Un*
Shields Daily News
Southern Echo
Sportsman
Staffordshire Sentinel
Sunday Life
Sunday People
Sunday Post

Bibliography

Sunday Tribune
Sunday World
Sunderland Daily Echo and Shipping Gazette
Thanet Advertiser
Thomson Newspapers
Western Morning News
Woolwich Gazette
Yorkshire Evening Post
Yorkshire Post

Websites

Arsenal Supporters' Trust arsenaltrust.org
BBC Sport bbc.co.uk/sport

Other

Arsenal TV Online

Index

Adams, Tony, 122, 134, 135-136, 142, 145, 148, 152, 154, 163, 170, 175, 187
Addison, Colin, 93, 99
Allen, Jack, 23
Allen, Clive, 133
Allinson, Ian, 143
Allison, George, 32, 47, 48-50, 62, 63, 64, 69, 73, 78, 95
Almunia, Manuel, 182, 190
Anderson, Viv, 141-142, 147, 153, 160
Armstrong, George, 113-114, 121
Arteta, Mikel, 197-198
Atherton, Moses, 78

Ball, Alan, 98, 115-116, 119, 121
Baker, Alf, 21, 22, 23
Baker, Joe, 90, 105
Barnett, Geoff, 104
Barnes, Wally, 78, 85
Barnwell, John, 93
Bastin, Cliff, 31, 36, 43, 55-56, 58, 59, 63, 67, 162
Benayoun, Yossi, 197
Bergkamp, Dennis, 165-166, 167, 168, 169, 174, 181, 191, 193, 195
Bestall, Jackie, 66
Bigden, James, 9, 13

Blockley, Jeff, 117
Bracewell-Smith, Lady Nina, 207
Briercliffe, Tommy, 6
Bosman, Jean-Marc, 165, 169
Booth, Andy, 169
Bould, Steve, 122, 135, 145, 148, 151-152, 159, 163, 202
Boulton, Frank, 79
Bowden Ray, 23, 55, 59-60, 67
Boyer, Joe, 40
Bradshaw Harry, 3, 5-7, 11, 12
Brady, Liam, 116, 117-118, 119, 120, 121, 123, 124, 132, 139
Brain, Jimmy, ix, 21, 24-25, 35, 51
Brook, Eric, 112
Brown, Laurie, 80
Bowen, Dave, 85
Buchan, Charles, 17, 18, 31, 32
Bull, Walter, 29
Burkinshaw, Keith, 127
Burns, Tony, 104
Busacca, Massimo 192
Butler, Jack, 23, 32, 77

Caesar, Gus, 163
Callaghan, Ian, 90
Campbell, Kevin, 161
Campbell, Sol, 187-188, 189, 193
Caton, Tommy, 163

Index

Catterick, Harry, 115
Chapman, Herbert, 8, 17, 24, 27, 29-33, 34, 36, 38, 39, 40, 42, 43, 46, 47, 48, 49, 50, 55, 59, 60, 64, 95, 100
Charles, Mel, 80
Charlton Jack, 122
Charlton, Stan, 80
Chedgzoy, Sam, 27
Clapton, Danny, 87
Clay, Ernie, 91
Clough, Brian, 82, 104, 131, 141
Cole, Ashley, 186, 187
Coleman, Tim, 6, 14
Compton, Denis, 23, 72
Compton, Leslie, 51, 71-72
Copping, Wilf, 23, 50, 63-64, 65
Crayston, Jack, 50, 56, 63, 65-66, 67, 78, 80
Cross, Archie, 5
Cudicini, Carlo, 159, 176
Cygan, Pascal, 193

Dalglish, Kenny, 137
Danskin, David, v, 1-2
Davidson, Randall Thomas, 16
Dein, David, 96, 150, 169, 172, 178, 205-206
Desailly, Marcel, 177
Devlin, James, 8
Dibble, Andy, 140, 147
Dick, John, 8-9
Dixon, Lee, 135, 145, 146, 148, 151, 152, 153-154, 186
Docherty, Tommy, 80, 89, 112
Drake, Ted, 44, 47, 50, 54, 55, 58, 61-62, 69
Ducat, Andy, 10-11, 15

Dunn, David, 190
Dunne, Jimmy, 35

Eastham, George, 80, 89, 91-92, 93, 199
Edelman, Keith, 204
Edu Gaspar, 181, 182
Elcoat, William, 5, 8
Emery, Unai, 200, 203, 204, 209-210
Eriksson, Sven-Goran, 167, 188
Eto'o, Samuel, 182, 190

Fabregas, Cesc, 183-184, 197
Ferguson, Alex, 142, 145, 167, 173, 183
Ferguson, Hughie, 27
Fiszman, Danny, 205, 206, 207
Fotheringham, Jim, 80
Friar Ken, 96, 151
Furnell, Jim, 93, 104

Gallas, William, 194
Garbutt, Billy, 14
Gazidis, Ivan, 203-204, 209
George, Charlie, 52, 100, 109, 110, 111-112, 121, 127
Gooing, Bill, 6
Graham, Dick, 82
Graham, George, 96, 99, 107, 111, 114, 122, 134, 135, 138, 140, 141, 143, 145-146, 147, 140, 153, 155, 157, 161, 162, 163
Grant, Cyril, 76
Gravesen, Thomas, 189
Greenwood, Ron, 130, 132
Grobbelaar, Bruce, 153
Groves, Perry, 143, 146

215

Groves, Vic, 85
Gudjohnsen, Eidur, 189
Guendouzi, Matteo, 210
Gullit, Ruud, 168

Halliday, Dave, 24, 34
Hapgood, Eddie, 23, 31, 44, 47, 50, 53-54, 67
Harper, Bill, 27, 31
Harvey, Colin, 115, 151
Harvey, Ian, 144
Hastings, Sir Patrick, 17
Hauge, Rune, 146
Healy, David, 190
Henderson, Jackie, 80
Henry, Thierry, 162, 177-178, 184, 193
Herd, David, 80, 87-88
Hibbs, Harry 83
Hill-Wood, Dennis, 95-96, 99, 100, 101, 118, 133
Hill-Wood, Peter, 95-96, 145, 165, 194, 205
Hill-Wood, Sir Samuel, 95-96
Hodgson, Roy, 179
Holton, Cliff, 80, 81-82, 84
Howe, Don, 94, 100, 131-132, 138, 141, 145, 163
Howell, Dennis, MP, 115
Hulme, Joe, 31, 36-37, 58, 87, 105, 139
Humble, John, 4, 6

Irving, Sam, 27

James, Alex, 31, 33, 51, 55, 57-58, 73
Jack, David, 24, 31, 40-41, 51
Jack, Bob, 41, 59
Jackson, Jimmy, 5, 9
Jensen, John, 146
Jennings, Pat, 127-128
Jeppson, Hans, 85
Jones, Bryn, 50, 73-74
John, Bob, 21, 22-23, 77
Johnson, Walter, MP, 115
Jones, Mark, 81
Joy, Bernard, 47, 67-68
Julians, Len, 80

Kanu, Nwankwo, 174, 179-180
Keegan, Kevin, 137, 156
Kelly, Bob, 40
Kelly, Eddie, 111, 116
Kelsey, Jack, 80, 85-86
Kelso, Phil, 6, 7, 11, 12, 14, 46
Kendall, Howard, 115, 163
Keswick, Sir Chips, 203
Kennedy, Ray, 100, 106, 109-110, 111, 113, 117, 127
Keown, Martin, 143, 163-164, 186
Kluivert, Patrick, 175
Knighton, Leslie, 17, 18, 19-20, 21, 22, 24, 77
Koscielny, Laurent, 199-200
Kroenke, Josh, 208
Kroenke, Stan, ix, 96, 197, 205, 207-208
Kutner, Steve, 160
Kyle, Peter, 14

Lambert, Jack, 24, 31, 34-35, 58
Lauren, 181, 185-186, 187
Laurens, Julien, 210
Law, Dick, 192
Lawrance, George, 3, 4

Index

Lawton, Tommy, 37, 70
Leavey, George, 3-4, 6
Le Saux, Graham, 171, 191
Lee, Francis, 91
Lee, Gordon, 125, 126
Lehmann, Jens, 182, 188, 189-190, 193
Leno, Bernd, 210
Lewis, Dan, 27-28
Lewis, Reg, 69-70, 76, 84
Lichtsteiner, Stephan, 210
Linward, Billy, 6
Limpar, Anders, 146, 157-158
Lishman, Doug, 83-84
Ljungberg, Freddie, 152, 160, 175-176, 180, 182
Logie, Jimmy, 81
Lombardo, Attilo, 168
Luiz, David, 210
Lukic, John, 153, 155, 169
Lydersen, Pål, 146

Macaulay, Archie, 78
McClelland, John, 103
McCulloch, Billy, 80
Macdonald, Malcolm, 106, 120, 125-126
McEachrane, Roddy, 6, 12-13
McKechnie, Ian, 103
McKenna, John, 17
McKinnon, Angus, 13
McLeod, John, 80
McLintock, Frank, 93-94, 97, 100, 107, 114
McNab, Bob
McNichol, Duncan, 5
McPherson, Ian, 81, 83
Makelele, Claude, 190

Male, George, 39, 51-52, 54, 67, 71
Mancini, Terry, 119, 121
Mangnall, Dave, 79
Mandley, Jack, 71
Manninger, Alex, 156
Marden, Reuben, 81
Marshall, James, 66
Matthews, Stanley, 60, 78, 83, 109
Maude, Mary, 208
Mee, Bertie, 94, 97, 98, 99-100, 102, 105, 107, 109, 112, 115, 116, 117, 121, 123
Mee, George, 99
Merrick, Geoff, 125-126
Merson, Paul, 143-144, 151, 158, 161
Milne, Billy, 22, 77, 99
Milne, Gordon, 101
Mislintat, Sven, 203
Monti, Luis, 54
Morgan, Alf, 83
Morgan, Stuart, 109
Morrell, George, 12, 14-15
Moss, Frank, 44-45, 79
Mountfield, Derek, 151
Moyes, David, 197

Nasri, Samir, 197
Neil, Andy, 32
Neill, Terry, 98, 101, 113, 114, 116, 120, 124, 125, 126, 128, 129, 131, 132, 133, 138
Nelson, David, 76
Nelson, Sammy, 101, 102, 111
Nicholas, Charlie, 130, 134, 137-138, 149
Norris, Sir Henry, 3, 4, 16-18, 19, 20, 21, 95

O'Flanagan, Dr Kevin, 103
O'Leary, David, 101, 118, 121-122, 123, 146, 148, 151
O'Neill, Martin, 166
Ormerod, Brett, 156
Overmars, Marc, 180, 181, 182, 183-184, 189, 191, 192, 195

Pak Ji-sung, 194
Papastathopoulos, Sokratis, 210
Parker, Tom, 31, 38-39, 49, 51, 71
Parlour, Ray, 159-160, 169, 179, 186
Pelé, 86
Petit, Emmanuel, 168, 170, 171-172, 174, 181, 185, 187
Pires, Robert, 166, 175, 180, 181-182, 185
Platt, David, 167-168, 169, 175
Platt, Ted, 85
Prutton, David, 191
Powell, Barry, 101

Quinn, Niall, 143, 149, 161, 163

Radford, John, 105-106, 110, 127
Ramsay, James, 35
Raul, Sanllehi, 200, 203
Reid, Peter, 152
Revie, Don, 87, 115, 121
Rice, Pat, 101, 107, 123, 152, 169
Richardson, Jimmy, 23
Rideout, Paul, 158
Rioch, Bruce, 108, 162, 166, 167, 168, 169, 202, 206
Rix, Graham, 101, 118, 123-124, 132

Roberts, Herbie, 32, 42-43, 67
Roberts, John, 111
Robson, Bobby, 131
Robson, Jock, 26, 27
Robson, Stewart, 141
Rocastle, David, 139-140
Ronaldinho, 156
Rooney, Wayne, 194
Roose, Leigh Richard, 14
Rooke, Ronnie, 70, 75-76, 78
Roper, Don, 78, 87, 88
Russell, David, 34
Rutherford, Jock, 23

Sammels, John, 105, 106, 119
Sands, Percy, 9, 22, 46
Sansom, Kenny, 102, 133-134, 136, 141, 148
Sagar, Ted, 44
Satterthwaite, Charlie, 13
Schmeichel, Peter, 182
Seaman, David, 146, 155-156, 157, 159, 175, 189
Selley, Ian, 150
Senderos, Philippe, 193
Sexton, Dave, 94
Shankly, Bill, 90, 110
Shanks, Tom, 6
Sharp, Jimmy, 14
Shaw, Joe, 46-47, 49, 50
Sidey, Norman, 67
Simpson, Peter, 94
Smith, Alan, 143, 147, 148, 149-150, 153, 155, 161
Smith, Jim, 134
Smith, Lionel, 85
Sørensen, Thomas, 192
Spink, Nigel, 167

Index

Stack, Graham, 45
Stapleton, Frank, 106, 118, 119-120, 130, 134
Storey, Peter, 97-98, 107
Strong, Geoff, 89-90
Struth, William, 48
Suarez, Denis, 210
Šuker, Davor, 177
Summerbee, Mike, 97
Sunderland, Alan, 118, 124, 129-130, 132
Swift, Fred, 67
Swindin, George, 79-80, 85, 89, 92, 113

Talbot, Brian, 118, 131-132, 133
Taylor, Graham, 108, 116, 145
Taylor, Peter, 120
Thomas, Michael, 147, 153
Torreira, Lucas, 210
Toure, Kolo, 188, 193-194
Tyson, George, 139

Uphill, Dennis, 82
Usmanov, Alisher, 206, 207

Valencia, Enner, 200
Vallance, Jimmy, 83
Vallance, Tom, 83, 84
Van Bronckhorst, Giovanni, 187
Van Gaal, Louis, 173
Van Nistelrooy, Ruud, 186
Van Persie, Robin, 191-192
Vialli, Gianluca, 180
Vieira, Patrick, 168, 169-170, 171, 172, 182, 183, 184, 186, 187, 202

Waddington, Tony, 92
Waiters, Tony, 113
Walker, Des, 169
Wall, Bob, 111
Wallington, Mark, 119, 123
Watkins, Elijah, 1
Watson, Dave, 151
Wenger, Arsene, 96, 108, 135, 136, 140, 144, 148, 154, 156, 157, 159, 162, 164, 166, 168, 169, 170, 171, 172, 173, 174, 175, 176, 177, 178, 179, 180, 181, 183, 184, 185, 188, 189, 190, 191, 192, 193, 194, 195, 196, 197, 198, 199, 201-202, 203, 204, 205, 206, 209, 210
West, Gordon, 111
Westcott, Ronnie, 67
Whitefoot, Jeff, 81
Whittaker, Tom, 47, 50, 58, 66, 77-78, 81, 83, 85, 87, 95
Wilberforce, Mr Justice, 91
Williams, Gwyn, 124
Williams, Stuart, 86
Willis, Dave, 58
Wilshere, Jack, 195-196
Wilson, Alex, 79
Wilson, Bob, 103-104, 106
Winterburn, Nigel, 134, 135, 140, 145, 146, 147-148, 152, 159
Woodcock, Tony, 130, 137, 139
Woods, Harry, 24
Wright, Ian, 146, 149, 161-162, 166, 168, 169, 175, 205
Wright, Billy, 90, 92, 93, 94, 97, 99, 100, 103, 105, 113